ENDURING OTHERWISE

HAUNTINGS: QUEER/TRANS STUDIES IN RELIGION

Series Editors: Ashton T. Crawley (University of Virginia), Tamara C. Ho (University of California Riverside), and Melissa M. Wilcox (University of California Riverside)

Hauntings publishes leading-edge work at the intersection of trans studies, queer studies, and the study of religion that presses past the established boundaries of those fields and of existing scholarship in queer and trans studies in religion. The series editors seek manuscripts that expand or explode the current boundaries of queer and trans studies in religion through engagement with new and under-explored topics, genres, and theoretical approaches. In particular, books in this series engage in innovative research, methods, and writing to explore the unacknowledged spectres of power—the hidden, ephemeral, ghostly, and evanescent structures—that haunt these fields and the cultures on which they focus. Hauntings foregrounds incisive and intersectional scholarship that explores the dynamics of power that continue to haunt the mainstream(s) of the fields from which it draws. These dynamics include race, colonialism, class, caste, religious minoritization, and trans exclusion.

Books in the Series

Enduring Otherwise: Muslim Queer and Trans Worldmaking in Indonesia
Ferdiansyah Thajib

Fear of Queer Taiwan: Anti-LGBTQ Movements Between Taiwan and the U.S. Religious Right
Ying-Chao Kao

Enduring Otherwise

Muslim Queer and Trans Worldmaking in Indonesia

Ferdiansyah Thajib

New York University Press

New York

NEW YORK UNIVERSITY PRESS
New York
www.nyupress.org

Library of Congress Cataloging-in-Publication Data
Names: Thajib, Ferdiansyah, author.
Title: Enduring otherwise : Muslim queer and trans worldmaking in Indonesia /
Ferdiansyah Thajib.
Description: New York : New York University Press, [2026] | Series: Hauntings: queer/trans
studies in religion | Includes bibliographical references and index.
Identifiers: LCCN 2025021141 (print) | LCCN 2025021142 (ebook) | ISBN 9781479839322
(hardback) | ISBN 9781479839339 (paperback) | ISBN 9781479839346 (ebook) |
ISBN 9781479839353 (ebook other)
Subjects: LCSH: Muslim sexual minorities—Indonesia.
Classification: LCC HQ73.3.I5 T43 2026 (print) | LCC HQ73.3.I5 (ebook) |
DDC 306.7609598—dc23/eng/20250615
LC record available at https://lccn.loc.gov/2025021141
LC ebook record available at https://lccn.loc.gov/2025021142

This book is printed on acid-free paper, and its binding materials are chosen for strength
and durability. We strive to use environmentally responsible suppliers and materials to the
greatest extent possible in publishing our books.

The manufacturer's authorized representative in the EU for product safety is Mare
Nostrum Group B.V., Mauritskade 21D, 1091 GC Amsterdam, The Netherlands.
Email: gpsr@mare-nostrum.co.uk.

Manufactured in the United States of America

10 9 8 7 6 5 4 3 2 1

Also available as an ebook

For Bernd

and

for all who are enduring the unendurable

CONTENTS

Introduction

In early 2018, many months after I had completed my fieldwork in Indonesia, as I was at my laptop struggling to write up my PhD thesis at home in Berlin, an alarming update popped up in my social media newsfeed. It was a report about a police raid on hair salons run by *transpuan* in a district in Indonesia's northwesternmost province of Aceh. Transpuan is a shorthand term for *transgender perempuan* (transgender woman).[1] During the raid, twelve transpuans from five different hair salons were rounded up. The police beat them, shaved their heads, and stripped them of their clothes in public. They then ordered them to wear men's clothes. The twelve transpuans were placed in police custody, although they were released the next morning following pressure from legal aid and human rights activists in the province.

In Aceh, hostility toward sexual and gender minorities was common during my research from 2013 to early 2015. While I was there, local legislators drafted Qanun Jinayat, a local criminal bylaw that was issued as part of the implementation of Shari'a law that began in 2001 when the national government gave permission for local Acehnese authorities to operate their own legal system. The situation for sexual and gender minorities in the region continued to worsen following the passage of this new criminal law in October 2015. The law subjected those allegedly involved in consensual same-sex practices to maximum punishments of flogging 100 times in public, a fine of 1,000 grams of gold, or 100 months in prison. Less than a year later, the wave of hostility toward people with nonheteronormative sexualities and transgender expressions swept through many other parts of the country. They were violently targeted by mob violence at the behest of their neighbors and local vigilantes. Police raided their private gatherings and their premises. People were beaten up, arrested, and imprisoned based on allegations of same-sex activities. Increasingly, nonheterosexual and gender nonconforming expressions have become taboo and those who practice them are persecuted in public spaces, such as city streets, universities, and cultural centers, as well as on the internet and through other media.

My first reaction upon finding out about the police raid in 2018 was panic. The incident took place only a few kilometers away from one of my field sites, a peri-urban node that I call Namu.[2] For ten months, my research activities had centered on a hair salon that I called Salon Primadona. The owner of the salon, a twenty-seven-year-old transpuan named Maya (a pseudonym), was kind enough not only to allow me to participate in everyday life in her salon but also to use it as a space for interviewing some of her employees and friends. She also offered the salon as a place for me to live for the duration of my research. This allowed our relationship to grow beyond the conventional researcher-research participant relation. When I saw the news of the police raid, I immediately grabbed my phone to contact Maya via WhatsApp.

Maya responded right away and reported that at that very moment a number of friends and herself were all inside a rented minivan heading out of Aceh. The group included her five employees and six close friends who either owned or worked in hair salons in Namu. Over the following weeks, we maintained contact with each other, mainly to organize logistical support in a temporary shelter, the location of which remained undisclosed, even to me. During this period, on a couple of occasions I asked Maya whether she and her friends were considering the possibilities of settling somewhere outside Aceh. Her answers to my question were similar each time: they had considered this option but would rather wait and see how the situation evolved.

About eight weeks later, Maya and her friends decided to return home. When they returned, they learned that gender nonconformity (defined in an official letter issued by the local government as "imitating the opposite sex") in hair salons had been officially banned in a number of regencies across Aceh, including Namu. The impact of this draconian policy caused a major breakdown of the dynamics at Salon Primadona. Maya told me that since the ban, she and her friends have avoided having group meetings or spending time in the hair salon beyond normal working hours. The Shari'a police, or Wilayatul Hisbah, were regularly inspecting her hair salon to check if she or any of her employees were breaking the municipal government's prohibition on wearing women's clothing. Life inside the hair salon as they knew it had drastically changed.

The story of Maya and her friends' return to Namu and their insistence on staying there, even though they knew they could no longer live in the same way as before, is a prime example of a broader pattern within Muslim queer and transgender lives in Indonesia, where everyday hardships are marked by periods of violence and social exclusion. Because public spheres in Indonesia increasingly display antagonistic responses toward sexual and gender minorities, this book is concerned with understanding those affected by this chronic violence feel.

What compels individuals to continuously inhabit spaces of ambivalence despite their physical fatigue, mental exhaustion, and emotional pain? What happens when one's idea of a good life has consequences that are inherently harmful? Why do people whom society considers to be morally abject persist in using the language of morality that has been weaponized against them? Why do outright rejection and discrimination not deter marginalized individuals from occupying public spaces? Why do these actors persist in seeking ways to be together, even if being together does not necessarily make them less vulnerable to violence? These questions, which emerged from a long-term ethnographic engagement in Indonesia, guide the book's attempt to bear witness to the affective experiences of those who continuously dwell in the impasses and promises of queer and trans religiosity within a predominantly Muslim society—an intersection mainly perceived across world religions as a site of profound dissonance.³

Much has been written about this tension, including in various online and offline think pieces, personal writings, and documentary films, as well as publications by a diverse number of collective initiatives. In Indonesia, as is the case in other regional contexts where there is a growing influence of conservative Islam across a range of public spheres, this tension is based on popular interpretations of Quranic passages and hadith (the sayings and practices of the Prophet Muhammad) that purportedly forbid homosexuality and gender nonconformity.⁴ Indeed, the experiences of Muslim nonheterosexual and transgender people have been taken up as subject matter by scholars from a range of academic disciplines all with differing theoretical assumptions, methodological techniques, and cultural contexts. My ethnographic research, however, has been deeply informed by my observations as a Muslim queer who has lived large parts of my life in Indonesia.

The impulse to pursue this research first emerged in the early 2000s as I witnessed the rise of violent campaigns against sexual and gender minorities in Indonesia's public sphere. These campaigns often happened as sporadic violent events. Vigilante groups, customarily adorned with Islamic symbolism and attributes, started conducting protests and raids on social gatherings held by and for people expressing alternative sexualities and genders.[5] However, this had not always been so.

During the three-decade-long authoritarian rule of President Suharto, which ended in 1998, pernicious vitriol against sexual and gender minorities occasionally surfaced in the public sphere. However, it remained confined to elite political circles, expressed through censure and specific discursive arenas such as religious debates.[6] It was only after the fall of Suharto, a period known as Reformasi, that these sentiments began to escalate into more visible displays of emotional intensity and physical aggression. This development contradicts the more long-standing, familiar stereotype that depicts "'Indonesian culture' as 'tolerant' of homosexuality and transgenderism."[7] It also reveals the subtle, slow, and drawn-out process of sedimentation of violent acts that served to privilege certain ways of being over the practices and behaviors of sexualized and gendered others. The durational nature of these controversies has compelled me to think along with Lauren Berlant, particularly her conceptualizations of "systemic crisis" or "crisis ordinariness"[8], ideas that describe how violent social events are no longer felt as a momentary catastrophe but rather as things that gradually become routine and normalized, rendering them seemingly mundane and insignificant.[9]

At the same time, stories of Muslims who inhabit the interstices between Islamic piety and nonnormative sexualities/genders continue to emerge. In the context of everyday life in Indonesia, these phenomena have been substantiated by empirical studies on what today would be called nonbinary genders within Muslim communities in Sulawesi,[10] the presence of a transpuan Islamic boarding school in Yogyakarta,[11] as well as covert homosexual activities in more traditional Islamic boarding schools in different parts of Java.[12] These findings suggest particular modes in which different actors inhabit seemingly incommensurable differences between living religious and nonnormative ways of life. How do the people who dwell in this seemingly irreconcilable gap feel? How do they emotionally deal with social realities that continue to pit their faith practices against their desires and ways of living? How do they choose between these two incommensurate ideas, and what happens if, for a number of reasons, there are no options to choose from? These were the conundrums that occupied my thoughts at the beginning of my fieldwork.

During my research trips in the period 2013 to 2015, mainly in Aceh, Jakarta, and Yogyakarta, I moved between different urban and peri-urban nodes of Indonesia. In these three regions, I engaged with interlocutors that included Maya and four other individuals I will introduce further on as the main protagonists in this book. An abundance of strong and mixed emotions accompanied our field interactions, which were made up of recorded interviews, casual conversations, and occasional group hangouts. These moments were filled with both joy and warmth and despair and feelings of uncertainty. At times when issues of religiosity popped up in these interactions, a bundle of uneasy feelings would surface. Mostly they were conveyed verbally, sometimes through wordless expressions mediated by mimed or bodily gestures. At other times, there was only a piercing silence. These moments seemed to intimate the boundaries of what was sayable and thinkable among a people subjected to the hostile opposition of religious doctrine and nonnormative sexualities and gender expressions.

A recurring thread weaves through the otherwise seemingly standalone life stories shared in this book. While these accounts detail experiences of personal and collective loss and despair, they coexist with efforts to hold onto hope for a good life despite emergent social realities that routinely demonstrate the opposite of such expectations. Taken together, the narratives are bounded by the impasses and promises of inhabiting queer and trans religiosity, each of them following distinctive affective pathways. Some protagonists were haunted by ongoing existential dilemmas. Some tried to navigate them by either moving toward or away from religious practices and values. Many times, they dealt with various forms and feelings of failure and exhaustion but continued on without necessarily knowing where that would lead. As much as these narratives have compelled me in my own research process, they have also sharpened the focus of this research to illuminate how Muslim queer and trans worldmaking, as a process of fashioning worlds through inhabiting them, operate through the affective dynamics of enduring otherwise.

Enduring Otherwise

The English verb "to endure" carries a range of closely related meanings centering on long-term experience with hardships and painful situations: to carry on despite the obstacles; to put up with something unpleasant; to undergo physically and mentally injurious or difficult situations without yielding, sometimes due to a lack of other options; to remain firm under suffering; to hold out; to last.[13] The concept of endurance has traveled through different disciplinary contexts and thematic fields, along with their different emphases of meaning. Originally, the term was developed in response to modern endurance sports at the turn of the twentieth century. Researchers studying field exercise physiology and sports sciences examined the physiological and psychological factors that influence the human body's ability to exert physical force over a prolonged period.

In more recent times, especially since Elizabeth Povinelli's work on contemporary liberal governance in settler-colonial contexts—particularly in Australia and the United States, the notion of endurance has gained traction in analyses of how marginalized communities continue to live under conditions of systemic challenges, chronic oppression, and structural violence.[14] Povinelli argues that as the "ability to suffer and yet persist," endurance denotes forms of life that inhabit the tension between the political potentials of human agency and their limits.[15]

On an experiential level, endurance as a phenomenon emerges through interconnected temporal, embodied, and agentic dimensions of human experience. As a temporal trope, endurance implies the suspension of time, in which situations of prolonged struggle against dispossession and marginalization seem to be without end and can extend across generations, incorporating both historical legacies and future aspirations. In this scene of living, the flow of time seems to stop, bringing endurance closer to the notion of living in suspended time to its limits.[16] For many subjects who endure the ongoing presence of hardship and vulnerability, these circumstances are often felt to be slow, sluggish, and stagnant. They can be conceived of spatially as the state of reaching an impasse or being stuck.

These aspects constitute the ways endurance manifests as an embodied experience, where infliction, debilitation, and exhaustion take hold as its most perceptible visceral and corporeal markings. They affect not only the individual bodies that endure but also the relations between these bodies. As Povinelli argues, endurance in life is "a realm that includes affective, physical, and social conditions that can depress the brain and immune system, rupture organs as well as bonds with families and friends, and orient violence inward."[17]

Across a spectrum of agential capacities, endurance is often emplaced between two other categories that reflect forms of human action in preserving life: survival and resilience. On one end of the spectrum is survival, which is understood as a capacity to ensure one's existence by overcoming immediate threats. Academic discourse, in particular, frequently reduces survival to passivity. Too often lives in their basic biological sense of existence, or "bare life," as Giorgio Agamben describes them, are interpreted as a living condition deprived of any political dimensions.[18] However, survival requires effort and is never a passive or insignificant act.[19] While the tangible outcomes of such efforts may appear minor, they can be traced in the seams of everyday life as evidence of past and present injustices.[20]

The counterpoint to survival is resilience, which denotes the capacity to bounce back, adapt, and recover from adversity. This term has been adopted by global institutions as a strategic framework for engaging community participation in the alleviation of poverty and the politics of securitization. As Sarah Bracke writes, "In a neoliberal political economy, resilience has become part of the 'moral code': the 'good subjects' of neoliberal times are the ones who are able to act, to exercise their agency, in resilient ways."[21] The key distinction among survival, resilience, and endurance then is that survival pertains to what has to be done, resilience concerns what can be done, and endurance considers what "ought to be done" in the pursuit of preserving life.[22]

Reflecting on the chronic conditions humanitarian aid workers confronted in Palestinian refugee camps, Ilana Feldman addresses the ethical and political quandaries of endurance in social projects that aim to "help people live better with circumstances they cannot change."[23] Feldman underscores the value of endurance as an imperative in situations of prolonged conflict where humanitarian assistance faces a reality where "nothing you can do seems likely to have much effect."[24] She also highlights how endurance ultimately remains fraught with a profound ethico-political conundrum both for the humanitarian actors and recipients: "Is continuing to live enough of a goal when there is so little opportunity to thrive? Can lives be really valued when they are not valued equally?"[25]

While Feldman's line of questioning is informed by the occupational demands of preserving the lives of others, the ethico-political conundrums by the communities involved in my research faced are deeply shaped by the everyday urgencies of self-preservation. Alternatively, then, the prime ethico-political concern of this book is the question of how, through gestures of endurance, people make the effort to help *themselves* and *each other* to live better with circumstances they cannot change. The more pertinent questions framing this inquiry are: What do the protagonists of this book consider *enough of a goal* as they continue to live a life with less opportunity to thrive? What counts as a valued life for those whose lives are continuously devalued as unequal?

This book traces how, within the longue durée of violence targeting Muslim sexual and gender minorities, endurance serves as a fecund site for worldmaking actions. My claim departs from the more commonly held view that due to its often-tenuous nature, endurance limits political agency. In her ethnographic work in a Spanish village besieged by finance-led capitalism, Hadas Weiss posits that endurance is nonpolitical because it focuses on ongoing efforts to get by rather than on an orientation toward the future.[26] Similarly, Ghassan Hage, writing about populist discourse in Australia, argues that while endurance is often regarded as a virtue—a refusal to see oneself as a victim of unchangeable circumstances—it ultimately diminishes political imagination.[27]

However, drawing inspiration from the growing literature on religious women's agency,[28] I take issue with some assessments of endurance as defined through narrow conceptions of agency rooted in the secular "humanist desire for autonomy and self-expression."[29] Saba Mahmood writes in her work on the women's piety movement in Cairo that "agentival capacity is entailed not only in those acts that resist norms but also in the multiple ways in which one *inhabits* norms."[30] For these women, inhabiting norms involves more than rhetorical and rational reasonings; it involves "affective modes of assessment" that "regard subordination to a transcendent will . . . as [their] coveted goal."[31]

While Mahmood's arguments are more focused on the discursive tradition and bodily practices that shape women's religious participation, Sara Ahmed's argument about "queer feelings" is pertinent for defining what inhabiting norms means among nonnormative subjectivities.[32] Ahmed argues that by neither embracing nor rejecting hegemonic social structures, queer lives involve a continual reworking of the very structures that the subjects, willingly or not, inhabit. This is by no means an easy feat. As Ahmed shows, the effects of not fitting the norms can also include a generative discomfort: "Discomfort is not about assimilation or resistance, *but inhabiting norms differently*. The inhabitance is generative insofar as it does not end with the failure of norms to be secured, but with possibilities of living that do not 'follow' those norms through."[33]

This perspective, which suggests the constant failure of queerness to fully fit (hetero)normative scripts alongside their inability to completely break ties with them, reflects attachments that open up different possibilities of living. The challenge that religious women's agency and the queer politics of emotion pose to established liberal assumptions, then, is to disengage from the oppositional subject in theorizing agency and to instead focus on contingently emerging forms of social life and self-conduct. In her work, which propelled the so-called post-secular turn, Rosi Braidotti further troubles these assumptions by challenging us to move beyond equating "political creativity/agency with negativity, or unhappy consciousness."[34] Not only does such an intervention displace the autonomous subject from its hegemonic form, it also allows for the consideration of multiple affirmative and creative forms of subjectivity and consciousness beyond those defined by oppression and marginality. In practice, this means that instead of political and ethical agency remaining dependent or oppositional to the current conditions, it becomes instead "affirmative and geared to creating possible futures. . . . Ethical relations create possible worlds."[35]

Echoing the various critical engagements by authors who aim to debunk the readymade accounts of agency as well as Elizabeth Povinelli's notion of "anthropology of the otherwise," the forms of enduring this book elaborates on take form as ways of living differently alongside dominant modes of being.[36] Writing about how urban poor communities in the Global South survive in the city, AbdouMaliq Simone poetically describes how otherwise possibilities emerge through the modality of enduring:

> Endurance depends upon the continuous fascination of discovery—the willingness to suspend the familiar and even the counted-upon in order to engage something unexpected. This engagement may sometimes simply reiterate a commitment to what already is, where the person decides that it is better to stay put with what is familiar. At other times, effort is made to find a way to make what is discovered useful, to incorporate it into one's life or see it as another vehicle to be occupied, and where time and energy is transferred from one way of being in the world into another.[37]

Many of the protagonists in this book enact a form of endurance resonant with this view. For them, inhabiting the mundane routines of dealing with life's daily grinds renders efforts to live alongside and against what Berlant calls "crisis ordinariness" as a means of hinting at the potential of creating other ways of being in the world. Hence the *otherwise*.[38]

As Ashon T. Crawley describes it in *Blackpentecostal Breath*, the otherwise "announces the fact of infinite alternatives to what *is*. . . . Otherwise possibilities exist alongside that which we can detect with our finite sensual capacities."[39] Riffing on Crawley, enduring otherwise connotes forms of life deeply entangled with constraints—both constant and violent—while remaining invested in practices of making worlds for overcoming these very constraints and interrogating what can be done differently. The spaces of otherwise that are of interest in this book do not represent a radical rupture with actual social formation nor are they autonomous from established religious norms. Instead, they emerge from the ordinary conduct and everyday narratives produced by the subtle acts of making, unmaking, and remaking the ethical and political possibilities—for oneself and with others—while inhabiting a world of chronic violence.

As I will show, viewed through the lens of affective dynamics, Muslim queer and trans worldmaking involves enacting capacities to endure past and present difficult personal situations and unjust social circumstances while conjuring worlds that do not yet exist. As a concept, the otherwise offers an intellectual, ethical, and political means of critically conceiving a generative relation that cannot be known in advance, one that exceeds categorical thinking and eludes reductive explanation.

While this book mainly draws on ethnographic material collected in Indonesia, these experiences are likely to be shared elsewhere by people who find themselves deeply enmeshed in the tensile intersections of gender, sexuality, and religion. Approaching Islamic practices and discourses in terms of social affinity, institutionalized authority, and self-cultivation through the many lenses of queer and trans worldmaking forms an arena where violent tensions not only prevail but also shapeshift. The affective narratives and experiences this book focuses on reveal how imbricated they are with religious practices, feelings, and attachments—best described using the term "*keyakinan*," or faith.[40] This emic term downplays the exaggerated dichotomy between institutionalized religiosity and personalized spirituality.[41] Joseph N. Goh articulates this in his seminal work on Malaysian trans men, where he argues that faith is expressed through material and spiritual practices that connect individuals to the "ultimate reality," defined as "the sense and meaning that cradle the visible materiality of human existence."[42]

In this book, the protagonists' engagements with faith—as both a source of and a manifestation of endurance—often take shape as a double bind. While some appear to be made by choice, others seem less voluntary. Many shared stories with me of having to reckon with the constraints of an Islamic conservative tradition that prohibits same-sex intimacy and gender nonconformity. These compelling forces of religion in Muslim queer and trans worldmaking reveal the more gruesome aspects of endurance. Enduring, in this sense, manifests through multimodal practices of withstanding, living through, putting up with, and suffering vulnerable and unpredictable relationships with normative violence, all within shrinking social spaces and limited material conditions. Most of the time, this is the only affective gesture that can be enunciated while dealing with stagnation and other states of disrepair. Endurance is far from a heroic act; it is fundamentally tied to forms of struggle to last over time during painful experiences without being decimated by them.[43]

On the other hand, by continuing to continue—alongside the risk of losing the necessary ground for survival, coupled with chronic exhaustion—the book's protagonists are also impelled by faith as they strive to lead a good life. Thus, enduring painful realities is not about denying or dismissing the suffering they bring, but about embodying and enacting values that keep open the possibilities that such conditions will not remain as they are. Religion becomes both a personal and collective source of enduring otherwise through affective meaning-making and spiritual healing.

Both cases show something important about the role of religion in the ongoingness of enduring otherwise in Muslim queer and trans worldmaking. The following chapters detail how these affective experiences diverge from the binary terms of resistance and subordination to the norm.[44] They explore how in enduring the tensile relationship between religion as lived experience and hegemonic structure, the protagonists open up more capacious possibilities for ways of being and belonging to queer and trans communities of faith.

The English word endurance does not have a literal translation in Indonesian, so its meaning is conveyed implicitly in my interactions with the protagonists of this book. However, I draw the meanings and ideas of endurance from Indonesian words that share an affinity of meaning, such as *bertahan* (to dwell or withstand), *menjalani* (to undergo or live through), *menderita* (to suffer), and other terms that convey a sense of the physical, mental, and affective labor involved in dealing with adversity.

The core argument of this book shares an epistemic affinity with scholars who attend to the heterogeneous ways that affects, emotions, and feelings open up new political possibilities for actors who are struggling with ongoing violence, structural inequalities, and other protracted forms of social marginalization.[45] It is also aligned with scholarship that investigates how queer and trans sociability has been historically intertwined with affective experiences of injury, social exclusion, failure, and all sorts of bad feelings.[46] I am aware that presenting a severe outlook on queer and transgender lives in Islamic contexts carries the risk of backfiring, particularly because such portrayals are often misused to justify imperialist, racist, and Islamophobic agendas.[47] As Nikita Dhawan points out, however, it remains crucial to address both Western and non-Western worlds related to the degradation of sexual and gender minorities.[48] This becomes even more crucial as the politics of essentializing violence gains more ground worldwide. It is both theoretically urgent and practically necessary to critically examine questions of inequality, particularly in light of the constantly shifting politics of gender and sexuality in different parts of the globe.

The framing of the global order into a "Global West versus the rest" or a Global North versus Global South has been based on differences in the political, legal, and sociocultural treatment of sexual and gender minorities. However, this binary view is losing explanatory power in light of the recent propagation of socially conservative programs and their attendant anti-queer and anti-trans rhetoric that traverse the purported divides. In some Global South countries such as Uganda, Malaysia, and Indonesia, the emergence and escalating persecution of sexual and gender minorities are the products of the continuing extensive links between local elites and Western conservative forces that were established during colonial times. This is substantiated in Rahul Rao's research on the co-production of homophobic discourses between Ugandan and U.S.-based Christian evangelicals.[49] His account challenges the simplistic view of Ugandan culture as uniquely homophobic, especially since the 2009 Anti-Homosexuality Law, and argues that "the Ugandan story reveals 'homophobia' to be more opportunistic, sometimes functioning in the service of imperial collaboration and at other times expressing a decolonial impulse."[50] The ways that marginalization of gender and sexual minorities is perpetuated across different regions globally demonstrates how the political dimensions of gender and sexuality remain deeply shaped by colonial legacies.

In writing this book, I have sought to adhere to the ethnographic impulse of staying true to the heartbreaking material that constitutes the research findings.[51] This book is not an attempt to give voice to the silenced and it is equally not about glorifying the protagonists' heroic struggle against structural violence or dramatizing their suffering to produce a trope of victimhood.[52] Instead, my focus is on understanding the complexities of Muslim queer and trans worldmaking within religious structures and beliefs that implicate violence. This ethnographic inquiry thus serves as testimony for how endurance becomes both a means of continuing to continue and a way for the protagonists to remake the world. How do people live otherwise in situations in which they are deprived of the possibility to do so? How does endurance provide a way of becoming something other than being utterly undermined by circumstances that one cannot change?

Affective Dynamics

This book focuses on affective dynamics as an entry point for carving out an ethnographic understanding of how Muslim queer and trans worldmaking in Indonesia emerges as a mode of enduring otherwise.

The concept of affective dynamics is best understood as a constellation of bodily experiences and enactments linked to the arousal of affects, emotions, and feelings. To clarify how this concept is applied in my analysis, I detail here how affects, emotions, and feelings function as distinct yet interconnected phenomena.

Affect is broadly understood to refer to a state or domain involving certain processes that are actualized when bodies register physiological arousal.[53] The resulting impression from these sensuous and material configurations is, however, imprecise and incomplete. Although affect theorist Brian Massumi's definition of affect underscores its operation as vital forces that exist beyond discursive meaning, language, or semantic capture, my understanding of affect is grounded in its display as observable situations.[54] Appearing to be excessive, ephemeral, and nonconscious, affective intensities remain contingently entangled with their material expressions, such as narrative, everyday speech, facial expression, bodily gesture, movement, tone of voice, or even silence and immobility. Even though affect-related experiences are not always transparently represented or clearly predetermined by language or discourse—at least at the level of observation—affect is conditioned within the boundaries of matter and meaning.[55]

The second component, emotions, are bodily sensations through which experiential registers are always-already-organized socially and culturally coded meanings and narratives.[56] Emotions are embodied social and relational processes. As Thomas Stodulka, Samia Dinkelaker, and I have discussed elsewhere, the expression and labeling of emotions is tied to cultural repertoires and can motivate actions and interactions and be conveyed by a person without necessarily changing their physiological state.[57]

The third component, feelings, refers to the subjective processing of bodily arousals, which shapes affects and emotions into objects of self-awareness.[58] Some feelings may evolve into emotions, while others are related to "extra-emotional" bodily sensations such as hunger, thirst, and pain or arise from embodied social interactions. Additionally, there are subtle and elusive feelings, such as those described by the term "gut feeling."[59] In Indonesian, "feeling" is translated as "*rasa*." The noun form is "*perasaan*" and the verb form is "*merasa*" (to feel). These are more commonly used than "*emosi*" (emotion) and "*afek*" (affect). The significance of rasa in daily social interactions has been explored by various Indonesianists.[60] Philosopher Franz Magnis-Suseno writes that in Javanese cosmologies, "rasa" encompasses a subjective experience that includes "the feeling of physicality and sensibility, the feeling of one's position in a field of interaction, and the feeling of unity with the universe."[61]

Within the triadic constellation of affects, emotions, and feelings, this means that while affects involve the materialization of bodily intensities, feelings register such forces as subjective experience and emotions are involved when a subject makes meaning from this experience through social and culturally constructed, shared, and circulated forms of expression.[62] These definitions all emphasize the relational aspects of affects, emotions, and feelings as biocultural processes.[63] The significance of these processes can vary based on the fluidity and proximity of meaning making and the communication practices involved as well as the spatiotemporal contexts in which feelings emerge as subjective experiences, emotions exist in between, and affects spread across bodies. However, in everyday life, these distinctions often blur as they intertwine in different ways and to varying extents. Hence, I use the analytical term "affective dynamics" to mark the active entanglements of affects, emotions, and feelings within processes of bodily arousal, the formation of subjectivity, and social interaction.

As I engage with the unfolding affective dynamics in my interactions with the protagonists of this book, I introduce two analytical tools. The first tool, *emotives*, aims to unravel the complexities of emotions and their expression. As defined by William Reddy, emotives go beyond mere verbal expressions of emotions to include speech acts that can generate, transform, conceal, or intensify affects, emotions, and feelings. They function as a mode of communication that actively influences the world.[64] Verbal articulations of emotions, however, are not the only prominent feature of my ethnographic material. Other features include various forms of bodily gesture, metaphor, digression, or subjunctive mood—or to put it simply, other forms of narrating wherein feelings were minimally described but were equally affective. To assist the analysis, I call this inchoate, ambiguous, and inarticulate emergence of intensity within narratives and interactions an *affective repertoire*. This tool helps chart how affects, emotions, and feelings circulate among the various subjectivities involved in co-producing ethnographic insights.

The Making of This World

More than two decades have passed since Lauren Berlant and Michael Warner, in their influential essay "Sex in Public," discussed the generative implications of queer worldmaking as a social project which opens up spaces for otherwise possibilities, characterized as "entrances, exits, unsystematized lines of acquaintance, projected horizons, typifying examples, alternate routes, blockages, incommensurate geographies."[65] Similarly, drawing on Nelson Goodman's exploration of "worlds" in language and literature, José Esteban Muñoz, in *Disidentifications*, adopts the term queer worldmaking as the "mode of being in the world that is also inventing the world."[66] For Muñoz, this mode of living involves persistent negotiation by marginalized subjects as they navigate dominant structures to reimagine possibilities for self-determination against the odds.

In this book, I aim to broaden the concept of worldmaking by examining how Muslim sexual and gender minorities in Indonesia live and reimagine possible worlds within their specific cultural, religious, and political contexts. Unlike the common approach among Anglophone scholars, who often prioritize "queer" or "trans" when exploring the intersections of Islam with alternative sexualities or genders, I place "Muslim" before "queer" and "trans" as analytical terms. This is particularly relevant in societies like Indonesia, where Islam is a central organizing force in both personal and collective life. This choice was inspired by a conversation with one of the book's protagonists, who questioned the common use of the term "queer Muslim," asking, "What if people identify themselves first as Muslim and then as queer?" This insight played a key role in shaping an analytical framework where Islam is not merely an intersecting aspect of identity with queerness or transness but a central, structuring element of the worldmaking process.

The term "Muslim" used in this book is neither monolithic nor universally applicable. As many scholars have emphasized, it embodies ambiguity, indeterminacy, and tension—both as a belief system and as a lived, normative, and discursive tradition.[67] In Indonesia, where over 85 percent of the population identifies as Muslim, this term encompasses a range of subject positions. The dynamics of pluralistic Islam in Indonesia have grown more complex in recent years, shaped by Islamic revivalism and conservatism following the Indonesian Reformasi in 1998.[68]

The political transition led to the emergence of various Islamic move-ments with differing agendas, including militants, liberals, moderates, and exclusivists,[69] alongside a rise in Islamic expressions in popular cul-ture[70] and religious piety in both personal and public spheres.[71] This context underscores the necessity of understanding the relational com-plexity that makes "Muslim" an evolving and open-ended framework.

The utilization of "queer and trans" as an analytical framework in this book warrants further explanation. This framing is made with awareness of the ongoing discourse in U.S.-based queer and trans stud-ies. As succinctly captured by Melissa Wilcox, these fields intersect most productively when they examine "spaces, people, texts, bodies, arts, and events that disrupt normative structures in order to understand and unsettle those norms."[72] However, the distinction between these fields remains crucial, primarily because queer studies tend not to fully engage with the material specificities of transgender people's experiences, instead using gender nonnormativity as an allegory for queerness.[73] While these insights have been generative, the decision to center both queer and trans in this book's terminology reflects the historical and geopolitical specificities of how these transnationally circulating concepts reshape worldmaking processes in the local context.

As an English loanword, the term "queer" began to gain traction in Indonesian discourse around the early 2000s, particularly within urban middle-class and activist circles.[74] Its uneven spread across urban and rural areas reflects the varying connections between local lesbian and gay communities and transnational queer discourses. Evelyn Blackwood notes that this process creates a space where individuals form communal bonds through a shared sense of *sama-jiwa* (same soul), grounded not necessarily in shared sexuality but in a common understanding of being similar types of people.[75] The term's local adoption is also tied to the increasing scrutiny of sexual and gender minorities in Indonesia. Gay activist Dede Oetomo explains that queer serves as a way to bypass the prejudice and social stigma attached to traditional gay and lesbian labels, describing it as "a more neutral and indirect term, akin to a *kromo inggil* [high Javanese] equivalent of gay in a culture that values euphemism and allusion in its discursive modes."[76]

Benjamin Hegarty traces the emergence of the terms "trans" or "transgender" in Indonesia to the mid-2010s, when activists adopted it to advance new forms of recognition.[77] By the late 2010s, terms like "trans" gained visibility through national online news and social media, encompassing identities such as *transpuan* and *waria* for trans feminine individuals, and *trans laki-laki, trans man*, or *priawan* for trans masculine people. Their adoption instigated intergenerational debates about their effectiveness in advancing social recognition. Similar to the discourse around "queer," the local embrace of the term "trans" reflects ongoing efforts to redefine societal acceptance and pursue self-determination through transnational connections.

* * *

After having explored this range of terminological designations, the question arises: what *world* is being made, unmade, and remade at the intersections of gender, sexuality, and religion in contemporary Indonesia? This book shows that enduring otherwise as the affective dynamics of Muslim queer and trans worldmaking is deeply about creating the space of possibilities within the specificities of *this* world that we inhabit rather than seeking out fixed new worlds as predetermined narratives or destinations.[78]

The world that lurks as the background of these projects, as I hinted earlier, involves a long history of complicated attitudes toward same-sex intimacy and gender nonconformity. Various scholars have explored the complexities of how same-sex eroticism and gender pluralism have influenced local social dynamics from the early modern period through the postcolonial era in Indonesia.[79] Throughout Indonesian history, same-sex intimacy and people with ambiguous gender were generally met by paradoxically lenient and indignant attitudes.[80] Rather than rehashing the entire discourse again here, I seek to highlight the continuities and changes that have shaped the heightened climate of rejection and repression toward sexual and gender minorities in present-day Indonesia.

In the 1980s, within a decade and a half after the rise to power of Suharto's authoritarian regime through an anti-communist purge, the state began tightening its regulatory grip in response to the increasing visibility of diverse local gender and sexual expressions, such as "*gay*," "*lesbi*,"[81] "*tomboi*," and "*waria*."[82] This shift occurred despite earlier political activity, including the establishment of the first waria organization, Himpunan Wadam Djakarta (Hiwad) in the 1970s, and continued into the late 1990s with organizations that advocated for sexual rights and reproductive health, many of which received international support for HIV/AIDS prevention.

In the meantime, Indonesian traditional cultures and belief systems have continued to strongly emphasize heterosexual marriage as a key marker of adulthood. This emphasis is reinforced by the New Order government's advocacy of the family principle (*azas kekeluargaan*), which centers on the heterosexual nuclear family. National media portrayals further contribute to viewing sexual and gender minorities as abject.[83]

Despite the political regime change in 1998, everyday heterosexism persists and has even escalated, as evidenced by increased surveillance and direct violence that targets sexual and gender minorities identified with the acronym LGBT (Lesbian, Gay, Bisexual and Transgender).[84] Since early 2016, anti-LGBT discourse—fueled by Islamic populism and neoliberal governance—has portrayed the family as the last bastion against what is framed as the "LGBT threat."[85] Defense Minister Ryacudu underscored this sentiment by defining the extreme danger of LGBT as its invisibility: "It's dangerous because we can't see who our foes are, but out of the blue, everyone is brainwashed."

In response to these alarmist narratives, feminist writer Intan Paramaditha highlights that they hark back to the New Order's framing of "OTB" (*organisasi tanpa bentuk*), or "organizations without shape."[86] This term was used to invoke the image of the nonexistent remnants of the Communist movement silently working to disrupt social order. The portrayal of members of the LGBT community as a national threat whose disruptive influence stems from their ability to hide within familiar settings of everyday life has made them a target onto which Cold War–era paranoid politics are projected.[87]

This is a world where Muslim queer and trans desires for acceptance are persistently met with mainstream responses that perceive them as threats. Despite the deep fractures in Muslim queer and trans people's relationship with it, this remains the only world they have. AbdouMaliq Simone writes about how the lived experiences of urban majorities in the Global South often hinge on the broken relationships to the world they inhabit: "What matters is *this* time, *this* instance, and what can be done with the tools we have now. What relations can be configured to access materials and capacities to act expeditiously, to minimize suffering, and reduce long-term damage?"[88] By remaining faithful to the brokenness of this world—enduring with little hope of moving forward or being accepted by broader society—Muslim queer and trans worldmaking becomes inherently open and anticipatory, creating a space for the otherwise, where something that may or may not yet exist can intervene.

Following the Heart

In recent years, scholars across various disciplines have introduced the term "affective ethnography" to describe burgeoning research practices that acknowledge the centrality of affect and emotions in knowledge production.[89] This book's approach is rooted in this contemporary scholarship, embracing the affective dimensions of ethnographic fieldwork as a guiding principle.

Two intellectual traditions ground this approach. The first is the anthropological discourse on self-reflexivity, positionality, and research ethics that gained prominence from the late 1970s to the early 1990s.[90] The second can be traced to the efforts of feminist anthropologists to reclaim emotions as valid ways of knowing both the self and the world.[91] The call for greater attention to affect in ethnographic research gained critical momentum two decades later, advanced by a number of psychological anthropologists.[92] While their arguments vary, they converge on the importance of ethnographers' affective practices and emotional experiences, which not only offer insights into the life worlds, people, and spaces they study but also carry valuable methodological and epistemological significance when carefully and systematically addressed.

In a research practice that takes the affective valence of fieldwork seriously, to give accounts of how research interlocutors experience suffering, despair, joy, or mourning without making ourselves vulnerable as ethnographers is tantamount to exploitative research conduct. What is at stake here is "the risk of reproducing simplifying dichotomies by putting them into emotional 'hot seats,' and presenting the anthropological persona as 'cool,' and more 'reasonable' in abstracting 'thoughts' from 'feelings,' or 'culture' from 'nature.'"[93] Yet this approach is far from straightforward. As anthropologist Kathleen Stewart evocatively describes it, "This is a method that tries to move in the manner of things slipping in and out of existence. One that makes demands on visceral imaginaries and the sensoria. As an ethnographic method, this would be a mode of thought that tries to describe the things that also propel it. Its objects would be its subjects."[94]

In this book, I make explicit the heuristic import of affective ethnography, guided by the metaphor "following the heart" (or *mengikuti kata hati*),[95] a term that originates from the traditional opposition between the rational mind and the emotional heart. However, the aim here is to move beyond this simplistic binary and engage with following the heart as a mode of homing in on the researcher's "capacity to affect and be affected" in relation to all the elements of a fieldwork encounter, including its environments, places, situations, materialities, and people and the process of writing an ethnographic account.[96]

As we will see, many of the steps that I took in the course of fieldwork mainly depended on what to me *felt right*. This approach has colored my considerations of how to engage with social relations and material-spatial environments, who I formed close bonds with in the field, who I distanced myself from, and which methods I used to elicit stories from the interlocutors. At the same time, this "feeling right" was never entirely based on my own experience but was generated through moments of sharing feelings *together with* others in the field. Following the heart therefore emphasizes the epistemic value of affective dynamics in the field by prioritizing relational and embodied ways of producing knowledge.

More than Dots on a Map

As noted earlier, I conducted my fieldwork in three locations: Aceh, Jakarta, and Yogyakarta. In anthropological terms, this approach is known as "multi-sited ethnography." The process of constructing an ethnographic object in this context involves literally following people, things, metaphors, narratives, lives, biographies, and conflicts.[97] I adapted George Marcus's "modes of following" by aligning them with the "heart"—the affective impulses that guided my research, deeply shaped by my personal biography and the cultural, political, and historical contexts of each field site.

My fieldwork spanned a total of fifteen months. I spent around six months in Aceh and divided the remaining time between Yogyakarta and

Jakarta. My initial motivation to conduct research in Aceh stemmed from a personal desire to connect with my ancestral roots. Raised in Jakarta in an aspiring middle-class family, I spent much of my early adulthood in Yogyakarta, also on Java. My paternal grandparents had migrated from Aceh to the more densely populated island of Java in the late 1960s in search of better opportunities. Before beginning my fieldwork in 2013, I had never visited Aceh, and my initial impressions of the region were shaped largely by stories passed down from my elders.

Growing up, it was common for people in my surroundings to make assumptions about my cultural heritage as an Acehnese, identifiable through my given first name, Teuku, an ethnic title typically given to a male born into a noble family in the region. I remember blushing when I was asked, "Have you been to Aceh? Do you speak the language?" During my teenage years, I spent much time following the news of the armed conflict between the military and armed combatants who demanded a fully independent Nanggroe Aceh Darussalam. This conflict, ongoing since 1976, prompted a longing in my young mind to better understand my cultural heritage. The desire to connect with Aceh grew stronger after the December 24, 2004, tsunami that devastated much of Banda Aceh and the northwestern coast.[98] As the region began recovering, the thirty-year civil war ended in 2005, following the implementation of Shari'a in 2001. Since then, reports of corporal punishment and human rights abuses have increasingly shaped global perceptions of Aceh as "radicalizing," "dangerous," and "backward."[99] These factors led to warnings before my research journey. My supervisors advised against visiting Aceh, citing safety risks. Colleagues urged me to stay alert and to leave at the first sign of danger. In the remaining parts of the book, my discussion of Aceh will evidence how the disparaging imaginaries about the region are redressed by the communities I encountered in the field.

The second site, Yogyakarta, was a place that I had considered for quite some time as my home, at least for ten years until I moved to Berlin to undertake my PhD program in 2012. It was here that I began my queer activism by organizing a queer film festival from 2005 to 2009. The festival ran without major issues in a city known for its public tolerance—until one evening in 2009, when a group of vigilantes stormed one of the festival venues.[100] This protest marked the beginning of a new wave of violence against sexual and gender minorities in the city.

It is this complex intermixing of biography and the feelings generated by bearing witness to, and to some extent, experiencing the shifting situations of Yogyakarta and Aceh that motivated me to connect and juxtapose these sparsely distributed points on the geographical map as designated sites for my study. Such geographical units are not comparable by scale. Yogyakarta (or Yogya in short) is an urban environment, part of the Yogyakarta Special Region, while Jakarta, the capital city of Indonesia, forms part of the massive Jabodetabek (Greater Jakarta) urban agglomeration. In Aceh, I conducted fieldwork in two peri-urban towns, Namu and Rancong, which are administrative towns in adjacent regencies on the northern coast of Aceh. The towns are only an hour apart by motorbike and I rotated my research stay between Namu and Rancong, commuting between them when possible.

Midway through my fifteen months of fieldwork, I added Jakarta as a third research site. Initially, Jakarta was a brief stopover between trips to Yogyakarta and Aceh. This shift occurred after my research in Aceh faced unexpected hurdles. A serious nerve-related illness forced me to return to Jakarta for recovery at my mother's home. Two months later, still recuperating, I returned to Aceh only to find that my relationships with key contacts had faded due to my prolonged absence and lack of communication. Feeling exasperated, I began to question whether continuing my fieldwork in Aceh was a viable path forward. After sharing my frustration with a colleague, their feedback prompted me to revisit the stories I had already collected, combing through them for overlooked insights or aspects that needed deeper scrutiny. This process brought to mind narratives shared with me during my coming of age as a Muslim queer in Jakarta, long before my formal research had begun. Reflecting on these earlier experiences not only reignited my determination to continue in Aceh but also transformed my fieldwork into a personal return to formative relationships in Jakarta.

This distress over lost connections in Aceh and the decision to add Jakarta as a research site is one example of many emotional experiences that accompanied my fieldwork. Various other affective responses engulfed me through this time: the elation when a community embraced my presence in the field, the anxiety when people failed to reply to my invitation to meet up or the boredom of waiting until they become available, intermingled with the disappointments over unkept appointments, feelings of isolation and loneliness produced by new environments or the thrill of going to new places and meeting new faces, and feeling apathetic due to physical exhaustion and the constant mental meandering between all these different emotions. These are all part of "field emotions" that are familiar to many anthropologists and had been shared in various ethnographic reports.[101] To me, however, these accounts can do more than just nod toward the self-reflexive project of ethnography. As researchers who share presence in the lifeworlds we study, we deepen our understanding of the experiences of those we encounter in the field by attuning to how affectivity is inscribed in our embodied realities.

Vulnerable Entanglements

Another key aspect of following the heart is how it informed my methods for gathering empirical material in vulnerable research settings. As I sought to establish contact with potential research participants in each of the three locations, different challenges arose. What constitutes a "first encounter" varied across localities, shaped by contingent factors such as privilege, vulnerability, social networks, and language. During fieldwork, I primarily communicated in Indonesian because most people in each area speak it in addition to their local languages, such as Javanese or Acehnese. Although I had lived in Yogyakarta for nearly ten years and had gained a good passive understanding of Javanese, I never felt comfortable speaking it due to its hierarchical structure, which includes ngoko (low), madya (middle), and krama (high) speech levels, each reflecting varying degrees of intimacy and respect based on social status. Even though some relatives on my father's side are fluent in Acehnese, I never had the opportunity to learn it properly.

Correspondence with people in my hometown, Jakarta, and my adopted hometown, Yogyakarta, was relatively smooth due to my long involvement in the local queer scenes. However, my experience in Aceh was quite different, even though I used the snowball method, following up on contact suggestions from LGBTQ activists in Yogyakarta and Jakarta. During the early stages of fieldwork in Aceh, my attempts to establish reciprocal exchanges often fell short, even with the use of researcher self-disclosure. By sharing personal and professional details,

I aimed to "level the playing field" and build trust with potential participants, particularly in vulnerable or hard-to-reach groups.[102]

However, in Aceh, many of these efforts were met with subtle refusals,
such as unreturned messages or, in some cases, direct antagonism. One
individual, for instance, declined participation due to suspicions that my
research was an attempt to create scandal. Despite being Indonesian, the
fact that my research was hosted by a German university led to concerns
about my association with a "Western-biased" approach and misrepre-
sentation of Acehnese Muslim culture. This strong reaction reflects
broader social practices of silence and secrecy conditioned by Aceh's
post-tsunami and postconflict geopolitical position within Indonesia.[103]
Another cause of this climate of discretion is the widespread sense of vulnerability shared among sexual and gender minorities in Aceh in the
face of increasing stigma and public persecution. I acknowledge that my
research topic entails the risk of what scholars have described as "stigma
contagion," where the researcher may share the stigma with participants,
potentially exposing them to unwanted disclosure and further risk due to
the taboo nature of the research.[104]

Even in more favorable situations, I remained sensitive to how my
questions were received. For instance, in my interactions with gay individuals in the field, I employed the common practice of "everyone is in the
know" (*tahu sama tahu*), a tacit understanding that avoids direct reference.[105] When possible, I used indirect language related to behavior or
attraction, such as "*aku kayak gini*" (I'm like this) or "*tertarik sama lelaki
lain*" (attracted to other men) or the term "*sekong*" (a self-referential
term derived from "*sakit*," meaning sick, used to reappropriate negative
views of homosexuality). These more nuanced terms allowed me and the
research participants to engage meaningfully with the subject matter
without getting caught up in debates over terminology.

My interactions in the field with lesbian subjectivities took a different
course. While there was still a tacit understanding that we "knew" what
we were discussing, these conversations involved less self-description
and fewer allusions or euphemisms. One exceptional case is my field
interaction with transpuan, who appeared more comfortable with direct
self-expression, likely due to the historical visibility of trans femininity
in Indonesia's urban life under the New Order regime.[106] As indicated
by the many undulating forms of connectedness that occurred during

my research encounters, ethnographic rapport is shaped by gendered relations.

The ethical tensions of following the heart influenced my choice of tools for gathering ethnographic material. While some material in this book comes from audio-recorded conversations, most derives from informal discussions. The use of audio technology was limited, as many research participants feared for their safety if our recorded conversations were made public. It goes without saying that I have followed anthropological convention, using pseudonyms and altering identifying details.

Recorded or not, some of the protagonists described our conversations as *curhat* sessions. Curhat is an abbreviation of *curahan hati*; literally, "to pour out one's heart," that is, to unburden oneself by having a heart-to-heart talk.[107] The curhat moments proceed in a contingent rhythm emanating from the intersubjective sharing of time and space between myself and the research participant. During these intimate exchanges, we often took turns discussing our feelings about past, present, and future experiences. Such intimate interactions usually demanded my full presence and deep listening as an ethnographer, so I avoided taking notes in situ. Instead, I documented new insights from these conversations by writing them down in the field diary in between field encounters.

* * *

By invoking biographical threads rooted in my cultural background and the vulnerable settings of my encounters with the book's protagonists, I foreground how, through following the heart, we can make affective experiences epistemologically productive without veering into the "confessional tales" style of ethnography.[108] This method has allowed me to broaden my understanding of the "field" in ethnographic research beyond spatial and temporal bounds, turning it into a compound world where affective responses to people, objects, places, and situations coalesce. These responses are shaped by past, present, and future relationships, blending relational and political dynamics as both our self-understanding and our understanding of others evolve.[109]

Anthropologists have long valued serendipity as a productive aspect of ethnographic fieldwork.[110] But rather than framing these influential yet unplanned moments of gaining insight as the materialization of fleeting external forces, I consider following the heart a research device that cultivates the researcher's capacity to remain attuned to what we feel during, before, and after fieldwork; how we are affected by encounters with others; and how others are affected by us. It involves letting emotions, affects, and feelings guide the research process, shaping our engagement with field interactions and the insights they offer.

These junctures remind us that as ethnographers, we share an affective continuum with our interlocutors, even as these connections manifest differently. Listening to and bearing witness to emotionally charged narratives entails navigating the complexities of our own cognitive and interpretive limits. Translating them into writing involves capturing their depth while conveying the emerging affective dynamics in a way that speaks to those who have not experienced them firsthand. Following the heart is not about abandoning "rational" research techniques in favor of emotional impulses; rather, it is about continually adapting and reinventing our research practice as our bodies not only become affected by ethnographic encounters but also co-shape them affectively.

The Chapters

As the multiple hearts of this book, the following chapters are configured as a fleshing out of the broad spectrum of affective dynamics enacted by Muslim queer and trans worldmaking in Indonesia in enduring otherwise. The chapters are intentionally organized to move back and forth between personal life stories and interpersonal interactions—to intercept the multidirectionality of affective dynamics that infuse the ethnographic findings.

Chapter 1 illuminates how Muslim queer and trans worldmaking is permeated by the affective dynamics of *konflik batin* (inner conflict). As a psychologically nuanced catchphrase in popular discourse, "inner conflict" captures perfectly the lived experiences of many Muslim sexual and gender minorities who experience significant emotional and mental turbulence resulting from their failure to reconcile their conflicting subjectivities. This chapter draws from the life stories of three protagonists, Rizky, Tino, and Anna. Each of them shares distinct experiences as they struggle with inner conflict throughout their life, many of which are recurring moments of moral breakdown. These affective dynamics are also suffused with mental health issues, gendered hierarchies, and queer intimacy. They shed light on the ways enduring the double bind of queer desires and religious aspiration become both a source of frustration and exhaustion and a modality for adjusting mental and sensual capacities in order to live on.

In Chapter 2, the affective dynamics of navigating inner conflict are relayed in an intersubjective field of interaction. The chapter focuses on the ethnographic material collected through participant observations in two group interactions in Aceh, in the transpuan community in Namu and in a gay community in Rancong. It examines how the affective dynamics of moral and ethical engagements in Muslim queer and trans worldmaking in Indonesia have emanated through interpersonal relationships as members of both communities cultivate forms of moral participation that go beyond simply resisting or submitting to dominant religious norms.

Chapter 3 takes a detour into the life stories of two protagonists: Maya, who we met at the opening of this book, and Ali. Both of their personal narratives are interwoven with accounts of violent events experienced in different life stages. Ali's story is centered on his hardships in self-identifying as queer while growing up in a religious family, while Maya's story centers on her daily exposure to communal forms of normative violence. These actors have adopted different tactics for putting up with situations where change for the better seems unattainable. They do this mainly by working through their memories of past violence and by holding on to present circumstances that are inherently unpredictable in order to create temporary moments of intimate attachment as social projects for making everyday life bearable.

The discussion of responses to violence is extended to a collective setting in chapter 4. In this context, the term *komunitas* (community) has been alternatively envisioned as a modality of collectivizing amid ongoing structural marginalization and the harmful gestures of hetero- and cisnormative societies. This chapter illuminates the various ways Muslim queer and trans worldmaking processes engage with the affective repertoires of safety, care, and belonging by drawing on two case studies: the trans community in Aceh and a queer of faith activist camp in Yogyakarta. Both accounts delineate how community configurations are built not only through sentimental affinity but also by shared experiences of enduring protracted violence.

The book concludes by thinking through how affective dynam-ics shape endurance as an everyday mode of engaging with otherwise possibilities—a way of living that recognizes life's inherent harms while striving to undo them. The conclusion offers insights into how this mode becomes a means for fostering ethical relationships that involve staying with pain as a way of worldmaking. It also considers the potential of endurance as an epistemic tool, deepening the ethical practices of affective ethnography. The chapter ends with a final story that recasts the cunning of endurance in Muslim queer and trans worldmaking—one that both hints at what lies beyond its horizon and offers new possibilities for others to live on or, if I dare say, even thrive.

1

Inhabiting Inner Conflict

In contemporary Indonesia, people frequently assume that Muslim sexual and gender minorities are constantly subjected to emotional and mental turmoil. This is exemplified by the catchphrase "*konflik batin*," or inner conflict, that is used to depict the psychological makeup of Muslims with alternative sexualities and gender expressions. In Islamic discourse, "*batin*" refers to an inner or metaphysical realm that is intertwined with local cultural concerns. People often use the duality of "*lahir*" (surface/outer) and "*batin*" (depth/inner) as an ontological distinction to define an individual.[1] The word "batin" is also used as a simplified reference to the metaphysical dimension of a person's being, or something akin to a soul. The common use of the term "konflik batin" reflects the dominant view that pits nonhetero and cisnormative ways of life against Islam in an irreconcilable opposition. "Konflik batin" thus becomes a trope for the inner states of those who fail to make peace with themselves; it characterizes Muslim queer and trans experiences as univocally conflicted and marred by negative emotions of self-contempt, self-manipulation, or hypocrisy.

Woven through the life stories of Rizky, Tino, and Anna, the three protagonists in this chapter, the stereotypical notion of konflik batin is contorted by ruminations on past and present events as well as future imaginings. Each narrative portrays repeating moments of moral ambiguity while making explicit the roles of affect, emotions, and feelings in inhabiting the tensile relationships with religious prescriptions. In this context, inner conflict as a metaphor for Muslim queer and trans experience appears as more than just a figure of speech or abstract concern: it connects personal and social ways of being and doing in the world.

Various scholars have described the emotional states of navigating conflicting situations as feelings of ambivalence. In her study of the U.S.-based AIDS activist group ACT UP, Deborah Gould articulates a structure of ambivalence delineating nonheterosexual subjects' lives as contradictory feelings that emerge from tensions between nonnormative sexualities and heteronormative demands.[2] In a similar vein, Dina Georgis's work, which engages with the affective dimensions of Arab queer experiences, dives into the dilemmas and double binds shaped by colonial violence and struggles for recognition. Her work focuses on how conflicting feelings can be engaged both within and against dominant narratives.[3]

This structure of ambivalence also relates to another cluster of emotions rich with moral undertones. The works of Samuli Schielke offer a conceptual framework for understanding the emotional landscapes that emerge within religious contexts characterized by ambivalence. In his research on Muslim communities in everyday life, Schielke points out the fragmented and ambivalent nature of the moral subjectivities of people (mostly Muslim heterosexual men) who are grappling with tensions between religious commitment and deviance.[4] From the perspectives of those whose lived experience are detailed in this book, a structure of ambivalence connects to a complex set of emotions laden with moral inflections.

Ambivalent ruminations about what is deemed good or bad, right or wrong, true or false, as well as discussions about realizing or failing to uphold values compounded by religious discourse are recurring themes in a number of narratives in this chapter and the next.[5] As Cherryl Mattingly points out, moral selves emerge through narratives shaped by the struggles and dilemmas of trying to make judgments amid ambiguous circumstances of everyday life.[6] Drawing on Hannah Arendt,[7] Mattingly further argues that how through this moral practice, everyday spaces can become "spaces of possibility, ones that create experiences that are also experiments in how life might or should be lived."[8] In other words, spaces of otherwise.

In anthropology, numerous scholars both emphasize the importance of distinguishing between morality and ethics and recognize the difficulties involved.[9] According to Didier Fassin, morality refers to the set of values and norms that define acceptable or unacceptable behaviors in a society.[10] Morality is considered external to the individual and is imposed on them through socialization. In contrast, ethics refers to the internal, subjective process through which individuals determine how to conduct themselves in the pursuit of well-being. Through self-reflection, people develop their own understanding of right and wrong. While morality is seen as a fixed framework, ethics is an ongoing process of virtuous thinking and behavior. Fassin argues that morality represents the social rules individuals are expected to follow, whereas ethics involves inner reflection and choices that guide their actions. In everyday life, this distinction is often blurred and religious institutions are commonly associated with both moral judgment and ethical formation.[11] Although this chapter and the next retain the theoretical framings that distinguish moralities, ethics, and political actions as distinct categories, they also explore what happens otherwise in between and beyond these categorical distinctions.[12]

At the same time, queer theory has traditionally avoided discussing "morality." According to Heike Schotten, this stems from historically long-standing forms of oppression directed at queer subjectivities in the name of morality: "It is this loyalty to and solidarity with those "below" that renders queer theory's anti-morality an emancipatory commitment rather than . . . [a] reactionary one."[13] This perspective aligns with Naisargi Dave's analysis of queer activism in India, which highlights the centrality of ethics as a creative and disruptive response to moral codes and obligations.[14] In these approaches, morality is essentially equated with social normativity and stability. But since religiously infused moral world views shape the self and social life of the protagonists in this chapter and the next, it is worth rethinking and engaging with this category in queer terms. How can religious-based conceptions of morality be queered? How are moral selves formed within Muslim queer and trans worldmaking? What otherwise possibilities are emerging from enduring ordinary lives that are inherently marked by uncertainties? Attending more closely to the lived experiences of inner conflict contained in the following three life stories provides some clues and tentative answers to these questions.

Rizky's Willful Hesitation

It was September 2014 and Rizky was just turning thirty-three years old when I met him one evening in a café in central Jakarta. We had become close friends since getting to know each other in early 2000 through a social networking website widely used by members of the gay community in Jakarta. When I met Rizky the first time, he was still a student at a university in Bandung, West Java and worked part-time as a photo model, whereas I just had finished college and had recently landed a job working as a journalist in Jakarta. Although during our initial encounters we were both single and looking for a partner and we shared a lot of similar interests, it did not take long for us to realize that we were better off as friends than lovers. Since we both lived in different cities, we did not meet that often, especially after I moved further away to Yogyakarta in 2003 to attend study for my master's degree. But this geographical distance never really became an issue in our companionship. We took turns visiting each other in our respective cities and spent time together catching up and discussing a range of topics that ranged from personal experiences, popular culture, and family matters to more metaphysical issues related to religion and life philosophies.

During our intimate interactions that we referred to as our "quality time," there were occasions when he would convey his stories with a particular moral and spiritual fervor. This was often demonstrated by the way he responded to my venting when I experienced difficult situations. When I was doubtful or sad, he would try to console me by telling me to pray or by reiterating the phrase "God will not burden a soul more than it can bear."[15] These responses indicate his deeply spiritual approach to life. On the other side, throughout these years of knowing each other, I have also witnessed Rizky's struggle to reconcile his desire toward the same sex and his religious aspirations.

Aside from firsthand knowledge of both aspects of Rizky's life, which strengthened my resolve to ask him to participate in this study, I was particularly inspired by his thoughtful response to my invitation. While he had some prior awareness of my work, it was not until our meeting that evening that I was able to properly introduce the intention of my research to explore the affective experiences of queer Muslims in Indonesia. Rizky was the person mentioned earlier who questioned why I was using "queer" as the primary signifier rather than "Muslim."

The Cost of Moral Breakdown

We met on a Saturday night so that we could stay up late talking without having to worry about getting up for work the next morning. Rizky was then working in a media agency as a media planner. Since moving to Jakarta in 2003, Rizky had been employed by three different companies in this field. While he was still a university student, he often told me that his dream job was to work in a more socially oriented sector, such as in nongovernmental organizations focusing on environmental or political issues. Several years had now passed and he continued to cling to this vision and often mentioned his feelings of being trapped as a "corporate slave." Rizky and I share such future ambitions with a generation of urban youth from the aspiring middle class that lived through the fall of Suharto's authoritarian New Order regime in 1998. Ariel Heryanto notes that the attitudes of the "progressive" middle class, such as those represented by university students, generally maintain a critical distance from the New Order construction of success or productivity that is oriented toward economic gains and a consumer lifestyle. Rather, the so-called "progressive" people in Indonesia are increasingly inclined toward the pursuit of self-worth and moral authority through forms of social engagement.[16]

However, Rizky considered himself lucky to enter professional salaried work in the capital and to attain a secure career relatively smoothly despite intense competition for office jobs among university graduates, especially since he did not have a degree due to a disruption during the last stage of his college study in 2005 as well as his troubled relationship with his boyfriend at the time, Arga. Prior to breaking up with Arga, Rizky believed he had control over his life and was a good person despite occasional mistakes:

> I truly believed back then that as long I have no ill will towards others, despite my own faulty conducts, *I think things couldn't go wrong* [in English], because I am doing good, the way is shown to me. But when my relationship with Arga turned bad, it really *consumed me* [in English]. I was so stressed out, I failed my classes and I really thought that everything is falling apart due to the breakup. I had even fallen ill—but you knew that already, didn't you? And then I ended up never finishing college. I had no

idea what my future would look like after that. In my mind, it would be really difficult for me to get a job, it really hurt my ego badly, I hit rock bottom and I did not know to whom I could run to. So, all this led me . . . towards my growing belief toward . . . God.

Rizky recounted that a few months after his breakup with Arga, he often had a chronic headache that he described as "vertigo that would endure for 24 hours a day." He went to several doctors to see if there was anything wrong with his head, but a definitive diagnosis eluded him. In a desperate attempt to find healing, Rizky even went to see a *ruqyah* practitioner. Ruqyah is an Islamic spiritual healing that uses incantation or Koranic recitation for exorcism. This method has been used more recently as conversion therapy for Indonesian Muslims with same-sex attraction.[17] But his condition remained unchanged. The headache lingered for a long time after that but then it gradually "faded away by itself" (*hilang dengan sendirinya*).

Another unsettling turning point in his life happened about six years later. While on a one-year scholarship to attend a community college in the United States, Rizky experienced another episode of deep depression. By that time, he had been employed by a media company for two years, so the news that he had been awarded this scholarship was a pleasant surprise. With this opportunity, he could earn an academic qualification that would support his aspiration to work in socially oriented professions. During his first few months abroad, he would occasionally contact me on Skype, telling me how content he was with his life there. In between his study, he made time to visit different cities, where he occasionally made new friends, maybe even falling for a couple of them. He was elated at the prospect of staying longer in the United States after completing his study there.

When he told his parents about this idea, instead of clearly telling him no, they began to excommunicate him. This triggered a chain reaction that was similar to what he had experienced in Bandung: skipping classes, withdrawing from other people, and feeling unwilling to leave the house. After receiving mental health support from the college he was enrolled in, Rizky was eventually able to finish his study and return to Indonesia. In retrospect, he concluded that his experiences in Bandung and the United States were symptoms of a major depression: "I came to understand that this could happen if you subconsciously blocked your-self from things that potentially could stress you out, things that you actually had to face." He also attributed his four months of "24/7 vertigo" in Bandung to his depression. I asked him to clarify what this condition entails: "Were you feeling sad or anything like that?" His answer was a clear "no":

> Maybe because I blocked it, maybe I could not admit that I failed to come to peace with myself, I was disappointed, I was down, I was . . . hurt. Maybe I was not accepting that . . . that this is not fair. It is not supposed to be like this. If you are right and others are wrong, then that person who is in the wrong should be the one who is miserable. If it did not happen, there had to be payback, someone had to make up for it. . . . So when Arga refused to deal with my demand to deal with our troubled relationship, just like when my parents refused to listen to what I have to say . . . what I felt was . . . mostly anger. I blocked everything out.

Rizky's explanation of mental blockage as due to his inability to make peace with himself brings into view the model of inner conflict. The effects of Rizky's emotional struggle with his loved ones not only took a psychological and somatic toll, they also considerably undermined his social interactions and his moral selfhood. These latter effects are mainly manifested in his sense that he had breached expectations of being a "good" and "right" person—not only in the eyes of others but also in his own view. The stories Rizky shared represent the repetitive nature of affective breakdowns, marked by depressive moments and mental block-ages as a part of his struggle to become a moral person.

The memory of these dismal experiences seemed to linger, hanging heavily over our conversation that night and preventing Rizky from talking more about what a viable future might look like. However, I wit-nessed a glimmer of hope in his solemn expression of "growing faith towards God" as a way of coping with these breakdowns. As we will see, Rizky became more drawn to learn more about Islamic values and teachings despite these feelings of inadequacy and failure.

As we moved deeper into the conversation in the coffee shop that evening, Rizky asked what prompted me to involve him as one of the research participants. I explained that it was because of how I perceived him: since we became close friends, I had always seen him as a spiritual person and I wanted to understand how he viewed that impression. In response he said:

> *I would say, most people I know are spiritual to a certain extent* [in English]. . . . But maybe, compared to those in my circle, I tend to question things more. I have more inquiries, although somewhat slow. . . . So I would say yes, I am more spiritual than I was eight or ten years ago.

By "eight or ten years ago," Rizky was referring to the time period when he developed a deeper interest in God and in Islamic teachings, particularly after experiencing severe depression. However, he disagreed with my assessment that he had become more religious after that specific event, stating, "I wouldn't call myself religious, as I'm not sure what it truly means to be religious. But if it means fully adhering to and embracing my beliefs, then I believe I'm still far from that."

Rizky grew up in a non-devout Muslim household in the Lampung Province of Indonesia. His family did not emphasize religious teachings in his upbringing. His father served in the military. His parents enrolled him and his two sisters in a Catholic primary school for their elementary education. Rizky explained that although his family did not focus on religious instruction or observance in his upbringing, they did aim to instill its foundational values. It was not until after the personal turmoil in Bandung that he began to independently explore religious matters. He started paying closer attention to sermons and engaging in conversations with individuals whose perspectives on Islam he deeply respected. Over time, he came to understand that the reasoning behind his father's approach to certain issues and values was rooted in underlying Islamic principles. Rizky realized that he shared many of these values, even before fully recognizing them:

> It made me realize that: "Oh, these things have been there all along." The reasons behind why certain things worked the way they did were already explained and anticipated in Islamic teachings. All the problems I had faced—their causes, effects, and potential solutions—become clear when you look at what has been said. To avoid those problems, we just need to follow the guidance blindly; without having to understand all the

reasoning behind it. You don't need to have all the proof or do somersaults to believe. Islam and the Quran have always offered insights to help us with whatever we're going through. It's there, if we choose to accept it.

Rizky stressed how his understanding of the absoluteness of Islam as a religion was not imposed upon him externally, such as by doctrinal teachings or family education, but was an organic process that he sees as deeply ingrained in his own life experience. Despite his own characterization of cultivating faith as self-discovery, Rizky still regarded his desire for following the Islamic teachings as somewhat "superficial"; he did not apply enough effort to study them deeply:

> I don't really follow it as comprehensively as I wanted it to be. By "it," I am not referring to some kind of a "calling." It is more like a reminder or a chance to learn more. Partly because I have no intention to find out more about it. I try to ignore some of the most crucial aspects most of the times because I'm afraid. Because . . . although I believe that Islam provides the one absolute truth, I'm afraid that the more I learn about it, the more guilty I will feel. So although I try to learn more and more about religion, I can only do so partially. . . . It's because I'm afraid once I know the whole truth, I will have to believe it. Whether I follow it obediently or not isn't the main issue. But once I know it, whatever it is that is written there [in the Quran], if I got the right interpretation, I would have to absolutely believe it then, I am certain of that.

When I asked him to elaborate on what guilt means for him, he replied: "The guilt arises because I understand right from wrong to some extent, yet despite this understanding, I do nothing to move closer to the full truth." Rizky's trepidation stems from a yearning to improve his religious practice and attitude. His fear is not directed toward his attraction to other men as something considered sinful and deserving of God's punishment. Rather, it is the fear of feeling guilty. Rizky's fear of guilt reflects a recurring emotional pattern arising from his ambiguous commitment to perceiving Islam as the ultimate "truth" while also anticipating the potential of feeling guilty due to his inability to adhere to the moral codes that may accompany such an understanding. The disjunction implied by Rizky's affective repertoire of "fear of feeling guilty" also reveals his understanding of the relation between faith, knowledge, and ritual practices that David Kloos describes in his monograph on Muslim laypersons' ethical improvement in Aceh. According to Kloos, "The more knowledgeable a person becomes, the more responsibilities he or she acquires, and the more likely (or grave), his or her sins become."[18]

Rizky's fear of not being able to live up to the moral responsibilities of his faith is tied not only to his self-awareness that certain acts are considered an offense against God's will but also to his failure to make use of this knowledge for his own moral improvement. One of the most significant challenges confronting Rizky in his pursuit of moral selfhood stems from his inability to find a common ground between his personally held view of Islam as inherently truthful and his ambiguous stance on matters pertaining to same-sex behaviors and queer identities.

Brotherly Love

When I met Rizky that night, he had been with his partner Donny for over two years and they had been living together in a residential high-rise in one of Central Jakarta's most densely populated areas. While his parents in Lampung remained unaware of his relationship with Donny, Rizky never deliberately hid it from his two sisters and their husbands, to whom he disclosed that he was living with Donny. Rizky tended to avoid direct discussions with his siblings on the topic of homosexuality, but from time to time the occasion would arise. One time he had an email exchange with his brother-in-law Firman regarding the issue of homosexuality in Islam. Firman had sent Rizky an online article saying it was forbidden. Rizky replied with links to articles presenting alternative perspectives regarding homosexuality in Islam, pointing out how God never forbids love. Rizky did not take offense at the communication from his brother-in-law, instead preferring to interpret it as a well-meaning reminder of the Islamic teachings and a gesture of care and concern. To a certain degree, Rizky concurred with his brother-in-law,

> although this is still an assumption since I haven't found out about the whole truth yet. It is forbidden. It's forbidden. Men are not supposed to be with other men. I cannot rationally explain why . . . this is a matter of faith. Again, I am open to learning what the Quran says about this; if it

says that loving another man is okay, I would believe that, and the same if it says otherwise. At this point, one thing I believe is that the sex [act itself] is the issue. . . . It's no more or less wrong than having extramarital sex with someone of the opposite gender. That's the problem with same-sex practices.

Rizky was referring here to *zina*, the Islamic doctrine that prohibits premarital and extramarital sex between Muslims. As Linda R. Bennett explains, zina in Islamic law refers to fornication or illicit copulation: "In dominant interpretations of Shari'a, zina is also understood to include the following acts: rape, incest, extramarital affairs, prostitution, premarital sex and statutory rape, and homosexual relationships."[19] While the Quran does not explicitly mention homosexuality in its references to zina, popular interpretations consider it *haram* (prohibited) for Muslims.[20] The conflation of zina and same-sex practices further compounded Rizky's skepticism regarding the use of sexuality and sexual orientation as markers of identity:

To me, terms like gay, queer, or whatever, all of them are just labels. *If I had to describe myself, I would say I'm a man who is sexually attracted to men* [in English]. This does not necessarily mean that I am not interested in women, though. I'm not sure if I am, and if I am, it might not be sexually. . . . And yes, I do enjoy having sex with men [laughing uncomfortably]. But the thing is, what has been bugging my mind is not the sex itself. I knew already that even if I find the truth, I would still engage in the sex.

When I asked him why he would still actively have sex even if he had embraced the "truth," he replied that sex would be the last thing that he gave up doing:

What has kept me from following through . . . from trying to learn the truth . . . is my relationship with Donny, whom I love, whom I care about. I worry that if we split up, he'll be left with no one. I don't have the heart to leave him.

Rizky believes that his sexuality is not determined by fixed identity labels like "gay" or "queer," which assume a bounded, self-contained individual.

Instead, he emphasizes the relational aspects of his sexuality, explaining that in any given context, he could also be emotionally attracted to the opposite sex. He often said to me, sometimes jokingly, that he might end up marrying and fully committing to a woman. For him, what matters most are the emotional ties, mutual attraction, and respect between him and his potential partner rather than conforming to societal expectations. By upholding a form of personhood that is tethered to desire, Rizky seeks to maintain the possibilities of becoming otherwise.

At the same time, this scenario also indicates the varying moral and cultural factors that often accompany shifts in different life phases. Throughout my adult life I often encountered other Muslim gay interlocutors who would intimate a foreseeable future of leaving "this kind of life" (cara hidup seperti ini). The phrase "this kind of life" in this context has a number of meanings: from same-sex activity to the general idea of socializing in the gay world.[21] Aspirations of departing the gay life typically entailed envisioning moments of closure, ranging from entering a heterosexual marriage to severing existing relations with their peers to naik haji (make a pilgrimage to Mecca).

While it may appear that the logical first step toward "leaving this kind of life" would be discontinuing sexual intercourse, Rizky approached it differently. Although he agreed with the view that homosexuality was sinful, he was not compelled to give up having sex with men in order to become a better Muslim. This stance is substantiated by his explanation that "the same-sex part will be the easiest to resolve, as you don't really need to be committed in a partnership just for the sake of channeling your lust. No strings attached." Hence, he remained sure that even if he could no longer be with other men, he could still channel his desire through other means, such as masturbation. However, one of the greatest challenges hampering his aspiration of becoming a better Muslim was his intimate entanglement with Donny, his current partner. This dilemma can be traced back to his description of the differences between erotic/sexual, romantic love and comfort love/companionship:

> If it's just about lust, as I said, it's easier to control. But what if it's not about the sex? How could you blame me for caring about someone? I think if it's just about giving someone a hug to comfort them, that's fine by me. The problem arises when . . . I start becoming emotionally attached, when

I start investing emotionally. You begin to treat it as a relationship, like being lovers [*pacaran*]. That doesn't feel right. Take my friends Sani and Daud, for example, who officiated their [gay] marriage in the U.S. For them, it's about the intention of becoming a couple [*niat berpasangan*], which is different from simply caring about someone or being close to someone, like a brother. I can be intimate [*dekat*] with Donny but not in that kind of relationship.

Rizky distinguishes between sexual, romantic, and companionate forms of love, distinctions that can be found across cultures.[22] As hinted above, his ideal notion of same-sex relationships between Muslims departs from the framework of gay coupledom. He emphasizes instead a form of loving that he described as "closeness and intimacy among brothers." At this point I noticed how Rizky was struggling to articulate what he meant, and I could only empathize with how difficult it must be to reflect on these profound concerns while at the same time sharing them with me. As if seeking my approval, he said:

> Love, as long as it is understood in terms of brotherly love, or whatever terms fit because in Islam . . . I think the proper term would be . . . compassion [*kasih*], right? So relationships between fellow Muslim brothers are not forbidden. It is even encouraged to care for others. The problem for me is what is being enacted. The sex, or even if you don't act upon it, but just lusting after others . . . that's when it becomes a problem. But after some time, at least in my own experience, [same-sex] relationships often evolve into something more than just about the sex, they become more about emotions [*emang lebih emosional*]. Then if at the end it is just a matter of emotion, like caring for your own brothers, do you really need to frame it as a coupledom?

The conflicting notions of romantic love, sexual fulfillment, and what he describes as brotherly love are rendered more complex when he brings emotions into the picture. To reiterate, his main concern is not same-sex practices per se, in the way they are understood to be a "pure" physical activity. Rather, Rizky's concern is pointed toward the moment when emotion becomes significant and shifts the physical quality of the encounter into one more conducive to a dating relationship (*pacaran*) or a coupledom (*pasangan*). Such framings, he believes, are contradictory. As an alternative, he is increasingly drawn to practices of homosocial care and affection, the "brotherly love" that can be read as closer to the Islamic ideals of love among fellow believers based on the Prophet Muhammad's reported hadith.[23]

Rizky's employment of brotherly love as an affective repertoire appears to be a makeshift solution to the conflictual notions of love, compassion, care, and intimacy caught up in the tension between faith and queer sexuality. In the meantime, Rizky's journey toward becoming a better Muslim remains suspended. Despite his quandaries about being in a same-sex relationship, he and Donny stay together as a couple, due both to his emotional attachment and to his feelings of moral responsibility. As indicated earlier, Rizky's moral and affective bargain is one of many forms of inhabiting the seemingly irreconcilable gap between queer intimacy and faith. Our focus here has been on the internal aspects of Rizky's inner conflict, particularly his attempt to cultivate piety and moral selfhood. The next section will examine how inner conflict can inflect social interactions.

Tino's Troubled Masculinity

I met Tino by chance. Our first encounter took place in December 2013 when I arrived for the first time in Rancong, a pseudonym for a small town on the northern coast of Aceh province. Rancong was on my list of places to visit during my initial trip to Aceh for a number of reasons, the first one being that this is where my late paternal grandmother grew up. My only knowledge of the place at that time was that association with the name. The second reason was that some of my contacts in Banda Aceh regularly mentioned Rancong when I asked about where more dynamic queer communities were located in the province. Before I visited Rancong, I had requested contact information for new potential acquaintances in Banda Aceh, and one informant had provided the phone number of Rafi, a person they thought might be able to introduce me to the queer community in Rancong. I called Rafi to introduce myself and provide details regarding my planned visit to Rancong. I also inquired if he would be interested in meeting in person. Rafi stated that he would be glad to, as he was unemployed at that time and thus had considerable free time.

A few days later, I embarked on a journey from Banda Aceh to Rancong via public minivan transportation, a mode of transit commonly used to connect larger cities to rural regions in Sumatra. When I arrived at my accommodation, I attempted to reach Rafi by phone but he did not answer. Instead, I received a text message apologizing for his inability to meet because he needed to leave town for a job interview. It suddenly dawned on me that I knew no one else in the town. Despite my genealogical ties to the place, there were no known relatives or kin living there. So almost desperately, I asked Rafi if he could introduce me to one of his acquaintances. This was when Tino entered the picture. Rafi provided Tino's contact information, indicating that he had already explained my plan to Tino and Tino had agreed to speak with me. On the phone, Tino sounded understanding yet cautious; he suggested that I take the evening for rest and said he would visit me at the hotel in the morning.

The following day, I felt a sense of relief when I saw Tino arrive at the hotel lobby. He took me to a coffee shop near the beach. Through the first cups of sweetened milk coffee, Tino and I exchanged some background stories. At the time, Tino was in his early thirties and worked as an announcer in a local radio station in Rancong, a profession he had pursued since graduating from a university in Yogyakarta in the early 2000s. His visibility in the local scene also led him to occasionally take on freelance jobs as a master of ceremonies (MC) at various public events. His main reason for returning to Rancong was to care for his aging mother. Tino explained that his willingness to help me was influenced by his past experiences as a student in Yogyakarta; he saw our interaction as an opportunity to reconnect with that phase of his life.

Tino is a quick-witted fast talker. With his deep voice, he talked about different subjects at a pace that I often failed to keep up with. After having our coffee, he drove me around the town on his motorbike[24] and we made several brief stops so he could introduce me to his different circles of friends. He also took me to his workplace at the end of what felt like a very hectic day and asked me to sit across from him in the studio while watching him work. It was not until June 2014 during the fasting month of Ramadan, and only after I had been in Rancong for a few months, that Tino was finally able to share with me his life story in greater detail.

Cruising Shame

As the sun set, the call for Maghrib prayer—marking the time for *buka puasa* (breaking the fast) during Ramadan—resounded from the mosque loudspeakers just as we arrived at a noodle shop in the center of Rancong. We ordered two bowls of sugary drinks, as was customary during the fasting month as they provide a quick energy boost after a whole day of fasting. We were also waiting for Rafi, who had said that he would join us after attending the fast-breaking event at his new workplace, one of the private national bank branches in Rancong. While stirring his cold drink, Tino admitted that he was not in the mood to see Rafi that evening; the day before, he had had a heated argument with him.

The quarrel between Tino and Rafi took place while they were waiting to break their fast and had decided to kill time together by going for motorbike ride. Tino was driving the motorbike while Rafi was sitting on the back. As they passed through the spot where the youth of Rancong hung out near the beach, Rafi saw two men passing next to them on a motorbike. Rafi seemed to be attracted to these men and instructed Tino to speed up their motorbike so he could flirt with them. At first, Tino followed the instruction, but then Rafi started to gesture to these men in a cajoling way. This gesture made Tino upset and he decided to turn his motorbike the other way while scolding Rafi. "That will be the last time I will be in that situation like yesterday again with him, it is really, really embarrassing [*sangat-sangat memalukan*]," he said.

I had seen Rafi make similar gestures on other occasions when we roamed through the town on motorbikes. Tino was also present during these occasions, but usually we would just laugh about it. So I asked Tino why he was particularly upset because I thought he was used to seeing Rafi's rather brazen ways of flirting with those he found attractive. Tino said:

No, but yesterday he was really vulgar [*vulgar sekali*]; he approached people who are good-looking in his eyes or those he found of interest. So he is really following what his heart tells him to do [*mengikuti banget kata hati*], thinking that this person can be seduced. I told him that this would be the last time he could do that. . . . It was really uncomfortable [*risih*]. I don't care if people call me a hypocrite [*munafik*] or anything, it is so uncomfortable. You saw it yourself, didn't you?

Tino's discomfort with Rafi's action seemed to tap into deeper concerns about self-expression and moral boundaries, concerns that he traced back to his past experience in Yogyakarta:

When I was still studying in communication, I was often filmed for campus assignments, and when I saw myself in those videos, my own effeminate side [Javanese: *menthel*] was a big no! I even condemned myself for it. Why was I so effeminate? Don't be too coquettish [*ceriwis*]. After that, I changed a lot, and now everyone says I am more charismatic on stage. I never exaggerate [*berlebihan*], except when I'm joking.

Tino described his feelings of being embarrassed (*malu*) and experiencing discomfort (*risih*) as primarily a result of Rafi's attempts at sexualized engagement (by means of cajoling) with other males in public spaces. Tino worried that being around Rafi might lead to other people questioning his own masculinity. This is something that he had been trying to avoid, for example by modifying any behavior that made him appear effeminate (*menthel*), coquettish (*ceriwis*), or exaggerated (*berlebihan*) and adjusting his daily conduct to conform with a more culturally authorized version of masculinity. His apprehension about Rafi's behavior is primarily anchored in the prominent use of the word "*malu*." This centrality of shame can be unpacked from two interlinked perspectives: the perceived "proper" role of emotion in various cultures across Indonesia and its contribution to the affective patterning of queer sociality in different settings.

Many scholars working on cultural theories that address emotions in Indonesian societies have asserted the integral role of malu (shame or shame-like emotions) in everyday interactions.[25] In her study on shame cultures in South Sulawesi, Indonesia, Birgitt Röttger-Rössler explains that the Indonesian model of shame is "organized consistently in social-relational or dyadic terms: The shameful behavior of one person always impacts on other persons as well; it also always diminishes and threatens the social integrity of others."[26] Röttger-Rössler's argument contradicts Thomas Scheff's view of shame as a negative self-assessment shaped by how one is perceived by others, as she asserts that in many Indonesian contexts, the display of shame is regarded as a virtue rather than a flaw.²⁷ Those who "know shame" and consistently demonstrate it in everyday interactions are well respected; in contrast, those who violate these norms and values can lose all claim to social recognition and support.²⁸ Elizabeth F. Collins and Ernaldi Bahar also highlight the productiveness of malu as a relational experience. They assert that not only does shame regulate interactions between people from different social ranks and age, it is also highly connected to notions of gender and sexuality:

> The Indonesian word for genitals [*kemaluan*] echoes the English expression "private parts." Furthermore, sexually provocative behavior by self or others should elicit malu. . . . Gender-inappropriate behavior causes both men and women to feel malu. A boy would feel malu if he behaved like a girl, for example by displaying tears in public.²⁹

Among queer studies scholars, shame has proven to be a particularly insightful area of inquiry.³⁰ Sara Ahmed describes how queer subjects often collectively share feelings of shame and self-loathing; these feelings are often perceived as the sense of failure before an idealized other and "experienced as an affective cost of not following the scripts of normative existence."³¹ In this perspective, shame is largely coupled with pride on a psycho-political spectrum that shapes and is shaped by the desire to "come out."³² Analyzing the rise of political homophobia in Indonesia at the turn of the century, Tom Boellstorff argues that within the Indonesian gay scene—at least until the recent past—"the fact that men engage in public sexuality . . . has not resulted in *malu*. . . . [It has] been greeted with curiosity and even titillation, or been casually looked down upon."³³

A closer examination of Tino's articulation of shame can provide us with further insight into the complex intersections between masculinity, emotion, and interpersonal dynamics. While it may be tempting to view Tino's feelings of shame, discomfort, and self-contempt as a reflection of his individual failings, his response points to a more pervasive underlying experience of staying with the pain of contradictions. Tino's account illuminates his inner struggles with both his social environment and his self-image due to an inability to conform to the prevailing masculine norms.

One aspect that stands out is the fear of potentially being recognized by individuals who may be familiar with his public persona as a radio announcer in the relatively closed environment of Rancong. In Acehnese culture, the intertwining of social status and shame is deepened when using the local term "*marwah*." This is a word that Tino also casually mentioned on several occasions in different situations: "*Jangan sampai hilang marwahku*" (I don't want to lose my marwah). Marwah loosely translates from the Malay word *maruah*, which simultaneously connotes dignity, reputation, and masculinity. Historically, this term was heavily reproduced during the thirty-year period of violent sectarian conflict in the region that ended in 2006.[34] In this case, Tino's fear of being stigmatized as a nonmasculine male intersects with his fear of losing face, which in concrete terms could jeopardize his livelihood, including his freelance work as an MC. The second aspect points to the discourse surrounding gender in the local Aceh context. As gender studies scholars have highlighted, the centrality of Islamic discourse to cultural life in Aceh and more widely in Indonesia can be registered by the overlapping of sexed bodies and gendered social attributes.[35] Together, they represent the true manifestation of *kodrat* (God's will).

The acuteness of Tino's feelings of malu has been produced by his own and Rafi's failures to keep within kodrat as a mix of locally and religiously scripted gender roles. Tino states that he is much more casual and personal in nature when approaching other men in order to avoid the risk of being ashamed for transgressing normative masculinity. He prefers to get to know them first using digital platforms such as social media, where they can remotely share personal information. Once he senses there is a mutual interest, he proposes to meet in person over coffee. He also mentioned that during these initial dates, he would strive to appear masculine (*kebawa laki*) in order to impress them. I asked him how he makes them feel attracted to him and he responded:

> By caring [*perhatian*]. . . . I give him my full attention. If someone is in a relationship with me, no woman can match the way I show care for men. I also let the man know I like him once we've grown close. If I have strong feelings for someone, I will tell him, even if it means he might leave me—I

don't care. What matters is that I have freed my emotions [*memerdekakan rasa*] toward him, allowing my inner self to feel unburdened [*tidak tertekan batin*]. I was being up front but not vulgar. However, after taking the initiative, these men—well, some of them—took advantage of it. Once they realized I had feelings for them, they would start asking me to pick them up, drive them around, or even give them money to buy cigarettes. At times, it felt mentally painful [*sakit jiwa*]. Approaching a "normal" guy feels like a mental illness because you made so much effort.

In *The Gay Archipelago: Sexuality and Nation in Indonesia*, Tom Boellstorff describes how for various reasons many of his interlocutors preferred having intimate relationships with "normal" men. He defined this preference for masculine men as "hetero-gendered desires."[36] In the case of Tino, the everyday performance of this desire involved making an "excessive effort" to navigate the normative constraints around care as a gender-specific feeling (women are more caring than men) in the hope of garnering feelings of intimacy from the subject of his affection. Tino claimed that sometimes he would navigate the gendered boundaries built around the feeling-word "care" to the extent that he would risk being subjected to psychological abuse.

Tino's attribution of gendered roles in performing care can also be applied to the gendered dimensions of same-sex practices. In the Muslim queer community in Indonesia with which I regularly interact, popular conceptions of male homosexuality and the physical act of sex among men—sometimes including anal intercourse—also reflect a gendered hierarchy. As Nguyen Tan Hoang notes, in patriarchal societies, bottoming is considered as the same as being a woman who is penetrated and dominated. The top position is viewed as active, dominant, and masculine, while bottoming consigns one to a position of less privilege that is perceived as passive, submissive, and feminine.[37]

While rumors and jokes about who is top and bottom were common between me and Tino, Rafi, and their circle of friends in Rancong, in our one-on-one conversation Tino expressed that he generally avoids anal penetration during sex. As he clarified, this preference is not due to repulsion:

If people told me about their experience, I can even enjoy listening to their stories. However, I just feel that it is improper (*merasa tidak pantas*) if they ask me to engage with such acts with them. They seem overly sex-oriented, as if satisfaction can only be found through that. My childhood education might have contributed to this view. While attending an Islamic boarding school, I was taught that anal sex is an act more animalistic than human, and because I learned this at a young age, this belief has stayed with me for a long time. That is my last fortress (*itu benteng terakhirku*).

I asked how Tino would describe his role in a sexual relationship. My question was intended to better understand how Tino viewed himself within the dominant framework of top-bottom sexual positioning rather than as an endorsement of these dichotomies. He responded that he is a *vers* (versatile):

> I can embody either the feminine or masculine role in a relationship, without it being tied to sexual dynamics. This means I can either be pampering (*memanjakan*) or enjoy being coddled (*manja*). For instance, I might be with someone who presents as top but suddenly acts cuddly around me. He enjoys being hugged, touched, or resting his head on my thighs. In those moments, my demeanor shifts, I became a real man (*laki bener*), embracing the male role in the relationship dynamic.

Although Tino asserted that he never engaged in anal intercourse, his idealized forms of same-sex intimacy are still anchored within the power dynamics that divide gender norms along the axis of the top-bottom positionalities. This is indicated by how Tino identifies his role as "versatile" in the relationship. Although less commonly used within the local gay scene, versatility as a third category allows for "the switching of multiple positions, but not the transcendence of them."[38] The masculinist bias still stands out in Tino's self-positioning: he moves between active caring (*memanjakan*) that is an attribution of masculinity and the wish to be coddled (*manja*) that is considered an inherently feminine attribute.

While addressing his thoughts on gender roles and sexual intimacy, Tino moved through a number of moral registers, each of which became a site of inner conflict, bounded by his shame at being unable to fulfill gendered expectations. Despite Tino's strong desire to conform to dominant gender norms, his ongoing quest for queer intimacy is remarkable.

Failure to Hijrah

Later that evening as our conversation continued, the noodle shop remained empty save for the elderly woman who had been fixing our meals. Outside the traffic on the street was calming down, most people were at home with their family enjoying their meal time after fasting the whole day or were preparing to attend the mosque for communal worship, *tarawih*, held every evening during Ramadan. My conversation with Tino progressed to the next topic as I asked him what his greatest concerns were these days. He replied that he felt increasingly pressured by those around him asking when he would marry (with a woman). He said he was not too bothered that people were inquiring about his personal life; his main worry was that he had yet to figure out who or how he would marry:

> I felt very anxious [*galau*] at times like this. I also felt this way when I saw photos on social media of my friends, one by one, getting married or having children. Even now, when I see a very good-looking man on the street, I sometimes curse [*memaki*] at myself: Why do I like men? This happens, for example, when I'm riding home alone on my motorcycle after working late at night. Sometimes I scream out loud: Why does it have to be like this? On one hand, I can't be like everyone else and have a girlfriend like everyone else. But on the other, why do I act this way? . . . The odd one out [Javanese: *nyeleneh*].

Tino also explained that some of his friends in Rancong had "succeeded" in marrying heterosexually:

> On one hand, I feel so happy [*senang*] for them because they actually did it. Then there's me, who has always wanted to go completely *hijrah*. Hijrah can mean different things to different people. For me, "total hijrah" would mean still be in contact with you and Rafi, particularly those close to me, but no longer meet with others. Of course, we can still hang out at the coffee shop as usual, but I will no longer be *gemeretak, geletak-geletak* [phonetic description of effeminacy]. Am I right? Just stay focused; after

all, isn't marriage a form of worship? In any case, returning to our religious roots ensures salvation. You've set yourself free; now your only task is to nurture your wife and children. Why couldn't I do this right now? No, it's not that I can't. . . . Why haven't I done this yet? I've been doing this for 30 years now! Come on, Tino! Find the one! Find her! It's not like you'll get married two months once you find her. It could take a year or more. That is why I am happy for those who've been able to return to "normalcy." I am especially happy for those who've been able to have children. They made it. I believe this is what it means to achieve the perfection of life [*kesempurnaan hidup*].

Hijrah in Arabic means "a physical migration." In Islamic tradition, it refers to the historical event when the Prophet Muhammad and his followers escaped persecution and fled from Mecca to Medina in 622 CE. When I started my fieldwork in 2013, the term "hijrah" had not yet gained the widespread usage that it currently holds. It was not until approximately 2018 that hijrah began to be referred to as a societal movement in Indonesia.[39] The Hijrah movement, part of the broader transnational Islamic revival, is reflected in the growing religious devotion among many Indonesian Muslims that is accompanied by visible lifestyle changes.[40] These include changes in clothing for both women and men; alterations in appearance (such as women wearing headscarves and men growing beards); and changes in habits, such as abstaining from activities considered haram or forbidden under Islamic law, like music, tobacco, and alcohol. The movement has gained significant traction among Indonesia's younger generation, driven largely by celebrities and a new wave of Islamic preachers.

Rizky, described above, had been contemplating leaving the gay scene but was prevented from doing so because of his ongoing attachment to his boyfriend. In contrast, Tino, envisioned "hijrah," which he defined as staying away from his current circle of friends, especially those who frequently engaged in "effeminacy" (phonetically described as "*gemeretak, geletak-geletak*") in their everyday interactions. Another complex set of affective layers and meanings is implied in Tino's views. On one level, Tino aspires to return to his idealized version of "normalcy," that is, heterosexual marriage and a reproductive family as a model of a "perfect life." For him, however, one of the major obstacles in achieving this personal transformation is his own inability to save himself from his self-image as the odd one out (Javanese: *nyeleneh*). However, simply knowing that heterosexual marriage would fulfill his religious duties and social expectations does not provide Tino with enough modalities that would enable him to fulfill his desire for hijrah.

I had learned that Tino prayed devoutly every day, and I wondered if he included in his prayers this desire to transform himself toward piety. Tino answered my question with assurance:

> Always! I pray that God will straighten me up [*meluruskan aku*]. But until now there is no result yet. I know some people who perform the *istikharah* prayer by crouching down and crying, but that is not my style of prayer. Everything has a process, I know that, but why this process never yields results eludes me. People do not just work all the time; they need to be paid at the end of the month. But I have not received my payment until now. I just keep working on it so that I can be straight, but I never got my result. The longest that I have managed to hijrah was four months. I did it when I was still in college.[41]

During the four months of hijrah during his study in Yogyakarta, Tino managed to avoid sexual engagement with other men. This underscores the importance of time in Tino's personal struggle toward becoming a better Muslim. His narratives are consistently colored by a certain tone of optimism: his belief that through time (and God's intervention) he will eventually find a solution to his dilemmas. In the meantime, as we sat there mulling about what the future would bring, Tino once again expressed hope, as if forgetting the difficulties that had concerned him just moments before:

> It [the future] is unknown to me, Fer. Right now, what I do know is that I want a partner with whom I can share a dynamic relationship— someone I can discuss my work with and spend time hanging out with my niece. I haven't found anyone like that yet. Perhaps if I lived in a bigger city, it might be easier to meet this type of man—someone I can connect with intellectually while maintaining a sense of balance. Ideally, he would get along with my friends, be pious, and join me in various activities, like attending book fairs. An old friend from Yogya once advised me to stop

overthinking these matters. She suggested that my inability to find a guy like this might be a sign from God that I am not meant to be with other men.

Tino's account brings us full circle to the paradox of ambivalence. His longing for the ideal boyfriend seems to be more pressing, thus interrupting his long-term vision of a good life based on heteronormative ideals. Instead of what may appear to be self-sabotaging behavior or idiosyncratic inconsistency on Tino's part, I see a double movement: his desire for an ideal boyfriend and in parallel, his acknowledgment of the constraining conditions as a compelling aspect of one's worldmaking attempts. This circumstance resonates with Sara Ahmed's description of "how ordinary attachments to the very idea of the good life are also sites of ambivalence, involving the confusion rather than separation of good and bad feelings."[42]

One of the main sources of Tino's ambivalence lies in his longing in the present for a dynamic (same-sex) relationship and his future aspiration of hijrah and the normative construction of perfect (heterosexual) life. Indeed, our conversation that evening was but a glimpse into a much more complex process of affective dynamics of constructing a moral self within the intersections of queer intimacy and religious norms. For Tino, religious values and teachings are felt in one moment as oppressive shackles, and at other times they are invoked as a source of moral freedom. The expression of sexual desire and the quest for intimacy that is typically valued in progressive liberal discourse as a form of personal growth appears as a psychic burden to Tino in his daily attempts to attain the perfect moral life.

By exploring Rizky's personal journey of attaining moral selfhood and Tino's emotional troubles that are ingrained in heteronormative and patriarchal understandings of masculinity, I have shown how some Muslim queer worldmaking entails inhabiting the structures of ambivalence in the cultivation of piety. This sets the stage for examining the story of a protagonist who distanced herself from the formal and practical dimensions of Islam as a way of enduring inner conflict.

Anna's Unfinished Business

I came to know Anna through Eva, a German PhD student who happened also to be in Yogyakarta conducting her fieldwork. Eva knew about my research focus; she and I had been colleagues since I initiated my research proposal in Berlin. It was Eva who proposed to introduce me to Anna, one of her closest friends in the city and, according to Eva, an ideal participant for my research. I agreed to Eva's proposal and she arranged a meeting for the three of us at a coffee shop in Sagan, a gentrified area in the center of Yogya.

I joined Eva and Anna at a table in the front terrace of the coffee shop and we began to swap stories. Anna is originally from West Sumatra and moved to Yogyakarta for a graduate program at the local university in 2009. At the time of our meeting in November 2013, Anna had already finished her master's degree and, with a business partner, had initiated a creative agency for business consultancy in advertising. In addition to that, Anna was actively involved in organizing a queer youth camp on faith and sexuality that had been held every year in Yogyakarta since 2012.

At our first encounter, although the memory is somewhat blurry, I remember how quickly I was drawn to the way Anna introduced herself as an "ex-Muslim queer" who no longer performed religious duties. While I was still forming my response to what she said, Anna went on, disclosing that she had previously worn the hijab when she was still living with her family in West Sumatra. However, she stopped wearing it after relocating to Yogyakarta. Anna's story made a deep impression on me and I understood then why Eva was so insistent that I get to know her. It was clear that she had a strong sense of self-worth—at least outwardly—that sparked my curiosity to know more about her life. I finally got the chance to talk with her again a few months after this initial meeting. Our second meeting took place on a notably humid evening in August 2014 in a more private setting at her workplace, which is located in Baciro, a dense housing area in Yogyakarta.

Feeling "Always Wrong"

During our initial encounter, Anna made another striking statement. After I explained what I meant by Muslim queer in my research context, she responded:

> I felt that it is impossible to be queer and be a pious Muslim at the same time. Back when I was still actively praying, I kept having this weird

feeling here [pointing to her abdominal area]. I don't know . . . in my mind, I would never be able to be truly clean in front of God when I pray. One time, for example, I had a huge fight with one of my former girlfriends, and afterward, I was so sad and confused that I started to ask God so that my then girlfriend would continue loving me despite what had happened. I did this through praying and a few days later we got back together. I really wondered why God had listened to my prayer. It doesn't feel right at all.

Anna's response is revealing in several ways. On the one hand, her articulation about the impossibility of being Muslim and queer echoes the broader discourse concerning the irreconcilability of religious belief and queer intimacy. At the same time, her confusion—prompted by the perceived impossibility of reconciling her religious identity as a Muslim and her desire for the same sex—played out not only as an inner conflict, or a feeling of a double bind. Anna also noted that she had experienced a gut-wrenching unease upon having such thoughts alone. This situation resembles a catch-22—damned if you do, damned if you don't—colloquially referred to Indonesian as *perasaan serba salah*, which roughly translates as "feeling of always being in the wrong."[43]

Out of fear of losing her girlfriend, Anna had asked for a divine solution through praying. However, because of the Islamic doctrine that censures same-sex intimacy, she then perceived this action as unintelligible. This narrative is interwoven with an Islamic grammar of spirituality that distinguishes the individual as a duality of lahir (external) and batin (internal). From a phenomenological perspective, the subjective experience of emotions and their embodiment is characterized by the location of feelings in the foreground or background of bodily experience.[44] Sometimes localized bodily sensations are what comes to the foreground in emotional experiences, as Anna illustrated when she indicated her abdominal region, where she felt difficulties reconciling religious instructions, spiritual needs, and queer intimacy.

The lingering effects of these contradictory feelings partially shape her self-identification as an "ex-Muslim queer." In some respects, Anna's narrative distinguishes her from Rizky and Tino. Unlike them, she distances herself from the formal and practical dimensions of religious life, such as ritual worship. Rizky and Tino fully embrace Islam as a belief system, despite the perceived discrepancies with their sexualities. In Anna's case, not adhering to religious prescriptions does not necessarily mean abandoning her faith in God. Anna used the term "being comfortable with herself" (*nyaman dengan diri sendiri*) to describe her feelings after discontinuing her religious practices.

She conveyed this affective repertoire during our second meeting in her workspace. The advertising agency was nearly empty that evening, with only me, Anna, and her coworker Tania sitting in an office approximately three by four square meters. Tania was working behind a desktop computer and it seemed that both were trying to meet a deadline. I asked Anna if I should come back another time if my presence was distracting, but she just laughed and assured me that it was fine: "Here in this agency, every day is a deadline, so it does not matter if you come now or the next day, I can make time for you." After telling me about how tired she was from her workload during the day, Anna's face brightened when I suggested starting with my questions so she could continue her work afterward. I began by mentioning how intrigued I was by her self-description as an "ex-Muslim queer" during our first meeting and how I had been wondering about the significance of religion for her. Speaking candidly, seemingly unaware that Tania might overhear our conversation, Anna said:

> Religion isn't so important to me. Actually, I still haven't reached my final solution about it yet. But this doesn't mean that I am an atheist or that I don't believe in God. I still strongly believe that there is a great energy that governs everything. . . . Perhaps this energy is what others call God, but for me, that term God is associated with the normative. In short, religion for me is simply a means to connect with this "great energy." But I wonder: does this energy reside within us or exist outside? Is it something each of us carries inside, interacting with other energies making things happen, or is it truly external? Many religions depict God as an external being that governs, watches, and controls us. But I question whether it might actually be within us after all. . . . This is why I don't use the term "God"—because of its religious associations and its perception as an external being.

When considering Islamic religious prescriptions, Anna's perspective is bound by various sources of tension. One key source is the Indonesian grammar of religious life, which requires the existence of an institutional framework. State policy expects all Indonesians to believe in one God and formally affiliate with one of the six official religions[45] or an officially recognized local beliefs (*aliran kepercayaan*) to access full civic rights. Those without religious affiliation are often labeled as communist, a label that led to nationwide massacres and incarcerations during the political turmoil in Indonesia from 1965 to 1966. Although there have been efforts by civil society forces since the political regime changed in 1998 to reduce the stigma against people who do not follow any of the official religions, the stigma attached to being an atheist or agnostic remains strong.

The second tension arises from her strong opposition to the idea of God as a normative construct that exerts complete control and governance over every aspect of our lives. Her reflections on spirituality challenge the prevailing framework that portrays God as an external source of authority who either rewards or punishes individuals based on their actions. By using the term "God" interchangeably with "great energy" and depicting her connection with this energy in terms of relationality, Anna questions the authority of religion as an institutional framework governing inner experiences. She highlights that this energy both exists within or outside of different bodies and manifests in the connections between these bodies.

In their case study of LGBTQI Muslims in Britain, Andrew K. T. Yip and Amna Khalid emphasize religiosity as an inner experience rather than strict adherence to religious doctrines. They note that many of their participants view spirituality as a personal "connection with the divine or supernatural energy incorporates a sensory dimension."[46] According to their research participants, spirituality is a sensation that engulfs them, providing a feeling of completeness, fulfillment, and connection to another force or energy. It is seen as something that is embodied rather than institutionalized. Similarly, Anna firmly describes her spirituality as an embodied relationality rather than being based on a "belief system" with cognitive and institutional connotations.

When I asked Anna about the ways and experiences that help maintain a connection with the divine in daily life, she responded cautiously. Although she criticized the common notion of prayer as a way to ask for salvation, forgiveness, and happiness, Anna saw it as a chance to express gratitude for everything she receives in life. However, she also mentioned that she usually requires a specific object or item to serve as a conduit or means of communication between herself and God in order to pray:

> In this sense, I am not so different from everyone else. The religions I know in Indonesia, all six of them, have this kind of materiality. Engaging with these objects allow me to get in touch with the immaterial. These objects can be anything. I don't have to go to the mosque to connect with the divine, I can do so in the church, a temple, or anywhere else.

This account highlights how the volatile nature of religious politics in Indonesia complicates Anna's attempts to distance herself from institutionalized religion. This structural constraint is evident in her ambivalent views on the use of religious symbols and material forms, not exclusively Islamic ones, as part of her spiritual practice.

Trying to bring her thoughts to a close, Anna told me that her quest to seek divine power is far from over:

> I don't think it will ever be finished. I'm not sure if I will become religious or not. Or if I will eventually come to believe in this external God. But based on what my life has taught me, something does exist, but it's not necessarily external. If it's external, it's not something that exists independently, on a different plane from us. It's within myself and in others as well. I'm not sure why some people continue to believe it exists outside of us. I sometimes feel the same way too. But I don't think that's the answer. It does feel a cop-out, so we can continue living without leaving too many questions unanswered.

Anna's reluctance to arrive at a definite conclusion carries subjunctive inflection. According to Byron J. and Mary-Jo Del Vecchio Good, subjunctivity is a narrative technique that allows the speaker to "maintain deep investment in the openness of the future, in its indeterminacy, in the presence of the potent and mysterious dimensions of reality."[47] Specifically for Anna, enduring the uncertainties of her present spiritual journey means engaging with otherwise possibilities by considering how the similarities and differences in the ways other people practice faith incongruously shapes her spiritual understanding. The weight of relationality becomes a recurring theme that connects her spiritual practices to the ways she navigates self-identifications regarding gender and sexuality.

The Comfort of Being Oneself

Compared to Rizky and Tino, Anna seems to speak about her gender identity and sexuality with less ambivalence. She attributes her positive view on both issues to concepts and theories that she learned during her master's degree program at the local university, particularly drawing inspiration from Judith Butler's concept of the performative aspects of gender identity.[48] She describes feeling *nyaman* (comfortable) with Butler's ideas because she finds them *cocok* (fitting) to her situation. For Anna, gender identity is only something that manifests in relation to others; it is a product of social interactions rather than an authentic internal essence:

> I don't think about it [gender] so much when I am alone. It always involves someone else. For instance, with the person closest to me, like my lover, there's a process of identification in our relationship. I have to consider how I position myself—whether I take on a masculine or feminine role—and negotiate that with her. The same applies in broader contexts such as at the workplace, in an organization, or within society. This positioning is rooted in principles of inclusion and exclusion. When people recognize me as a part of one group, they often exclude me from other social categories. So it is a matter of how I socialize [*bersosialisasi*], not about self-identification. Over time, this process of recognition also affects me. I internalize it [*masukkan ke hati*; literally, take it to heart] and it shapes my self-perception. But this process comes from relating to others, not from relating to myself.

Anna refers to Judith Butler's model of gender performativity, which understands gender as produced and naturalized through the repeated stylization of the body, shaped by social norms and the interplay between the inner self and external bodily expression in relation to an audience. Drawing on Butler's philosophical argument, she highlights the distinction between how her gender is perceived by others and how she perceives it herself. To illustrate her point about gender as relational, she mentions examples from her past and present relationships with other women. She recalls that before moving to Yogyakarta for her MA study, she did not fully understand the concept of gender norms but felt a desire to challenge them, even though she was not sure how. She reflects on her previous relationships, noting that one of her five former partners, in particular, was problematic:

> This one former partner, she was really feminine, and I was the more masculine one. She always saw me as the male figure in the relationship. I wasn't allowed to go shopping at the women's department and my hair had to be cut short. . . . Even during sex, she would imagine that I had a penis. This was something I couldn't accept.

She continued drawing comparisons with her other romantic partners, including her current one:

> When I asked my current lover: "How do you see me? A man or woman?" And her answer was: "Anna . . . I see you like Anna, I am comfortable with Anna." This made me feel accepted for who I am. I could cook if I wanted to, and I could also do things that men typically do, like racing. It wouldn't be a problem as long as I am being myself. That's what comforts me.

The strong presence of the emotive concept of comfort (*nyaman*) in her understanding of gender as a relational construct is noteworthy. According to Ruth Holliday, in Western queer cultures, comfort primarily relates to the state of achieving a "harmony of self-explanations and self-presentations" in which one's internal perception of themselves aligns with their outward expressions.[49] However, there is a clear difference between Holliday's analysis, which emphasizes the importance of matching inner self and outer appearances to achieve the comfort of queer identities, and Anna's desire to be accepted as her "authentic" self, regardless of whether there is alignment between her inner self and her outward presentation of her body. Instead of focusing on the concurrence between her self-perception of gender and how others perceive it, Anna's comfort stems from a desire to be authentic in both aspects.

Indonesianist literature has provided rich explanations regarding the historical framing of debates about authenticity in claiming citizenship that include gender and sexual identities.[50] In his recent monograph on the technology of trans femininity in Indonesia, Benjamin Hegarty explores how throughout the modern history of waria, comfort has functioned "as not only a prerequisite for but as synonymous with national belonging."[51] Hegarty further argues that "warias framed the body as akin to an interface between self and society" rather than as a site where inner and outer parts of the person are experienced as opposing forces.[52] In line with Hegarty, I interpret Anna's desire to represent a gender that is authentic to both herself and others as comparable to her understanding of her inner spirituality. Both emanate from and shift through bodily encounters, emphasizing alternative possibilities of being.

Anna's efforts to claim moral selfhood draw from her experiences of comfort. Similar to her relational understanding of spirituality, Anna sees gender identity as inherently tied to how others perceive her. Instead of constantly rebuking attempts to categorize her gender identity, she understands that "the authenticity of one's gender" will continue to shift through different social encounters. This view matches with Raewyn Connell's assertion that "gender is not fixed in advance of social interaction, but is constructed in interaction."[53] As Anna repeatedly stated, what matters to her is "being comfortable with oneself." To her, LGBT identity is something she considers only because of external reasons and is mostly a matter of friendship or work, not something she feels insecure about.

Like Rizky, Anna perceives sexual and gender identities as social labels that do not entirely dictate her sense of selfhood. The difference between Anna's and Rizky's narratives arises from the different circumstances that shape how they construct their moral identities. In Rizky's case, his understanding is linked to his belief in religious values and his desire to become a better Muslim. For Anna, in contrast, it is about embodying her true self. However, I noticed a quality of ambivalence in Anna's self-assertion of comfort. This is particularly apparent in the incongruities in her narratives, specifically how she internalizes the opinions of others around her, or of society at large, regarding religiosity and gender identity. At times, she seems to conform to these opinions, while at other times she expresses dissent.

If Anna no longer sees any contradiction between spirituality and gender identity or sexual subjectivities, what other sources of inner conflict emerge for her as a former Muslim queer? This question takes us to the last point of our conversation that evening.

Shrinking Heart

When discussing her personal views on religion and gender, Anna mainly described them as things of the past. The subjects of her present struggles came up only later in our conversation, when she whispered to me, as if not wanting her employee Tania to overhear: "I have mono-phobia." She further explained this to me as an acute fear of being alone. Curious to hear more about this condition, I probed Anna for more detail. "It's psychosomatic, my stomach or throat will hurt, and then my heart beats very fast." Additionally, she shared that she often fantasizes that others are speaking negatively about her when she is not present. She continued:

> In my mind, I visualize it like this: My heart [*hati*] that is already small, add to that acid, salt, anything that stings, that's how I felt when I'm alone. It used to be even worse. Imagine a sharp, huge rock placed on top of it, so heavy. . . . Psychosomatically, my heart starts beating very fast, I can't breathe, I couldn't stand. Some people name this feeling isolation, but I call it disconnection. What I need is a connection, not someone physically next to me, but someone who truly engages with me. So, even if there are people around, if there's no real connection, it doesn't help either.

Anna used the Indonesian metaphor *hati*, which I have previously discussed as being transculturally translated to the English word "heart," to express a high level of emotionality. She described her heart shrink-ing and experiencing pain to convey the different levels of emotional pain she feels when she fails to connect with people around her. Anna traced these emotional episodes back to her childhood in Padang, West Sumatra, where her parents divorced and she lived with her grand-mother while her mother battled depression and contact with her father was denied. At age fifteen, Anna left her grandmother's house to live alone in a boarding house, while her mother remarried a military man she did not get along with. Soon after, her mother committed suicide. Meanwhile, Anna still couldn't have contact with her birth father, who had since been diagnosed with schizophrenia. Recounting this experience, she said, "I feel that I was the saddest person in the world, I was just this singular being who is disconnected from everyone."

Using the affective repertoire of "fear of being alone," Anna illustrated how the affective dynamics of inner conflict develop within social relations. She associated the need to be connected with others to the painful memory of losing touch with her parents during her teenage years. Although she values relationality, she also feels ambivalent about it. Ambivalence, as an emotive, is not merely a description of her internal emotional intensity or the specific texture of her experiences of loss, isolation, and disconnection. Rather, it represents an ongoing negotiation of competing emotional forces. These affective dynamics contribute to the ambivalence Anna feels toward connection: while she values relationality, she is simultaneously wary of the pain and potential for further emotional loss that such connections might bring.

The salience of embodied relationality for Anna can be a source of emotional difficulties and, at times, enable her to keep going in the face of these adversities. This inner conflict mirrors the fragility of moral selfhood resulting from the dialectic between self and otherness. Anna's experience exemplifies how inner conflict in Muslim queer worldmaking takes place *beside* but not completely defined by polarized understandings of social or religious norms and by transgressive sexual and gender subjectivities.[54] Alongside this contentious gap, various other moral concerns may arise. In this sense, inner conflict as an affective form of Muslim queer worldmaking is necessarily an unfinished and incomplete process.

* * *

The inner conflicts Rizky, Tino, and Anna face are embedded in, and extend beyond, their struggles to reconcile religiosity with nonnormative sexualities and genders. The affective dynamics of constructing a moral self can vary considerably across biographical trajectories, individual desires, and value systems. Instead of simply replicating the prevailing heteronormative discourse that views inner conflict as a psychological burden, these individuals view it as a model for navigating multiple and sometimes conflicting emotions simultaneously. In their interactions with various scenes of life, encompassing competing moral discourses, mental health issues, gender hierarchies, spiritual healing, and bodily experiences, the protagonists continue to create and adapt numerous affective connections to diverse conceptions of a good life. By engaging with these affective experiences, they construct personal meanings regarding their changing subjectivities as well as their treatment of others and how others perceive them. Inner conflict gives rise to a moral self that is both fragile and contingent to scenes of living.

The impetus toward inhabiting inner conflict appears across various situations that, when combined, reflect repeated encounters with intense contradictions between multiple ideas and alternative possibilities. This brings to mind the notion of impasse, which Michael Jackson describes as a situation where "the unified experience of being in the world is fractured."[55] He suggests that an impasse represents not just a spatiotemporal state of being stalled or stuck but also one of potential. While impasses can slow or hinder well-being phenomenologically, there is also a sense of hope that emerges from this depleting condition. Lauren Berlant also highlights this productive capacity of impasse. She describes it as "a holding station that doesn't hold but opens out into anxiety, that dog paddling around a space whose contours remain obscure. . . . It marks a delay that demands activity. The activity can produce impacts and events, but one does not know where they are leading."[56] This captures the experience of suspended life, where one exists in a state of temporal uncertainty, neither fully advancing nor entirely immobilized, caught instead in an anxious anticipation that nonetheless demands action.

Confronted with inner conflict and its uncertain outcomes time and again, Rizky, Tino, and Anna make various efforts to endure. In doing so, not only do they adapt their sensory and mental capacity to endure, they also transform them. Their endurance becomes more than a response to fractured being; it constitutes an affective remaking of selfhood amid ongoing impasses and contradictions.

2

Moral Participation at the Margins

The sun was at its midday peak as I joined Tino and his friends for a brief getaway to the beach in Rancong. We settled into a shaded thatched hut, eager to escape the heat. What started as a relaxing afternoon with a few fresh coconut drinks imbibed directly from the husk and casual conversation filled with laughter turned into covert whispers as a young, affectionate couple entered the thatched hut next to where we were sitting and started to surreptitiously make out. The group unanimously agreed that such a display of public affection is morally unacceptable in Aceh and must be reprimanded. The conversations extended to the apparent inconsistencies in the implementation of Shari'a law in the region and comments on how hypocritical Acehnese societies can be when it comes to issues of sexuality.

This was not an isolated event. Later that same week, during a late-night motorbike ride, Rafi—who had first introduced me to this group—offered to give me a lift back to the boardinghouse. As we waited at a red light, he directed a harsh comment toward a female motorcyclist queuing next to us. He seemed annoyed not only by the fact that she was riding a motorbike alone at night but also because she was not wearing a *jilbab* (hijab) in a public space. His remark seemed to be a sexist and self-righteous, but he was also making an insinuation about the dubious implementation of Shari'a law in Aceh by pointing out that it is more about the local government's attempt to pay lip service rather than any genuine interest in elevating public morality.

Moments like these left me puzzled. This confusion arose in part because of the stories I had heard from Rafi and his friends about stigmatization and other forms of marginalization they experienced due to their nonnormative same-sex desire or gender expressions. Such views are deeply rooted in dominant beliefs that view such individuals as morally abject. As I continued my fieldwork and encountered similar situations in various places and communities, I realized that it would be insufficient to analyze this phenomenon solely from a dichotomous perspective that categorized these practices as either complicit or resistant or as belonging solely to hegemonic thinking or creative action.

Earlier, I showed how Rizky, Tino, and Anna experienced inner turmoil as they worked on their moral selves. This chapter extends those affective dynamics into an intersubjective field of interaction. It probes into the connections and frictions between moral judgment, ethical improvement, and the political imaginary of Muslim queer and trans worldmaking in communal settings. These circumstances were particularly salient when I listened to conversations between the protagonists and their close ones about everyday events.

As illustrated by the vignettes above, far from being simple conversations, these engagements are laden with moral, ethical, and political concerns. Hence, beyond the practical and cognitive patterning entailed in these processes, I focus on the affective dynamics that enable and shape particular moral and ethico-political enactments at the collective level.

* * *

It is crucial to clarify the conceptual frameworks surrounding the use of the term "community," or *komunitas*, as many of the book's protagonists refer to it. Various Indonesianists have explored the notion of community. In his work on Indonesian nonheterosexual subjectivities, Tom Boellstorff notes that his research participants typically referred to themselves as "people" (*kaum*), while komunitas was occasionally used as an English loanword.[1] However, following the fall of Suharto's authoritarian New Order regime in 1998, civil society activists increasingly embraced the term "komunitas" as a symbol of disillusionment with the government and political party systems. This term characterizes the spirit of political organizing from below, such as that heralded by the rise of the student movements that led the 1998 political reform.

Contemporary Indonesian societies also bore witness to how this term then pervaded both mainstream media and consumer culture, to the extent that critics viewed it as just one of a series of fashionable terms that had become devoid of political meaning. As cultural studies scholar Ariel Heryanto writes, the wide application of this term to describe the reemergence of the spirit of collectivism cuts both ways.[2] While acknowledging that the popular use of the term "komunitas" promises a utopian world where everyone belongs to each other, Heryanto cautions against taking this term at face value, as the community it was striving to enact often came with a price. The price of that belonging includes intolerance, exclusion, or uniformity and other instances where community "functions more as a threat than a promise—a threat of annihilation of those who don't align themselves with the 'community.'"[3]

Even though many of the komunitas I encountered in the field are primarily formed around shared identity markers such as gender, class, religion, ethnicity, and locality, it is important to also look at how the meaning of the term among sexual and gender minorities in Indonesia reveals a more complex case than a simple translation from the classical understanding of community. The coming together of individuals experiencing rampant marginalization as a komunitas reveals the inherently fractured and unstable aspects of communal life in Muslim queer and trans worldmaking.[4] This communal configuration is not only held together by deep emotional bonds rooted in shared histories, localities, and identities but also by the "rush of affect" that pulls individuals toward—and sometimes away from—one another.[5]

Building on this brief theoretical sketch, this chapter examines the affective forces and social contexts that bring individuals together to collectively address questions of moral valuation—what is considered good and right. It also explores how they collaboratively define what constitutes a good life for their communities through ethical judgment and consider the broader implications of their actions for the wider social network through political imagination. To illustrate these dynamics, I analyze two sets of empirical material collected in Aceh: a focus group discussion with the transpuan community in Namu and a hangout session with a group of gay men in Rancong. The use of a specific set of affective repertoires in these collective formations challenges existing moral norms and generates alternative understandings of morality. I introduce here the term "moral participation" to describe how the boundaries between multiple modes of being and becoming "moral" are blurred as they are mediated through a range of communal practices. In these situations, we can see that commitment to and enactment of a specific set of religiously coded moral values involves not only pragmatic and cognitive attachments but also affective ones.[6]

"Of Course It's a Sin!": Paradoxes of Trans Piety

My first interaction with the transpuan community in Namu occurred through Maya, whom we met earlier. Prior to meeting Maya in person, I had only heard her name mentioned by individuals I had met in the capital of Banda Aceh. They described her as the ideal person to connect with if I wanted to research the lives of transpuan individuals in the region. Maya was the founder and leader of a transpuan community organization in Namu that I will call Rumoh Aceh. This organization primarily focused on HIV care and prevention. Although Rumoh Aceh's activism was limited to the district level, as one of the very few transpuan organizations in Aceh, it had attracted attention from LGBT rights activists nationwide. Maya frequently traveled to the provincial capital of Banda Aceh or other cities across the country to attend workshops and meetings on behalf of her community group.

My first meeting with Maya took place one late afternoon in December 2013. Prior to that, we had been communicating through text messages and phone calls to arrange the date and location for our meeting. At first, she had suggested meeting at a coffee shop next to the beauty salon she operated, Salon Primadona. However, just before I left for the designated place, she called and asked me to go to her hair salon instead. When I arrived at the hair salon, which was roughly fifteen minutes' walking distance from where I was staying, Maya and her two friends were waiting on their motorbikes in the parking lot. She instructed me to jump on to the back seat of her motorbike. We drove to the town center, and on the way there, Maya informed me that we were heading to a coffee stall that was popular among the local "*hemong*" (a term commonly used in the local gay slang to refer to "homo" or "gay").

As we approached the coffee shop and rode slowly into the packed parking lane, my heart began to race. I felt the intense gaze of the other coffee-shop clientele (mostly male) as Maya and her friends parked their motorbikes. At the time, I wondered whether people were staring at us because of the presence of feminine figures entering the perimeter without headscarves during broad daylight or because our group mainly consisted of transpuan. After all, in Shari'a-regulated provinces, public spaces like coffee shops are predominately occupied by men.[7] This particular scene resonates with the gendered world of coffee shops in other places such as Cairo, described by Mark A. Peterson, where men of all classes frequent the coffee shops while only a few women, mostly from the upper class, spend time in newly feminized coffee shops.[8]

Under the watchful eyes of the other customers, we entered the coffee shop and took our seats in the inner part of the building. Maya then introduced me to her two friends, Dara and Arie, who were members of Rumoh Aceh and employees at Salon Primadona. I began by explaining my plan to conduct an ethnographic study on Muslim queer and trans worldmaking in Indonesia and expressed my interest in their involvement as research participants. Maya warmheartedly welcomed my idea and suggested organizing a focus group discussion (hereafter FGD) with the transpuan community in Namu, as she was also curious to see how her friends would engage with religious issues.

Little did I know that when Maya said that she wanted to have the FGD soon, what she meant was that it would be held later that evening. Maya and her two friends immediately became busy, making phone calls and sending text messages to invite members of Rumoh Aceh to gather at 10 p.m. that evening. According to Dara, it was important to hold the meeting in the late evening because most of their friends worked in the salon during the day and could attend after only business hours. I also overheard Maya saying on the phone: "If necessary, close the hair salon earlier so that you can join in time." The meeting was set to take place at Mami Yana's hair salon. Mami Yana was an esteemed elder in the transpuan community in Namu whose opinion was highly valued. Maya said we should go to Mami Yana's salon directly after we finished our coffee so that I could be introduced to her as soon as possible. Maya believed that gaining Mami Yana's blessing could help me establish rapport with the rest of the community members during my fieldwork in Namu.

While Maya and her friends were busy making phone calls, I began to feel nervous. I hadn't prepared any structured questions for the FGD since it was planned spontaneously. Meanwhile, Maya told me how curious she was about how her friends would talk about religious issues, as they had never engaged in that kind of discussion before. She added, "While for me personally, I don't really know why, but every time Islam is brought up as a topic of discussion, my body feels weak [*badanku terasa lemas*]." Maya's eagerness to know and the paralyzing inertia she felt when religion became a topic of discussion highlight the limits of what can be said and thought among individuals facing the apparent conflict between religious doctrine and nonnormative sexuality/gender subjectivity.

What happened next felt very quick to me. The four of us traveled to Mami Yana's hair salon, which was located farther west from the town center. I drove the motorbike with Maya in the passenger seat, following Dara and Arie's motorbike as they led the way. When we arrived at Mami Yana's salon, she was busy dealing with a customer, so she came out only briefly to shake my hand. We did not stay long and then had dinner at one of the satay food stalls on the Medan-Banda Aceh intercity road. We parted ways shortly after. I told Maya that I needed to return to my hotel to freshen up and prepare my questions for the FGD.

The FGD

Around 10 p.m., I returned to Maya's salon. Maya, Dara, Nanda, and Alia were getting ready. They locked the double doors of Salon Primadona and we headed to Mami Yana's salon. When we arrived, there were already around five other people waiting inside. The chairs were set in a circle, and a pot of tea and some glasses were ready on a corner table. As I was greeting each of the early attendees, two more people arrived. Eventually, there were fourteen people, including Mami Yana and me, crammed into the salon's lounge, which was only about 4.5 square meters in size.

The discussion began with Maya giving an introduction. She explained the purpose of our gathering that evening and introduced me to the group. Afterward, she asked me to explain why I was there. Nervously, I shared my intention, but my anxiety grew as some individuals in front of me started to giggle as soon as I spoke. Maya called them out: "Why are you all laughing?" Nanda, seated opposite me, explained through her giggles that they were laughing at Cut, a transpuan sitting quietly next to me. Apparently, her eyelash extensions were either too heavy or not properly attached, thus causing her difficulties in opening her eyes. Maya instructed Nanda to change seats with Cut so that the group could concentrate on what I was saying. Although I was not sure whether the transpuan group was able to continue focusing on what I said, I went on, explaining my purpose to the best of my ability.

The atmosphere became tense when I asked the group if I could turn on the audio recording machine to document the conversation. Mami

Yana replied: "No, I do not know who you are or where you are from, and from all of the waria communities in Aceh, why do you choose to come to this one in Namu?" I tried to answer her question by explaining again my background and the purpose of the research, but she remained unconvinced. Dara and Maya tried to support me by explaining to Mami Yana that recording conversations during research is a common practice and that it would be difficult to remember all the details without a recording. Despite their efforts, she remained adamant in her refusal.

To defuse the heated discussion, I suggested to Dara and Maya that we could continue the discussion without recording. However, I also asked the rest of the group, especially Mami Yana, if I could take some notes while they were speaking, saying, "I hope you don't see me as being impolite for taking notes." Mami Yana nodded quietly. I took her gesture as permission to proceed with the group discussion. Consequently, some of the details of the conversation that took place that particular evening I have recalled only partially. The quotes that follow are not direct transcriptions, but rather reconstructions based on my quick notes taken during the FGD, which I later expanded upon immediately after the session.

I opened the discussion by asking the group what thoughts came to mind when they encounter the term "*agama*" (religion). At first, the participants seemed a bit perplexed by this seemingly abstract question. After a few seconds of silence, Dara responded:

> Islam is a way of life [*pedoman hidup*]. It helps me separate right from wrong. But because we are transgender, having an outward appearance as man while feeling like a woman on the inside, naturally, as we grew up, especially in my experience, a feeling [*perasaan*] emerged within me. Have I sinned when I got to know a man and had sex with him? Then there is this fight in my heart.

Before Dara had even finished speaking, a participant, Luna, heckled: "Of course it's a sin!"

Luna's comment—implying that one is naturally a sinner—exemplifies the kind of disruptions that typify the informal interactions between members of the in-group and the wider Muslim community. It also serves as a constant reminder to the protagonists of their failure to achieve moral perfection in the eyes of God because their gender-transgressive bodies are always already associated with sinful desire.

Feeling sinful and fearing divine punishment are two aspects of affective regulation that individuals experience as they construct their moral selfhood in relation to larger spiritual powers. However, despite these seemingly debilitating conditions, most participants in the discussion continued to engage in worship. Mami Yana, speaking on behalf of the other attendees, emphasized the central role of Islam as a way of life among the transpuan in Namu: "All of us here still uphold religious norms and aspire to perform piety the best way we can. Although for some of us like me [who occasionally wear men's clothing] it is apparently easier in comparison to those who have a full female appearance."

Mami Yana was referring to the range of identification terms that exist among transpuan individuals in Aceh. In everyday parlance, "Makcik" is a Malay/Indonesian term to refer to adult women, similar to "Aunty" in English. But among the transpuan community in Aceh, the term "*Cik*" at the end of the word is also derived from the term "*banci*," which in Indonesian popular language has historically been used as a derogatory term for a transgender woman or effeminate man.[9] The term "Makcik" is used to categorize different types of transpuan through their physical appearance.

One end of the spectrum is represented by "Makcik Pak Jan," a person who still maintains a masculine appearance and only occasionally dresses in women's clothing. On the other end, there are "Makcik Pak Pere," who have embraced a feminine appearance through body modifications (such as breast implants and silicone fillings), hormone therapy, and women's clothing. In the middle of this spectrum, we find the "aspiring Mak Cik Pak Pere," who are typically younger transpuan individuals who occasionally adopt temporary feminine attributes such as wigs and padded clothing to create the impression of breasts.[10]

Maya supported Mami Yana's account of the centrality of Islam among transpuan in Aceh by encouraging Achiel, one of the younger participants who had been quiet throughout the discussion, to share her thoughts: "Tell Ferdi, Chiel! Share your experience of winning the Sari Tilawah competition [which involves a poetization of interpretation or exegesis of the Quran] in the district recently, tell him about your experience!"[11] Achiel appeared surprised and remained silent, indicating that she was not ready to tell the story. Uncomfortable in her silence, Cut, who was sitting next to her, jumped in and said:

> Actually, Achiel lives in the district next to Namu, so she's not originally from here. But she is quite well known among the people in this area, and they often call her names when they see her on the street. One day, she participated in the Sari Tilawah competition here, and when she took the stage, many people jeered at her, calling her "*Bencong! Bencong!*" Once she began reciting the Quran, people realized how talented she truly was, and she ended up winning the competition.[12]

Mami Yana responded to Cut's description of Achiel's background story with a sense of pride: "As you can see, although we are like this [*begini-begini*], all waria here know how to read and recite the Quran [*mengaji*], and we are also well informed about religious teachings [*paham agama*]." Inspired by Mami Yana's opinion, the other participants began to speak up one by one. Asri, for instance, said, "Yes, despite our situation, we strive to follow religious norms to the best of our ability. When we return home after having sex, we take a *junub* bath [to become ritually pure], so that if we were to die in our sleep, we would die *husnul khotimah* [with a good end]."[13] Maya provided further examples by mentioning how all hair salons run by transpuan in Namu close their doors and stop accepting customers each time the call for Maghrib prayer (around sundown) is announced. Another participant, twenty-eight-year-old Nanda, exemplified what Asri meant by following norms by sharing her thoughts about the proper ways of dressing: "For those of us who have a feminine appearance, we also wear a *kerudung* [veil], just like any other woman, out of respect for them." Asri then summarized the different remarks by stating, "What we emphasize here is maintaining a harmonious relationship with our social surroundings."

The conversation then shifted to a debate among the participants about the appropriate conduct when attending *salat berjamaah* (congregational prayers) in the mosque, specifically regarding their positioning among the rows of worshippers (*saf*). Some participants explained that they join the front rows directly behind the imam (prayer leader), which are typically reserved for male worshippers. Others mentioned that they stand at the back with the female worshippers, while a few choose to stand separately, in between the male and female rows. The participants were unable to reach a consensus about the right position of transpuan in the gender-segregated arrangements of the mosque. Each participant appeared to have a predetermined idea of where they should stand, shaped by their own understanding of gender embodiment.

These accounts were then challenged by a dissenting voice in the group. Luna addressed the group with a trembling voice:

> Yeah, but what I don't understand, even after all that we have done, is that when we go to the mosque with the genuine intention to repent [*bertaubat*], although we are already in *baju koko* [a type of male shirt worn for ritual worship], not wearing makeup, and when we arrive there, people still say: "Hey you, *banci*! The lower crust of hell! What are you doing here? Do you want to bring this mosque to destruction by coming here?" Why is that? Why do they keep laughing at us? Why do they con-demn us like that? People can be so righteous!

I heard uneasy chuckles coming from the group, and with a grin, Maya said almost apologetically to me: "You have to excuse Luna; she can be *emosi* [emotional] like that."[14] Maya continued, explaining that she pre-ferred to perform *salat wajib* [obligatory daily worship] at home rather than attending congregational prayers at the mosque, thus avoiding the risk of dealing with verbal abuse from others:

> Mind you, I am not doing this because I am stigmatizing myself [*menstigma diri*] as a sinner. But since the sight of waria praying in a mosque causes so much controversy, and in Islam we are taught that insulting someone is a sin, this is why I'd rather not go [to the mosque]. This way, I won't cause others to commit sin because of who I am. It's bet-ter to worship alone. To me, Islam is about my personal connection with Allah, not with society.

I asked the group what they would wear when performing salat. Maya replied:

> Although I myself am not a devout person, I would always remind Alia [her housemate and coworker], "Have you done your prayer for today?

Don't forget to do so. If you pray, do it in any way that is comfortable for you, you can wear male clothing or *mukena*" [a cloak that fully covers females and is worn at prayer].

Some of the participants immediately responded to what Maya said. One person remarked, "No, it is a sin [to wear female clothing]! You must be humble in facing God." Another participant said: "It is *haram* [prohibited] in Islam." A different participant exclaimed: "It's like toying with religion [*mempermainkan agama*]!" Nanda attempted to clarify what some of her friends meant:

> For praying, since it is not something to be toy around with [*main-main*]— we are facing Allah, aren't we? Then I will be authentically [*betul-betul*] a man when I practice salat. I don't wear my makeup, I remove my nail polish, no bra. Just a simple pair of short trousers, then a sarong. I usually wear a *peci* [a black cap widely worn by Muslim males in Southeast Asia], and I roll my hair to tuck it inside the peci. Because this is a really serious [*bukan main-main*] task.

I could hear some of the group members clearing their throats, indicating their tacit agreement with Nanda's remark. Meanwhile, Maya insisted that individuals should have the freedom to choose their own devotional clothing based on personal comfort: "This is the problem. We keep complaining when someone labels us as sinners, but among ourselves, we also call each other sinners. Why are we doing this to each other? Why can't we let each person decide how they want to pray?" The debate continued without resolution. Maya and the rest of the participants couldn't agree on the proper gender attributes for devotional worship.

As I glanced at the clock on the salon wall, I realized it was already past midnight. Sensing the fading energy in the room, I proposed that we should end soon. Before wrapping up, I asked if anyone had any final thoughts on our discussion. Maya responded with a lengthy monologue, seemingly addressing the rest of the group instead of directly answering my question:

> You see, Ferdi, by forming this community, we can at least help one another. If there were a scale to weigh our sins, even if we've made many

mistakes or indulged in our sexual desires by engaging in sinful activities, we are still doing our best to help others. We regularly give *sedekah* [alms] to orphans and assist those in our community who are in need, particularly our own family. This is all to save *pahala* [divine rewards] for the afterlife, which will atone for all sins committed. The strange thing is that despite spending so much to support our surroundings, we still manage to survive; our God-given fortune [*rezeki*] never runs out. God never sleeps. These are all God's trials, and we respond in different ways. When I die, I want to be remembered for my good deeds, nothing else. And when one of us passes away, we can all support one another as a community. Who else will wash our bodies after we die but our fellow waria?

Maya concluded her remarks by addressing the Muslim death ritual, emphasizing that washing, shrouding, and praying for the deceased are obligatory elements of Islamic funeral rites. Typically, the bathing rituals are performed by someone of the same gender as the deceased, although exceptions can be made for close relatives of the opposite gender. The death of a Muslim transpuan often brings such questions to the forefront, especially regarding who holds the right to perform the ritual washing of the deceased.

This dilemma came to public attention following the passing of Dorce Gamalama, a renowned Muslim transgender entertainer from Indonesia, in 2022. Dorce's journey of transition has been extensively covered by Indonesian media, which subjected her life to ongoing public scrutiny. In the weeks leading up to her death, she expressed a wish to be washed and buried according to women's rituals, affirming her identity as a woman. However, her wish sparked controversy: the Indonesian Ulema Council insisted she be buried as a man, while the Muslim mass organization Nahdatul Ulama supported her personal choice. In the end, her family decided to bury her as a man.[15]

Late that December evening, the group conversation drew to a solemn close as Maya posed an open-ended question about how to collectively navigate a world where the fate of transgender bodies remains uncertain, even in death. It was nearly 1 a.m., and most of the participants were ready for dinner. Except for Mami Yana and a few others, the rest of us headed to a food stall in the town center, a popular spot for Maya and her friends, known for its *mie Aceh*, a spicy curried noodle dish unique to the region.

Sins and Sensibilities

The quotes from the FGD illustrate the types of discussion that arose when religious issues became a central topic among the transpuan community in Namu. Many of the debates centered on making sense of sin, particularly in relation to how gender nonconformity complicates daily conduct and engagement with Islamic rituals.

In an article discussing the concept of sinning among "ordinary people" in Aceh, David Kloos writes that an affective framework serves as a key tool for understanding the tension between individual and communal responsibilities in judging bad behavior.[16] Many individuals, when dealing with their own sins or those of others, turn to the practice of salat as a way of seeking divine forgiveness. However, this practice often sparks debate among Muslims due to differing interpretations and the sociopolitical contexts surrounding it.[17] Despite these differences, most interpretations of salat emphasize the development of a direct, personal relationship with God based on lived experience.[18]

In contrast, the debate that took place among the circle of transpuan in Namu expressed concerns quite distinct from the majority opinion. This exchange is instructive, as it reveals the contentious nature of moral and ethical values attached to salat. For them, salat functions not only as a standard practice for performing Islamic piety and seeking forgiveness but also as a key reference point for determining what is considered morally and ethically acceptable. Moreover, it carries political implications regarding nonnormative gender expressions during prayer. This includes arguments about proper attire and uncertainties about one's position within the congregational arrangement in the mosque. The interaction at the FGD in Mami Yana's salon demonstrates that the transpuan group there relied on affective modes of assessment to convince themselves and each other about the proper way to conduct salat.[19]

The group's disagreement about what to wear during daily worship is influenced by Islamic values of humility and modesty.[20] These values affectively code cultural and social expectations, and Islamic edicts requiring both females and males to cover their bodies (*aurat*),[21] albeit in different ways.[22] Muslim transpuan subjectivities challenge clothing norms embedded in the gender binary and heteronormative assumptions, leading to different understandings of bodily expression and affect relate to the notion of sinning. In one perspective, Maya emphasizes the importance of authentic self-expression during salat and suggests that individuals pray in clothing they find comfortable, including wearing the female attire of mukena. In another perspective, salat is perceived as a spiritual place where one should remain humble and modest in the face of God. This condition requires one to be "authentic" by letting go of one's feminine attributes during salat and dressing according to the sex one was assigned at birth.

These conflicting opinions have led to concerns about how sinning is used to marginalize certain groups, as Maya pointed out. While some of the FGD participants, such as Luna, spoke of feeling injured by those who often insulted her as a sinner, the emerging debate within the group about the notion of sinning in response to Luna's experience also revealed how such discussions can perpetuate similar feelings of exclusion among those targeted by this hurtful speech. At the heart of the conversation was a question of moral acceptability: whether the choice of clothing during devotional worship should be seen as a personal responsibility rather than a tool for enforcing moral standards. By addressing the unequal power dynamics within the hegemonic use of the concept of sinning to undermine sexual and gender minorities, Maya raises an ethical question about how we should treat one another.

To answer this question, Maya shared her experience of ceasing to attend mass prayers in the mosque due to the prevalence of violent speech against the visibility of transpuan. She drew a clear distinction between her personal connection with God and communal forms of religious practice, a distinction echoed by some of the other protagonists discussed earlier.[23] Maya explained that her decision was not intended to justify the stigma attached to transpuan but was rather the due to her ethical consideration of preventing others from engaging in insults and abuse. Such actions are explicitly prohibited according to the teachings of the Quran.[24] Rather than asserting her individual autonomy, Maya's empathetic gesture of "not making others commit sin" demonstrates a form of ethical and political imagination that emphasizes intersubjective orientation. By avoiding implicating others in sin, Maya extends a sense of solidarity aimed at reworking power hierarchies perpetuated by gendered inequalities. Her concluding statement captures the relational quality of the collective meaning-making process in the FGD.

The discussion of sinning and its gendered embodiment in the ritual practice of salat sparks a consideration of the negotiation between self and other. In turn, this brings attention to the moral and ethical practices of those living on the margins of the society. Sinning and repentance are viewed as strategies for enduring violence and marginality as a collective while also fostering a sense of belonging through moral participation. To rephrase Maya's conclusion, one of the main purposes of the community is to care for one another. In this sense, morality is fundamentally concerned with sustaining relationships with others, a notion that resonates with the cultural models of emotions in many non-Western contexts.[25]

Moral Dimensions of Emosi

The FGD participants' understanding of morality in relation to individual dispositions and normative discourse is intertwined with the use of emotive and affective repertoires. Emotives can be observed, for example, in the suspicious line of questioning directed toward me and the narratives of pain and suffering group members shared. Additionally, there were expressions of pious self-identification that fostered a collective sense of pride and dignity.[26] While affective relationality is suggested by the atmosphere of intimacy within the group—passionate arguments, jokes, jeers, bursts of laughter, and vehement exclamations—group members did not explicitly articulate specific feelings. However, affective relationality did affect the group dynamic.

To further explore the entanglement between affective dynamics and moralities, we need to go back to the moment when Luna passionately shared her experiences of being insulted at the mosque. I could sense tension building in the group as Luna narrated her frustration. However, this tension dissipated prematurely when Maya quickly dismissed Luna's outburst by labeling her as an emotional person (*orangnya emosi begitu*). Interestingly, this was the only time emotions were distinctly named as such. Up until this point, although affects, emotions, and feelings were seamlessly woven into the group interaction, they had not been a topic of discussion. The difficulties in openly addressing these modalities indicate a particular set of moral conventions at work when it comes to expressing emotion. These were indicated not just by the strong emotive and evocative questions Luna raised in her story but by also her somber facial expression, her trembling voice, and the tears in her eyes. Maya's characterization of Luna as emosi, a loanword from the Dutch "*emotie*," suggests that Maya was concerned about the potential negative impact of continuing the discussion in such an emotional manner. This intervention highlights the complex nature of the meanings of the term "emosi."

It is useful to further consider the loanword "emosi" and its linguistic root within Western culture, where emotions are often associated with gender-biased meanings. This relates to the portrayal of emotions as "the irrational, the uncontrollable, the vulnerable and the female."[27] In her study on American culture, Catherine Lutz examines how emotion is often contrasted with rationality. This bias portrays women as inherently more emotional than men, thereby granting men greater power in the social order based on their presumed superiority in rational thought and cognitive behavior.[28] In contrast, Birgitt Röttger-Rössler presents a less oppositional view of gendered emotionality in Makassar societies in Indonesia, particularly in relation to shame.[29] She observes that men and women have different but complementary roles in sustaining and reshaping the social system. A key question for future research is how rigid gender norms shape the emotional expressions of gender-nonconforming individuals as they navigate existing social structures.

It is also interesting to note how the word has been vernacularized in Indonesia. According to Andrew Beatty, the loanword "emosi" refers to a "sudden access to negative emotion, implying a loss of control."[30] This term does not encompass a broad category of emotions. Beatty, citing Karl Heider's previous research on the landscape of emotion in Minang cultures, claims that rather than describing "real" emotion, the word "emosi" "made people think about emotion in an unfamiliar way."[31] In this context, the term "emosi" is used to indicate a combination of mixed emotions associated with "stirred affect and negative emotional arousal".[32]

Maya's remark to Luna suggests an attempt to dismiss emosi as an isolated anomaly rather than a shared experience. It seems that Luna's display of emotions disrupted the flow of our conversation that evening, leading Maya to offer moral advice. The other members of the group may have interpreted this as a reminder to regulate their emotions during discussion. I believe that Maya's reaction can be linked to the wounding and trauma-inducing qualities of Luna's remark. Dwelling on this painful incident could divert the group's focus from the main purpose of the discussion and expose them to a level of vulnerability they were not yet ready to share with me, especially considering my status as an outsider who had only recently gained access to the community.

Mami Yana's refusal to have the conversation audio-recorded hinted at their caution about sharing personal information with someone they knew little about. Maya's intervention can be read as an attempt to negotiate the limits of ethnographic opacity, and I remain sympathetic to this probable cause, although I never asked Maya the reason for her action that particular evening in December 2013. I present this account to underscore the intricate connection between how Maya and her friends reflect on, act upon, and cope with the constraints of moral norms in their interpersonal interactions. Emotions also serve as a moral compass, helping define the boundaries between the self and the other.

I have shown how forms of affective dynamics enable Muslim transpuan to cultivate moral selves and practice their ethico-political aspirations. However, the FGD interaction also showed how the community of transpuan in Aceh face limitations in their social interactions, which are often limited to a particular time and space, such as their hair salons. This is not to say that the community members are completely excluded from the public sphere. There were a few occasions during my fieldwork when we ventured beyond the hair salons. However, these occasions were more the exception than the rule, as being in public spaces carries the risk of stigma and discrimination for transpuan. This highlights the marginalization of social interactions and the everyday moral actions and ethical practices of individuals with nonnormative genders within the dominant moral order in terms of both space and time.

Nongkrong as Moral Participation

Our exploration of the collective moral practices of the transpuan in Namu was framed by the formal setting of the FGD. However, I encountered other forms of collective engagement with moral conduct among my research interlocutors in Rancong. Located just an hour's bus ride east of Namu, Rancong is the hometown of Tino, whom I introduced earlier. During my fieldwork in Rancong, Tino and I frequented various public spaces there, especially the *warung kupi* (coffee shop). In most of our meetings at these places, we were joined by a group of friends, primarily male, and spent many afternoons together chatting and joking. Occasionally, they would order coffee and food or quietly fiddle with their laptops or smartphones. As sunset approached, the warung kupi would usually close their front doors to comply with Shari'a law, which prohibits commercial activities during the prescribed time of Maghrib prayer. However, most of the warung kupi clientele, including our group, would remain inside, sitting quietly in the dark until the evening call to prayer of Isya was heard and the coffee shop reopened.

Sometimes we would visit different coffee shops or stalls for dinner. However, most of the time we would spend the rest of the evening together in the corner of a coffee shop I refer to as FM, located by the beach in the center of Rancong. On weekends, in addition to serving as a family restaurant, the place would provide live music entertainment for its customers. Accompanied by music played on an electronic organ, two or three people from Tino's group of friends were hired by the business owner to take turns singing popular songs in front of the café's customers as they enjoyed their meals.

FM is an example of the numerous other coffee shops that have mushroomed in Rancong that serve as the main public spots for leisure in Aceh. Spaces for leisure activities like shopping malls, cinemas, or karaoke bars, which are typically found in urban and peri-urban areas of Indonesia and attract a predominantly young, middle-class clientele, are not common in this Shari'a-regulated province. On Sundays and holidays, some individuals in the town might visit the beaches or other natural attractions for a picnic, while those who are more economically privileged may travel to other cities outside Aceh, such as Medan, North Sumatra, to access nighttime entertainment. However, during weekdays, coffee shops are the most popular sites for public leisure in the urban setting of Aceh. Warung kupis, in particular, serve as central gathering places for young people. It is worth emphasizing that women have limited access to these coffee shops. While some women do occasionally visit the coffee shops, especially during the day when they are accompanied by mixed groups of friends, family, or coworkers, male clientele across all social classes routinely dominate the space.

This gendered public space often helped conceal the (homo)sexualized aspects of interactions within the particular group of men I spent time with in Rancong. Despite their nonheteronormative sexuality, the gender-conforming appearances of my interlocutors in Rancong allowed them to blend in easily with the other men who frequented the coffee shops. Only by deeply engaging in conversation could I glean the content of group interactions, which often challenged the normative construction of masculinity. The group's embodied masculinity enabled them to socialize among themselves while navigating the risks of unwanted exposure of their same-sex desires to the wider public. To some degree, this group of gay males in Rancong enjoys relative flexibility in traversing and occupying different public spaces and times. This situation contrasts with the challenges faced by the transpuan community in Namu, who experience stigma and discrimination due to their gender-nonconforming bodies.

During the hangout sessions in Rancong, Tino and his friends engaged in "effeminate" (*ngondhek*) banter and jokes, often accompanied by gossip and personal stories (*curhat*) about their romantic or sexual affairs with other men. A notable example took place at FM one afternoon. Five people, including Tino and me, had been hanging out in the coffee shop since noon. An hour later, two of Tino's friends, Doni and Asta, arrived with their coworkers for their lunch break. When they saw us, Doni and Asta casually greeted us before joining their group, which was seated just a few meters away from us.

In the beginning, Tino and his three friends seemed to pay less attention to Doni and Asta. However, at some point, they started making jokes and mocking Doni and Asta for trying too hard to perform masculinity in front of their coworkers in order to blend in as straight. They laughed at Doni and Asta while commenting on how their gestures were way too effeminate (*ngondhek*) for a straight person. Some people at my table even playfully simulated an imaginary dialogue containing sex puns based on the movements of the lips of Doni, Asta, and their colleagues. They did all of these things boisterously without considering whether people in the warung could hear them or not. I could not tell for sure whether Doni and Asta or their coworkers could hear what was being said at our side of the table, as they did not react. However, considering our proximity, it is likely they heard some of these rather offensive jokes and chose to ignore them.

In his monograph about nonheterosexual lives in Indonesia, Tom Boellstorff discusses the role of *tempat ngeber*, or flaunting places, in the formation of *dunia gay* (the gay world).[33] This term refers to semi-private sites in public spaces where Indonesian gay men express and assert their desire for same-sex intimacy away from the scrutiny of family or workplace.[34] Notably, unlike Boellstorff's informants in Surabaya (East Java) and Bali, none of my research interlocutors in Rancong mentioned the word "*ngeber*." Instead, Tino and his friends often interchangeably used "*nongkrong*" (hangout) and "*ngumpul*" (get-together) to refer to their group activity.

Nongkrong, according to Alexandra Crosby, is a group activity that "creates a space, protected from the outside world, where social conventions and political stereotypes are loosened or even reversed; a space for taboos to be aired."[35] The dynamics within nongkrong involve what Benedict Anderson calls "direct speech," which is "made up of "gossip, rumors, discussions, arguments, interrogations, and intrigues."[36] Following the notion of nongkrong as a spatial practice across different social classes (mostly by male actors) that produces a public sphere and serves as a form of political participation through conversation, I argue that nongkrong for nonheteronormative Muslim subjectivities also operates as a communal event that establishes moral boundaries. Through the act of nongkrong as a semi-public practice, they willfully participate in drawing moral boundaries around certain social behaviors. One example of this is the following scene.

Anggun at the Papal Basilica of Saint Francis of Assisi

During one of our regular hangout sessions at FM on a rainy afternoon in January 2014, as we were sitting in the *lesehan* (ground-seating) section of the coffee shop, Tino asked me and three of his other friends whether any of us had seen the new YouTube video of Anggun singing in a Christmas concert held at the Papal Basilica of Saint Francis of Assisi in Italy. Anggun is a famous Indonesian female pop singer-songwriter who moved to France to pursue an international career in music and eventually gained commercial and global success.

Gossip, rumors, and conversations about female pop stars, both local and international, are common among the network of Indonesian gay friends I socialized with on a daily basis. These discussions usually focused on the latest controversies, hit songs, appearances, or fashion styles of certain public figures, mainly female, who are embraced by the queer subculture and considered gay icons. Anggun was one of the female celebrities linked to this prestige, alongside internationally renowned figures such as Madonna and Britney Spears and nationally celebrated Indonesian singers and *dangdut* performers such as Ayu Ting and the late Julia Perez.[37] These figures have been embraced by many sexual and gender minorities in the country because they represent glamour and strength in the face of adversity.

When Tino brought up Anggun during our conversation that afternoon, I expected it to be a typical chitchat about the media buzz surrounding her latest fashion statement or yet another successful performance on the international stage. As some of us had not yet seen the concert video Tino mentioned, we gathered around to watch it on a group member's tablet. While the video streamed, Iman, one of Tino's friends, interjected: "Why is she performing at the Vatican? Isn't she supposed to be a Muslim?" This question sparked a heated debate about the authenticity of Anggun's Muslimness. Others replied, "Maybe she did this to humiliate [*mempermalukan*], no, . . . to besmirch [*mencoreng*] the name of Islam?" Tino remarked, "Perhaps she is just being professional about it? She does it because someone hired her and she made use of the opportunity to leverage her own popularity?" Andi, a communication major at university, said, "Yeah, but I bet this also has to do with the pope trying to pit Muslims against each other. By appointing a Muslim singer in a Christmas concert, this must be one of his strategies for Kristenisasi!"[38] I was mainly quiet as a tried to keep up during the rapid exchange among the group of four. At one point, I asked if Anggun had publicly identified herself as a Muslim, but no one seemed interested in responding to my question. They all seemed baffled by how one of their favorite singers and a fellow Indonesian Muslim could perform Christmas carols in a basilica in a globally televised event organized by the Vatican.

This vignette depicts a typical get-together (or nongkrong) involving Muslim gay men at a coffee shop in Rancong. Through nongkrong, the participants not only express their sexual subjectivities and transgress normative masculinity, they also make claims about what constitutes the moral boundaries. Tino and his friends did not question the aesthetics of Anggun's performance or her revealing strapless dress, which can be considered immodest and unacceptable according to the Islamic female dress code. Instead, they focused on the possibility that Anggun's performance at a Christmas concert, where the pope was present, might represent an attempt at religious conversion or apostasy. The interlocutors did not consider alternative interpretations of Anggun's performance as a possible gesture of interfaith harmony (*kerukunan antar agama*), which is also common in Indonesian public discourse, especially among moderate Muslim intellectuals. Instead, they viewed her actions as a moral threat.

Tino and his friends' fixation on Anggun's performance stemmed from speculation that she was transgressing national and religious affiliations. The suspicion that her performance was a covert attempt at religious conversion reflects the distrust and fear among Indonesian Muslims, especially after the political reform in 1998, toward perceived threats to the identity and stability of the Muslim community. As Andi's comment on "*kristenisasi*" suggests, his concerns reflect the common usage of the term among Indonesian Muslims, which Melissa Crouch described as denoting Christian missionary practices viewed as unfair or deceptive. Such methods, Crouch explains, may include providing aid or material assistance to non-Muslims with the intent of converting them to Christianity.[39]

The feelings of disbelief, disappointment, and betrayal that surfaced in the interaction reveal the limits of the group's moral laxity concerning Muslim identity. They could participate in friendly banter around non-normative sexual innuendo and intimacy on a daily basis. They could enjoy celebrating female entertainers, such as Anggun, even though their clothing choices often strayed from religious norms. These celebrities could even serve as a means of expressing belonging to cosmopolitan lifestyles and rearticulating a certain trope of modernity. In these instances, morality appeared more secular and loose in its application. However, when Islamic identities were potentially challenged, what appeared to be flexible moral positions became subject to a wider historical and culturally specific discourse on religious conversion.

Neither Subversion nor Submission

The Anggun controversy illuminates how some Muslim queer individuals do not always adopt an agonistic framework in their interaction with hegemonic moral norms. This is evident in the negative emotional reactions to and growing apprehensions about Anggun's behavior, which they suspected was propagating a Christian message aimed at influencing others away from Islam. This reaction is closely tied practical concerns rooted in Islamic orthodoxy. This concept is related to the work of Talal Asad, who argues that the religious dimension of moral engagement reflects more than just a set of opinions; it embodies a specific relationship, one defined by power. Furthermore, he states that Islamic orthodoxy is present "whenever Muslims have the power to regulate, uphold, require, adjust correct practices, and condemn, exclude, undermine, or replace incorrect ones."[40]

A similar dynamic was present among the transpuan in Namu, particularly when some participants of the focus group discussion insisted on not "toying with religion" (*main-main dengan agama*). What constitutes the limit of moral legitimacy is different in each case. The moral reproach Tino and his friends expressed stems from their fear and suspicion of a conversion agenda; they believe that the act of an Indonesian Muslim performing for the Vatican church may jeopardize collective affinity to Islam as a source of true belief. Conversely, the moral reproach the transpuan in Namu expressed was rooted in humility and modesty as virtues that should be nurtured during worship. This pertains to a belief that one can commit to one "authentic" gender through proper gender-specific attire when facing God.

Some of the contradictions in these interactions remain unresolved, and this situation points to the difficulties in finding the balance between personal and religious ideals of morality.[41] The main point is not the success of such practices in establishing an "authentic" moral standing. Rather, the most important insight here is the potential for Muslim queer and trans subjectivities to heterogeneously and collectively inhabit the tensions between the moral codes that can be transgressed and those deemed nonnegotiable. It is tempting to view these actions through the lens of false consciousness that perceives sexual and gender minorities as internalizing and re-signifying the very norms that subjugate them.

This issue returns to the initial concerns in this chapter: whether these moral practices in Muslim queer and trans worldmaking are merely resignifications of, and submission to, dominant norms given their less explicit forms of making alternative meanings.

The community members' modes of moral participation differ from the liberal-progressive model of agency that Saba Mahmood describes as "encumbered by the binary terms of resistance and subordination," a model that "ignores projects, discourses, and desires that are not captured by these terms."[42] Instead of reproducing either/or arrangements, members of each community navigate moral norms and ethical judgements both individually and collectively in response to the specific situations they encounter. Although these interactions are marked by power asymmetries organized along gender lines, with gay males in Rancong having more access to public spaces than the transpuans in Namu, the two situations demonstrate significant overlap. In both cases, the moral participation of group members works within and against dominant moral codes engendered by religious doctrines, social norms, and political discourse. However, the practices of these different communities are made up mainly of improvisation, drawing on the everyday vernaculars of Muslim queer and trans worldmaking, such as same-sex desire, gender-nonconforming bodily gestures, styles of dress, popular cultures, and strategies for coping with stigma and marginalization. In this sense, moral participation in Indonesian Muslim queer and trans worldmaking is far more nuanced than any narrative that portrays these experiences as either subverting or reinforcing norms. Such a view risks oversimplifying these diverse spaces into a single defining category.

In a broader social context, the moral practices of these different communities and their emotional implications may not necessarily translate to better inclusion. But despite the bleak consequences of their actions, the actors involved persist all the same. The repetitive acts of articulating how one is being affected by the challenges of forming individual and communal relationships with existing moral values and codes are what configure the possibility of enduring otherwise in Indonesian Muslim queer and trans worldmaking projects. While such forms of moral participation are multifaceted and may appear ambiguous to those outside these communities, one thing is certain: being marginalized due to existing moral norms does not preclude these communities from being moral. The process of becoming a community relies on a wide range of bodily capacities, personal experiences, and ways of forming relationships with what is considered moral, ethical, and political. Muslim queer and trans worldmaking projects entail collective ways of dealing with individual moral struggles. Affective bonds between community members form in this way. From this togetherness, efforts are made to cultivate ethical sensibilities and envision political possibilities for inhabiting the world differently.

This chapter has shed light on the role of komunitas as a site of moral participation that emerges on the fringes of Muslim societies in Indonesia. Even though these communities functions as spaces for intimacy, reciprocity, and conviviality, they are also deeply rooted in shared experiences of vulnerability to violence and the desire to overcome common suffering. In the next chapter, I will delve deeper into the mercurial aspects of Muslim queer and transgender worldmaking, where individuals persist in living under the shadow of violence. Their stories shed light on how personal encounters with violent events are forged into spaces of otherwise. Within these spaces, questions about how life might be lived or should be lived are continually reworked and reimagined.

3

In the Shadow of Violence

Sexual and gender minorities in Indonesia include people who identify as gay, lesbian, queer, waria or transpuan, trans man, and other nonhetero and noncisnormative subjectivities who do not define (and/or do not have the privilege of defining) themselves in terms of identity categories. However, it wasn't until 2016 that this group was collectively labeled using the acronym LGBT and people in that category were portrayed as a threat to the nation. The Islamic newspaper *Republika* initiated this framing with a front-page headline on January 24, 2016, that proclaimed "LGBT Is [a] Serious Threat." The origins of this controversy can be traced to a Twitter post made in mid-January 2016 by the Muhammad Nasir, the minister for technology, research, and higher education. Nasir suggested that LGBT student organizations on university campuses should be banned, triggering an immediate and intense media reaction. Seemingly caught off guard, he attempted to soften his stance with less provocative statements. However, his remarks had already garnered significant backing from key government bodies, including psychiatrists and public figures, many of whom called for further exclusionary measures against LGBT people.[1]

The media storm that followed Nasir's comment reveals a shift in the nature of political power in Indonesia today. This event, which was dominated by the mass media, underscores the structural dynamics of Indonesia's liberalization and the complex negotiations between collective meanings and the emotions that drive them. While power is now wielded by a diverse array of actors, many of whom are adept at using media, it is clear that that those most in need of protection, such as sexual and gender minorities, are the ones who have been most harmed.[2] Emphasizing the mediated nature of the anti-LGBT controversies since 2016 is not an attempt to downplay the real-life experiences of lesbians, gays, waria, and others who face threats to their well-being; the far-reaching repercussions of the media campaign have intensified these threats.

Anti-LGBT sentiment, amplified through both mass and social media, spilled over into public spaces. Posters and banners began appearing in major cities like Jakarta, Bandung, and Yogyakarta bearing slogans such as "LGBT is a contagious disease: Do not let Allah's punishment fall upon us as it did to the sodomites and lesbians in the past," "Lesbians and homosexuals are barred from entering our territory," and "We condemn LGBT." Many of these messages, infused with religious demagoguery, were reportedly issued by nonstate organizations with Islamist backgrounds such as Front Pembela Islam (Islamic Defender Front), Gerakan Pemuda Ka'bah (Ka'bah Youth Movement), and Forum Ukhuwah Islamiyah (Islamic Brotherhood Forum). This rhetoric was compounded by more direct, often legitimized, forms of violence that targeted sexual and gender minorities across the archipelago.

Various scholars have identified the causes and impacts of the rise of anti-LGBT campaign in Indonesia since 2016.[3] As I have discussed elsewhere, this volatile public discourse is not unprecedented.[4] It emerged from the remnants of New Order ideology, which emphasizes a set of "family values" (azas kekeluargaan) defined by heterosexuality and the paternalistic nuclear family as the basis for national belonging. In this context, sexual and gender minorities are portrayed as abject[5], a public nuisance[6], and subject to censorship.[7] The social marginalization of those who don't conform to hetero and cisnormative logics became more explicit after Indonesian Reformasi in 1998.

Many believed that Reformasi would usher in an era of social justice and equality for the nation. This optimism was bolstered by early signs of democratization such as freedom of the press, electoral reforms, and regional autonomy. The civil society sector also grew as social justice activists expanded their influence. Some organizations made significant progress toward achieving equal rights and a dignified life for sexual and gender minorities. However, this hopeful moment was short lived. The transitional period following Suharto's fall also featured Islamic revivalism, which had been suppressed during his regime through tight control over religious expression and institutions. Since the early 2000s, phenomena such as the popularization of a pious lifestyle among the middle class, increased visibility of public piety in the media, the revival of Islamist political parties, and the increasing number of informal Islamist conservative groups indicate the central role of religious morality in remaking social, political, and cultural values in Indonesia.[8] This redefinition of public morality by state- and religion-based interests directly impacted the newly claimed political freedoms of sexual and gender dissidents that had begun to emerge.[9] Nonnormative genders and sexualities, which had previously been met with reluctant acceptance and occasional condemnation under Suharto's regime, began to face increased hostility from various nonstate Islamist organizations after 1998. One of the first major incidents occurred in November 2000, when a gathering of gay men and transpuans in Yogyakarta was attacked by local Islamic vigilantes.[10] Following this, more violent events took place, primarily in urban areas of Java.

The state has been complicit in these developments. Indonesian police forces have not only failed to protect the victims of these attacks but have also been perpetrators of violence toward sexual and gender minorities.[11] From 2000, a shift toward greater regional autonomy in the country coincided with the proliferation of discriminatory laws and regulations. In the name of upholding public morality, numerous provinces, districts, and municipalities across the archipelago gradually issued regulations that characterized homosexual behavior as "immoral" and punishable by law. Legislative changes on the national level further reflect this shift: the 2008 Anti-Pornography Law was the first to contain clauses later used against non-heterosexuals. The 2022 Criminal Code further criminalizes extramarital sex, disproportionately impacting gender and sexual minorities as well as women. This development counters the popular depiction of "'Indonesian culture' as 'tolerant' of homosexuality and transgenderism."[12] Instead, it reveals a subtle, drawn-out process of legitimizing certain ways of being while delegitimizing other ways of being based on sexual orientation and gender identity.[13]

The emergence of anti-LGBT campaigns in 2016 is part of the larger pattern of normative violence in Indonesia's modern history. Normative violence, a term coined by Judith Butler, refers to violence that is not only normative but also stems from the enforcement of societal norms. Butler considers normative violence to be the active feature of normative regulations that promulgate ideals used to render actions legible or illegible—or judged acceptable or unacceptable. Because norms "define the parameters of what will and will not appear within the domain of the social," they encourage violence against those who do not conform, while those who affirm the norms benefit.[14] Butler writes that norms exert violence in two ways: one is occasional and incidental violence tied to a particular manifestation of the norm and the other is the inherent violence of norms by virtue of their constitutive "worldmaking" and "reality-conferring capacity."[15] To delineate how normative violence shapes the affective dynamics of Muslim queer and trans worldmaking, this chapter follows the life stories of Ali and Maya.

Ali's Growing Pains

I first met Ali, a twenty-seven-year-old Muslim gay man from Yogyakarta, in 2007 while he was volunteering at a queer film festival I co-organized in the city. At the time, he was still a student at one of Yogyakarta's Islamic universities. Our collegial relationship continued on and off over the three years we worked together to plan film festivals. We often ran into each other at social events and other queer gatherings in the city, including monthly gay nights he organized with his friends at a local nightclub. Occasionally, I would spot him at Gang Buku, a local hangout that was one of the few spots in the city where gay men and transgender women could socialize and, at times, engage in sex work with passing clientele. During these encounters, Ali sometimes appeared dressed in female clothing and full makeup, or what some scholars refer to as *dandan*.[16] This usually indicated that he was there for sex work instead of just socializing.

Over time, through our sporadic collaborations and chance encounters, I learned that Ali was heavily involved in advocating for LGBT issues. His activities ranged from conducting HIV/AIDS campaigns with the local Indonesian planned parenthood organization (PKBI Yogyakarta) to leading a community-based LGBT rights group in 2011. Ali's peers often described him as pious. He was regularly called upon to lead prayer ceremonies at communal events, such as when we held a communal feast, or *slametan*, during the queer film festival.[17] Ali's image as a pious Muslim seems to have been shaped by his upbringing and his education. Our mutual friends often brought up Ali's educational background as an *anak pesantren* (a student of an Islamic boarding school), sometimes jokingly. Alternatively, he would be referred to as *anak kyai*, a phrase that highlighted that Ali's father was a well-known religious male figure (*kyai*) in his village.

One of the most memorable events that occurred between Ali and I transpired during the final queer film festival in April 2009. It was the fourth time the festival had been organized since I initiated it with a friend in 2006. After three years of co-directing the festival, I felt it was time for me to step back and give someone younger the opportunity to lead. I encouraged Ali to take on my role as director, promising that I would support him through the entire process. He accepted my proposal and took on the leadership role of organizer of the 2009 festival.

Despite a hostile protest some months earlier in Jakarta that year, the preparations for the festival had proceeded smoothly. The queer film festival in Yogya was part of a touring event that derived from the film festival held in the capital. A few days after the festival opened in Yogyakarta, Ali, Fitri, the director of the festival in Jakarta, and I gathered at one of the film screening venues, the French Cultural Center in Yogyakarta. It was late evening as we sat around the café in the cultural center preparing for the next day's screenings. The last film screening for that day had just finished and most of the audience had already gone home. The atmosphere that night was tense. That morning, both the manager of the French Cultural Center and the festival organizing committee had received a letter signed by the Forum Ukhuwah Islamiyah demanding that the festival be stopped. Rumors circulating among the festival organizers suggested that the festival could be attacked by this particular group at any time. Anticipating potential hostility, we requested a representative from the local chapter of the Legal Aid Institute (Lembaga Bantuan Hukum) to provide legal support throughout the night's events.

The anticipated moment came as dozens of men approached the gate of the center. Their faces were concealed with scarfs and they were waving banners and flags. Almost half of them brandished machetes, crowbars, and other sharp objects. They shouted angrily at the organizing committee and demanded that festivalgoers leave the event. Initially, I was gripped by a paralyzing fear when these men arrived. However, I quickly got hold of myself and asked Ali and Fitri to join me in meeting with the protesters' representatives to hear their demands. Udin from the Legal Aid Institute also attended the discussion as a mediator. The three of us sat around one side of a round table in the café across from five representatives of the protest group. The remaining protesters stood vigilantly behind them, observing the mediation process from beyond the iron picket fence that marked the perimeter of the French Cultural Center.

The situation escalated when the protesters accused the festival of recruiting gays and lesbians and labeled the organizers as promoters of vice that needed to be stopped. Fitri immediately tried to refute these claims, while I viewed them as rhetorical provocations. One protester then asked each of us if we were gay or lesbian. Fitri denied it, identifying herself as a heterosexual ally. Ali, visibly frustrated, spoke in a trembling voice, "Yes, but if I had a choice, I would never have chosen to be born this way!" Before he could finish, the opposing speaker interjected, "If you really don't want to be gay anymore, we could show you the way, but the first step is to stop the festival!"

Feeling disquieted by Ali's emotional outburst, I tried to steer our discussion away from this line of questioning. Realizing that prolonging the debate might be counterproductive and harmful to us as festival organizers, I sought to deescalate the situation by asking the protesters to state their main demands. I told them then that we would discuss these demands with the rest of the festival committee before collectively deciding on our response. After voicing their formal demands, the protesters agreed to leave the venue. But later that same evening, the police revoked the festival permit and the film festival was officially shut down for security reasons (*demi alasan keamanan*).

A closer look at the specific moment of Ali's emotional response to the demonstrators' accusations offers a glimpse of his internal conflict about being both Muslim and queer. The focus here is not just on understanding how individual bodies handle contradiction and how this tension might manifest as emotional breakdowns but also on the interactions that triggered Ali's response. This includes not only his vulnerable position in front of the protesters but also his relationships with his supporters—Fitri, myself, and the other festival organizers—who were present during the contentious discussion that evening.

Blossoming Against the Norms

Memories of that incident at the French cultural center returned to me as I met Ali again one dry and chilly evening in April 2014 during my fieldwork in Yogyakarta. We sat in a *warung susu* (literally, milk stall) on one of the city's busiest streets in the south. I'd had serendipitous interactions with Ali on a handful of occasions during the initial months of my field-work, but they were mainly in noisy night clubs, so we did not have much opportunity to chat. During one exchange, I mentioned that I wanted to interview him for my research, and he agreed to be interviewed.

Also during that encounter, he whispered to me, "Mas, I am now posi-tive, but I am healthy." He has always addressed me as "Mas," a respectful term in Javanese for older men, a practice shared by only a few of his peers; most others call me by my first name. I was struck by his casual-ness in sharing this news, especially since most people I knew living with HIV in Indonesia found it difficult to accept a positive diagnosis, let alone discuss it openly. Ali's openness about his seropositive status is unusual viewed against the larger historical backdrop of the HIV epidemic in Indonesia. Even though the disease has been present there for decades, since the 1980s, it still forces many individuals into silence and secrecy as survival strategies.[18] Despite the fact that on paper at least, antiretroviral therapy has been made available free of charge nationwide since 2006, the silence around HIV infection persists due to the moral and social stigma attached to HIV/AIDS and to local political conditions marked by discrimination and faltering healthcare systems.[19]

As we caught up that night at the milk stall, Indonesian pop-rock music blared around us, interspersed with the noise of groups of young people at nearby tables. I remarked how much healthier he looked, recalling how weak he had appeared the last time I saw him, about a year before I left for Berlin. He told me that he was now working for a private telephone service provider, saying, "The working shift is quite tough, Mas, but the salary is good. I feel much better now since leaving the activist circle. I just couldn't handle the stress anymore." I had heard rumors that Ali had resigned from his position as a director for a youth LGBT rights group in Yogyakarta in 2012, but I had not realize at the time that he had left the activist scene altogether.

Before delving into deeper conversations, I asked Ali for his consent to record our conversation. I preemptively apologized if any of my questions came across as intrusive or suggested that I was unfamiliar with his life. He agreed and began sharing stories about his life.

Ali's stories centered on his childhood and his ambivalent feelings toward his family. Ali is the youngest of four siblings; he has two older sisters and one older brother. He described his family as normative (*mengikuti ekspetasi masyarakat*), meaning "all my sisters wear *jilbab* [a headscarf], all are married, none are *neko-neko* [Javanese for acting out of the ordinary]. This is so different to me; since I was very young, I have been the most rebellious [*paling rebel*] out of the four." This "rebelliousness" often led to arguments with his father, a highly respected religious leader in their *kampung* (urban informal settlement). Despite these disputes, Ali acknowledged that his life is heavily influenced by his parents, especially his father, regarding the conduct of a "good Muslim." This included daily prayers and attending an Islamic boarding school. His decision to attend an Islamic university was also driven by family obligations:

> I am not that smart, so I didn't want to disappoint my family. I didn't insist on attending a prestigious and expensive university. For me, failing university would have added a huge moral burden [*beban moral*]. So I did what my family told me to do, which also saved them money.

Ali disclosed that the pressures from his parents extended beyond his formative years and into his adult life. Despite expressing discomfort with his familial relationship, Ali still lived with his parents at the time of our conversation. It is common for unmarried Indonesian young adults, particularly those from the working class like Ali, to live with their parents and siblings. Scholars have noted that the dominant norm of heterosexuality in a family home often negatively affects gays and lesbians by forcing them into lives of isolation and secrecy.[20] This is also generally the case for Indonesian gays. Tom Boellstorff notes that while the heterosexual family home affects Indonesian gay men differently based on class and status, it is predominantly a site where nonheterosexual practices and identities must remain hidden.[21]

Ali had developed a higher degree of confidence about exploring his same-sex desires after entering university. As a young adult, he was able to find solace and support through his own community. While finding supportive peers did not necessarily encourage him to disclose his sexual orientation to family members, he didn't entirely isolate himself or "close himself" (*menutup diri*) or keep his social life secret.[22] He didn't hide his active engagement with sexual rights issues in the city.[23] However, his involvement in Yogya's queer scene, such as the queer film festival organization, never gained approval from his family, especially his father. These activities frequently became a source of conflict between him and different family members.

One evening, after attending the International Day Against Homophobia and Transphobia (abbreviated as IDAHOT), which is commemorated annually every May 17th, he arrived home late. His father, angered by his tardiness, grabbed Ali's backpack bag to search through it for prohibited items such as cigarettes. When his father found a few packs of condoms that were distributed during the commemoration of IDAHOT inside his backpack, he shouted, "How many condoms did you use today?" (translated from Javanese: *Entek kondom piro kowe!*). The entire family heard this, casting a mercurial tone over the household for days. His siblings continued to bring up the matter; his sister accused Ali of being a sinner (*tukang maksiat*) while his brother-in-law scolded him, yelling, "You infidel! A graduate of *mu'allimin* [Islamic religious education], a son of a kyai, but hanging out with a bunch of homos!"[24]

The tension between Ali and his family members peaked in 2012 when his sister read his personal diary. She discovered Ali's private thoughts and feelings and what he wrote about his intimate relations with other men. Moreover, she found out he was HIV positive, a diagnosis he had received in 2010 but had kept secret for fear of worsening the already strained familial relations. Recalling his initial reaction to the diagnosis, Ali said:

> It was a really bleak time at the beginning. I was very negative and down. . . .
> I lost my balance [*hilang keseimbangan*]. What should I do? I hadn't finished college then, didn't have a stable job, and only did volunteer work here and there, but nothing permanent. I had these very destructive ways of viewing life. I started blaming many things, but now I realize that sometimes there are blessings [*anugerah*] hidden in ugly things.

Ali saw these events—his HIV diagnosis and his sister's discovery of it—as a blessing in disguise. They significantly impacted his troubled relationship with his family and his perception of life. After the diary incident, Ali ran away from home feeling enraged (*marah sekali*) and ashamed (*malu*) because his HIV status had been exposed without his consent.

For around two months, he stayed with different friends in Yogyakarta and also went to Jakarta to find a job.

During this period, his siblings tried to contact him via emails and text messages. His older sister, for instance, sent him an email asking him whether his "decision to be gay" (*memilih menjadi gay*) was final. When he confirmed that it was, she began sending him articles on popular psychology and Islamic teachings, trying to convince him that he had made the wrong choice and could still "return" to heterosexuality. Ali did not explicitly refute his sister's opinion in the emails but responded by sending her online articles that offered counterarguments.

After being away from home for two months, Ali received a text from his brother-in-law asking for an in-person meeting. They met at a hospital in Yogyakarta where Ali was collecting his monthly antiretroviral medication. Ali intentionally selected this location because he understood his brother-in-law would be unlikely to cause a scene in a public setting, even if their discussion became confrontational. In that meeting, Ali's brother-in-law asked him to return home, expressing his family's concern. Not long after, Ali went home, since by that time he had already run out of places to stay. He recounted that when he returned home,

> everything seemed quieter, as if nothing had happened. This is typical of my family. Every time there's a problem, it never gets resolved. Things just suddenly turn quiet [*hening*] again. Perhaps they do this to protect my father's *pride* [in English], since he is the only one in the family who still doesn't know about *this* [seropositive status]. But sometimes, I still can sense my siblings are watching me from afar.

This narrative underscores how the avoidance of conflict is indicative of the prevailing heteronormative family model, or "family values" (*azas kekeluargaan*). On one level, this model operates through the unresolved and tacit dissonance within Ali's family domain, that idea that "everyone knows" while family members discreetly monitor each other's conduct (in Indonesian, *tahu sama tahu*). One way to interpret the siblings' less antagonistic ways of addressing Ali after his return home to see it as a strategy to avoid the risk of him leaving again. However, I want to draw attention to Ali's perception that the seemingly less contentious domestic situation after his return was an attempt to protect the father's pride. The discrete atmosphere within Ali's family—stemming from the potential shame and disgrace that Ali's seropositive status could bring the family—further establishes an affective ground for his ongoing othering within the familial unit. How much does this tenuous atmosphere affect Ali's own sense of belonging to notions of family and home?

The Home for the Heart

Our conversation at the milk stall continued into the night as we ordered our second round of drinks. I asked Ali whether he was still devoutly performing religious duties as I knew he had in the past. He answered:

> Not so much anymore. I think I am more a spiritual person now than a pious [*taat*] one. I feel more comfortable [*lebih nyaman*] being in the middle [*di tengah-tengah*]. I am not one of those "Muslim fanatics" anymore. Maybe people still consider me as a Muslim, but I am more of a "Muslim KTP" [a term referring to someone who is listed as Muslim on their ID card but does not actively practice] since I no longer fully perform religious rituals.

By not fully performing (*tidak sepenuhnya menjalankan*) religious duties, he was referring to his lack of intention (*niat*) in practicing obligatory worship. While Ali would still go to the mosque for Friday prayers and would sometimes pretend to fast during Ramadan or perform daily prayers around his family at home, he only did this to avoid feeling guilty (*merasa bersalah*) for not fulfilling his parents' expectations. This lack of intention is something that he did not perceive until he grew older. As a teenager, he not only performed most of the five basic acts in Islam (*Rukun Islam*) wholeheartedly, such as conducting daily prayers and fasting during the whole month of Ramadan, but he also engaged in the habitual practices of *sunnah* (supererogatory act of worship following the example of the Prophet) such as the morning prayer of *salat dhuha* and the ascetic (*prihatin*) fasting ritual every Monday and Thursday. He pointed to several life events that had shifted his perception of Islam, mainly attributing them to his experience in the *pesantren* (Islamic boarding school):

> When I was in the pesantren, I studied very detailed rulings within Islam through an esoteric book called *Riyadhus Shalihin*. But in spite of its claim of comprehensiveness, I still did not feel accommodated. One specific ruling, for example, stipulates that females should not appear masculine and vice versa. . . . . If anything, learning about all this made me even less longing [*merindukan*] toward, well, maybe not God, but toward the religion itself.

Ali also realized that the problems he had at home with his family extended to peers and neighbors in the village:

> In retrospect, my upbringing [*pola asuh*; literally, "parenting patterns"], especially my father's parenting style, played a significant role. While my mom was generally more understanding, my father's tough upbringing was traumatic [*menimbulkan banyak trauma*]. Actually, it wasn't just my family, people in my surroundings also contribute to this trauma. If only they taught me that religion is full of love and compassion [*cinta kasih*], perhaps I wouldn't have turned out like this and might have embraced it more. But in the end, I hated it [*membenci itu*] because they forced it on me.

Ali's depiction of the trauma that shaped his identity mainly pertains to the pressures he felt growing up, especially from his father, who often mocked him for seeming "effeminate" (*kayak perempuan*). His junior high school years were pivotal, marking the time when he "started to realize" his sexual desire for other men: "I did not accept it then. It [the realization of being attracted to men] only came to me later as I gained more knowledge about these things. When I first found out, I was really *in denial* [in English]." Ali elaborated that his denial encompassed

> all kinds of bad feelings. I blamed everything else—God, my family. I couldn't understand why I was so different from others. Even when I tried to appear as "manly" as possible, I faced constant ridicule. Meanwhile, my friends didn't seem to struggle so much [*bersusah payah*] to get

acceptance. My father was never supportive. Even if I tried head over heels [*jungkir balik*], he still didn't care.

This last remark brought me back to the incident at the French Cultural Center in April 2009 when Ali had experienced an emotional breakdown. His statement to the group of protesters that he "did not choose to be born this way" conveyed more than just remorse or shame for being born with nonheterosexual desire. His statement also expressed a mix of difficult emotions, such as anger, envy, and frustration about being treated unjustly and about the lack of acceptance he had experienced for not appearing "manly enough." The overlap of shame, remorse, and feelings of injustice in Ali's narrative reveals a complex relationship between nonnormative sexual desire and gender construction. His nonmasculine behavior and his same-sex desire are intimately linked, contributing to his negative feelings and his desire to distance himself from the oppressive norms that induced these feelings in the first place.

Ali also told me about an incident that took place in May 2012 involving an Islamic vigilantes that raided the public reading of Canadian author Irshad Manji during her book promotion tour in Yogyakarta. The book launch was disrupted by a local Islamist radical group called Majelis Mujahidin Indonesia (Indonesian Mujahedeen Council) that used physical force, leaving some attendees injured, including Ali. This incident deeply impacted Ali. When he compared it to our encounter with protesters during the 2009 queer film festival in Yogyakarta, Ali said:

> The clash [*bentrok*] during "Irshad Manji" was the saddest [*paling sedih*] for me, even though at the time I was already distancing myself from practicing all the Islamic rituals. But in that moment, I felt like Islam was exclusively for heterosexuals.

Repeatedly witnessing and being the victim of attacks fueled by religious sentiment led to a loss of faith in Ali:

> People become judgmental when they believe in something too much. Ideally, religion should be a means to understand and open up one's heart. In reality, it does not work that way. . . . In the end, I have to adopt many

identities [*memilih banyak identitas*]. Yes, I am a Muslim. Yes, I am an ODHA [*orang hidup dengan HIV/AIDS*; person living with HIV/AIDS]. Yes, I am gay. We are not just one identity. For now, I am more comfortable being in the middle. I don't want to be too extreme when it comes to religion.

Ali's perspective aligns with his self-description as a "Muslim KTP" in contradistinction to the "Muslim fanatics" he describes. These descriptions underscore the moral complexities in his lifeworld, which can't be understood outside the frame of affective meaning-making. His self-identification as a nominal Muslim is diametrically opposed to the "extreme" others who not only put "too much faith" in religion but also impose their beliefs on others. Similar to Anna's account earlier, the increasingly pervasive conflict between sexuality, gender, and religious morality in Indonesia has led to significant reservations for Ali about his prior identification as a pious religious subject. In Ali's case, though, his identity as a Muslim remains intractable.

Ali's emphasis on "being in the middle . . . for now" and his reluctance to be defined by a single category as he navigates between multiple identities reveals his affective gestures of enduring otherwise. Holding fast to different possibilities for self-knowledge without seeking a definitive answer has become a driving force in his attempts to define and cultivate selfhood in the shadow of normative violence. This mode of enduring otherwise is most pronounced when he speaks about the uncertainties of his religious commitment. It is also reflected in his current focus on spirituality, which began when he started practicing meditation not long after being diagnosed with HIV.

Ali learned about meditation from an acquaintance in the local Yogyakarta chapter of PKBI, an organization that provides care and support for HIV patients and has been a significant part of Ali's engagement with sexual rights issues:

From this guy, I learned about kundalini meditation. Now I tend to believe these things more, but not completely, since I'm still in process. I also don't want to believe in it too much. I don't know if I'll think differently tomorrow. . . . Sometimes deep down in my inner heart [*hati kecilku*], I feel that every day my perspective is growing, that I won't stay stuck at the same point forever. . . . But I also fear that one day I might fully embrace this as the absolute truth as well. But who knows? Maybe one day I'll become more diligent again in praying again. . . . Who knows?

Ali's description of his "inner heart" portrays an internal conflict that aligns with the patterns discussed earlier regarding the affective dynamics of Muslim queer and trans worldmaking. His narrative reflects his efforts to derive meaning from past and present events while contemplating potential futures. Ali also contemplates the potential of leaving his current home with his family:

Personally, I really want to leave my family. . . . I want to have a new environment where I can be my true self [jadi diriku sendiri]. At home, there's just so much drama all the time. I want to be in a place where I don't have to pretend anymore, but on the other hand, it is hard [berat] to leave my family.

Ali continued speaking, as if to himself:

Yes, it is family. That's my biggest stumbling block [ganjalan terbesarku]. They never support me, but sometimes they empower me. . . . It's like, we are born as a clear transparent bottle, but it's our family who mold [mencetak] our character, sometimes to a point that we lose sight of our true self. All that remains are these residuals [kerak] sticking to us, layer after layer, accumulating over time. It takes so long to clean them off. And in the end, I become this person who, on the one hand, loves them too much, but on the other hand, hates them because they are the ones who made me so unhappy.

As he told me this, the employees at the milk stall began to tidy up the empty tables and chairs next to us, preparing to close for the day. Before parting ways, I squeezed in one last question with a more hopeful tone, not wanting to end the conversation with a sour note. "So, tell me," I asked, "What does true happiness mean to you? And how do you envisage it in the future?" His reply was simple: "My dream is to build a home of my own, with a steady partner. We can plan many things; together we can make a home for the heart [rumah hati]."

Ali's coming-of-age story in a contentious family life has many bends and twists that include the frustration and sadness of having to deal with physical and mental abuse from people in his close surroundings and from fellow Muslims. His journey is further complicated by the ambivalence he feels about his current interest in spirituality and his embodied attachment to Islamic rituals. The hardship of being diagnosed with HIV adds another layer of emotional struggle. Ultimately, all these affective experiences converge into his subjective understanding of well-being, encapsulated in the adage of "home is where the heart is," a concept that is paradoxically shaped both within and against the model of his own family home.

His description of himself as an empty bottle covered with layering residues (*kerak*) of normative discourses that operate through the parental control and familial pressure is poignant. Ali's persistence in inhabiting multiple identities between sexuality, seropositivity, spirituality, and piety are tethered to familial attachment. For Ali, the approval of any one identity by his family is less important than their acceptance of him in his entirety—to use Ali's terms, "to be accepted for who he is," a singular selfhood woven from plural identities.

The relationship between normative orders and alternative sexualities in Ali's story appears dramatic and pressing. It operates through the intimate and routine "brokerage" of modern Indonesian Muslim family life. The family, as reflected in Ali's story, triggers an affective repertoire of home-making that is shaped by his reflections on his past, present, and future lives. However, normative violence reaches beyond the scope of kinship and domestic spaces as well, as we will see in how a Muslim transpuan faces and deals with societal forms of normative violence.

Maya's Injurious Path

Maya, the transpuan from Aceh we met earlier, has endured a life marked by repeated violent disruptions that have profoundly shaped both her personal experiences and her work with the community. As the leader of the local transpuan organization, Rumoh Aceh, she has focused not only on HIV care and prevention but also on advocating for the self-determination and well-being of transpuan individuals in the region. While Rumoh Aceh's activism is limited to the district level, the group's status as one of the very few transpuan organizations in Aceh has garnered nationwide attention from LGBT rights activists. Maya often traveled to the provincial capital of Banda Aceh and other cities across the country to attend workshops and meetings on behalf of her community group.

My first encounter with Maya set into motion the focus group discussion with members of the transgender community in Namu. Our meeting in a coffee shop before the FGD in December 2013 marked the first of many conversations that followed. Maya took extra effort to ensure that my research stay in Namu was both productive and comfortable, even hosting me in her hair salon, her place of residence, during the later phase of fieldwork. Some of the most intimate exchanges between Maya and I occurred during my stay at Salon Primadona in the fasting month of Ramadan, July 2014. These exchanges mainly took place in her room, often late into the night, as we enjoyed the dry season's cool breeze from the slightly open door that connected her room to an unkempt balcony facing the Medan-Banda Aceh main road.

We usually chatted until dawn, with Maya lying on her bed while I lay on the guest mattress on the floor, against the occasional background noise of passing trucks and night buses traveling between the provincial capitals of North Sumatra and Nanggroe Aceh Darussalam. Maya's room was decorated with feminine touches such as pink walls, cartoonish bed covers, and stuffed animals stacked in the corner of her bed. Adjacent to Maya's room was the bedroom of Alia, her transpuan housemate and employee at the hair salon located on the first floor. Both sleeping rooms upstairs on the second-floor were separated by plywood panels. On the same floor, there was an open section that members of Rumoh Aceh often used to rehearse for traditional dance performances, such as for the IDAHOT commemoration held in Banda Aceh a few weeks before my arrival. This was the intimate setting in which we told each other our stories of the past and present events and our expectations about the future.

Earning Your Way Back Home

Maya's story traces back to when she was twelve and first realized that her gender was "waria." This realization occurred just as she started to actively engage in sexual activities with her male friends at elementary school in Kuala Batee, a subdistrict town where she grew up around eight kilometers east of Namu.[25] At the age of sixteen, just as she was about to begin her sophomore year at a local vocational high school in Kuala Batee, one of the teachers "outed" Maya:

> At the time I didn't want to "come out" to someone I respected because I was still unfamiliar with the concept of gender. . . . But then the teacher told me "I know you are *dandan* [wearing makeup] at night." And it was true. Since high school, I had been going the bus terminal with my makeup on to make extra money, and I also gave massages there. It wasn't just me, I did it with my friend Lita. We did this to help pay for our school tuition. It should have been irrelevant; my academic achievements [*prestasi*] shouldn't have been affected by this. But when they found out about my gender [*tapi karena tahu gender aku*], my achievement scholarship [*beasiswa prestasi*] was taken away.

This story illustrates the role of *prestasi* (a word that means both "good deed" and "achievement") as the normative mode of recognition in Indonesian society. Maya's scholarship, which was awarded to students with academic excellence, was terminated after her teachers discovered her gender nonconformity. The term "prestasi" also serves as a critical measure of social inclusion among sexual and gender minorities.[26] A person is deemed *berprestasi* (successful) if they achieve certain moral, economic, sociopolitical, or academic goals. They are thus deserving of recognition from others. Maya's story complicates this notion of prestasi as a manifestation of respectability. Her public display of gender nonconformity, which was seen as incongruent with hetero- and cisnormative moral standards, resulted in the loss of her academic merit. For transpuan, prestasi as an affective marker of belonging is always already experienced as a double burden. While achieving prestasi might help transpuan prove their worthiness to be included, they are often expected to work twice as hard for half the recognition that most (cisnormative) people receive. This pressure to consistently demonstrate exemplary conduct or achievement as a means of gaining social acceptability is not unique to Indonesian transpuan. A comparable case is noted by Peter Jackson in the Thai context, who notes that the term *kunla-gay*, meaning a "decent" or "respectable" gay man, emerged to describe those whose social acceptance is earned through their positive contributions to both family and society.[27] Queer and trans subjectivities in the region are thus often caught between external pressures and internalized demands to exceed normative expectations, compensating for the burden of deviance projected onto their lives by dominant social norms.

Prestasi can manifest not just as moral excellence but also material gain. In Maya's family, the latter appears to hold more weight in securing acceptance. This is evidenced by her experience after finishing high school. At seventeen, Maya undertook what is known as circular migration (*merantau*) by traveling to Medan, North Sumatra. Here she earned a living doing street-based sex work colloquially known as *mangkal*. During this time, Maya began regularly wearing makeup and women's clothing and also underwent some minor body modifications, such as silicone implants for her chest.

Merantau typically involves individuals leaving their home for a time in order to earn a living, seek knowledge, or gain experience. The migrant has the intention of ultimately returning home.[28] However, Maya's return home did not elicit the usual celebratory homecoming associated with this tradition due to her feminine appearance as a transpuan:

> Upon my return, they told me to leave and never come home again. My brother even struck me on the hand, saying, "What are you doing, *bencong*? You're going to hell! You should die!" . . . So I left again. I worked relentlessly. Day and night seem to reverse. During the day, I stayed home to rest, and when evening came, I would go *mangkal* [loitering for sex clients]. At the same time, I continued to send some of my income back to Aceh for my parents' daily expenses and to help my younger brother with his college tuition.

Over time, circumstances began to improve. It appeared that Maya's mother had sensed her involvement in street work. Although she never mentioned it directly, she sent text messages urging Maya to be cautious and not to come home too late. Her brother's behavior toward her also improved. Maya analyzed these changes in this way: "That was the weird thing. I am still waria; I did not change my appearance for them. So what does that tell you? My family loves me because of the money, right?"

Maya raises an insightful point about the conditional nature of familial acceptance for transpuan. Only after she provided stable financial support to her family did she receive better treatment, leading her to question whether familial ties are contingent on monetary provision. Maya had to bear immense personal cost as she navigated perilous conditions outside the home to earn her way back home. In her early adulthood, in addition to traveling to Medan, she moved between different places to engage in sex work, including Jakarta, Banda Aceh, and Ipoh, Malaysia. During these periods, physical assaults, sexual abuse, and other life-threatening events became normalized parts of her life.

Nightmare on Elsewhere

One quiet evening in the fasting month of Ramadan, Maya, her friend Andra, and I were in the lounge of the hair salon. Business was slow due to the mandatory temporary closure of all businesses during Ramadan, from the moment the call to prayer rang out over the mosque loudspeakers until sundown when it was time for Muslims to break their fast. This intermission lasted each day until the conclusion of Tarawih, the late evening congregational prayer held at the mosque during Ramadan at approximately 10 p.m. The salon's double doors would be left ajar for any clients who urgently needed hair treatment and could access it discreetly. As Maya extinguished her cigarette, she broke the silence and asked if she had ever told us about her experience in Ipoh, Malaysia. Andra and I shook our heads, prompting her to say, "I always want to cry when I tell people this story, but really what I had experienced when I was away from home was [sighing] . . . [silence]. Perhaps this is what people nowadays call 'human trafficking,' although at that time there was no such words, but I believe that was what I experienced."

Maya received our full attention as she recounted her story, using vivid bodily gestures to illustrate key points, such as mimicking the jump that she made to avoid immigration raids. I noticed Andra's mouth was hanging open in shock. Violence was Maya's everyday experience while doing sex work in Malaysia in 2010. The violence was inflicted upon her by clients, immigration officers, policemen, and her employers, the Mamak Ayam and Bapak Ayam, as well by fellow transpuans she worked with.[29]

One day, Maya's coworker, who slept in the cubicle next to hers, fell seriously ill and was unable to walk. Maya offered to help, but her coworker's condition deteriorated and she became delusional, even accusing Maya of trying to poison her. She recounted a particularly haunting memory: "One night while attending to a client [lying on the sofa, as she spoke, to reenact her position at that moment—demonstrating how her client lay on top of her] I caught a glimpse of the sick coworker's pale, thin face as she crawled under my cubicle door, reaching out for help." Maya shrieked as she told us this part of the story. "The next day, I overheard a conversation between the Mamak Ayam and Bapak Ayam; they were planning to ditch the sick waria in an abandoned public toilet on the outskirts of the city and leave her to die," she said. Fearing potential legal and immigration issues if the plan was carried out, Maya decided to escape and return to Aceh as soon as possible.

During the later part of my stay in Namu, Maya offered to let me stay in her room on a mattress reserved for guests. At first, I hesitated since I considered it unethical to sleep in the same room as my research participant. I asked whether I would disturb her privacy if I slept in her room, but she assured me it was no issue. She never slept alone; if no one else was around, she would ask Alia, her employee-housemate, to stay with her. "I don't dare to sleep on my own anymore, so you sleeping over is actually doing me a favor," she said, adding, "I think I still have this trauma over that night and the dying waria in Malaysia."

Our evenings usually involved long chats before falling asleep. Through these conversations, we learned more about each other. These informal talks provided me with vital insights into Maya's vulnerabilities in ways that would have been impossible to gain in a formal interview. Several times, I was awakened by Maya's shouts and her mumbling in Acehnese in her sleep, suggesting frequent nightmares. When I mentioned her sleep disturbances in the morning, she would merely smile and say, "Oh, really?"

Maya's expression of trauma is not limited to the haunting image of a dying friend calling out for help or the fear of sleeping alone. It also manifests in her sleep disturbances, which she seems unaware of. The term "trauma" was similarly used by Ali when describing his antagonistic relationship with family members, particularly his father. How does trauma operate in the everyday processes of Muslim queer and trans worldmaking? What are the connections between everyday articulations of trauma and the clinical category from which the term emanates?

In Maya's case, trauma appears to be part of the geopolitical conditions in Aceh after the thirty-year sectarian conflict under the Indonesian New Order regime that were compounded by the 2004 tsunami. Annemarie Samuels describes how postconflict and post-tsunami rehabilitation efforts popularized the term "trauma," which came to express a range of emotions tied to experiences of disaster or crisis.[30]

But after spending a considerable amount of time immersed in the daily lives of people like Ali and Maya who are susceptible to structural violence, I contend that trauma needs to considered beyond the scope of a pathological category generated by catastrophic events such as war, genocide, or natural disaster. This stance aligns with Ann Cvetkovich's invitation to consider trauma as an everyday phenomenon and part of everyday discourse that "sometimes seems invisible because it is confined to the domestic or private sphere. Sometimes it doesn't appear sufficiently catastrophic because it doesn't produce dead bodies or even, necessarily, damaged ones."[31]

Instead of reading trauma as a fully psychopathological condition, I focus on the everyday articulation of trauma as an emotive that allows the actors to engender different ways of meaning-making amid chronic violence. Maya's bodily gestures of trauma offer insights into more than just personal tragedy; they serve as a powerful reminder of the ongoing threats trans-feminine individuals face. These threats, often disguised as normalcy, encompass the past, the present, and the future.[32] Understanding Maya's trauma solely as a clinical syndrome, a passive response to memories of past violence, neglects or even dismisses the complex meanings attached to the lived experience of trauma. While I am not suggesting that this constitutes a wholly conscious act on Maya's part, her being haunted by these horrific events demonstrates the elasticity of trauma as a vernacular affective response to violence.

Trauma and Miracle

Trauma resurfaced in our conversation when Maya explained why she made a last-minute change to our meeting in December 2013 from the coffee shop next to her hair salon to another coffee shop further into the town center. She made this change after spotting a group of men she identified as ulama (religious figures) gathering at the neighboring the coffee shops. The sight of them made her feel *goni-goni*, a term in the gay lingo of Aceh that means afraid or paranoid.

I asked why the sight of this particular group caused her such fear. She explained that sometimes she overheard sermons amplified through mosque speakers that were delivered by some elements of ulama (*oknum ulama*). These sermons portrayed transpuan as a source of vice because they wore female attire to incite lust among men. Maya said, "To me, it seems as if the person giving the sermon is trying to provoke those attending the worship to attack us." This imagery of being the target of an attack by an angry crowd is a recurring theme in Maya's accounts of being afraid to go to crowded places: "An image forms in my head, where I feel like people are ready to strike me at any moment. That's why I tend to avoid such places."

Maya attributed these mental images to previous experiences of enduring physical abuses from anonymous mobs, particularly when she was still actively engaged in street-based sex work in cities like Banda Aceh and Medan in North Sumatra. I asked how she felt in such dire circumstances. She responded:

> In my head, I saw people plotting my death [*dibuat mati sama orang*] and I saw myself surrounded by fire. I don't know how to describe it. All I could feel was that my body felt weak and defenseless [*pasrah*]. But in the midst of all this, there was actually a *mukjizat* [miracle]—which is why I keep saying God loves Their people.

Maya then shared in detail her experience of the miracle (*mukjizat*), an Islamic theological term that refers to extraordinary divine interventions performed by prophets and messengers. This miracle happened on what would otherwise have been an ordinary night while she was working in Medan. That evening, a potential client approached Maya but refused to agree to her payment request, so she declined the offer. Offended, the man returned minutes later with a group of people on motorbikes who proceeded to assault Maya while her friends fled the scene, leaving her alone to be struck and kicked. She recalls that as a motorbike ran over her, she didn't feel any pain but was in a semi-conscious state. When the group of motorcyclists temporarily departed, Maya seized the opportunity to stand up and run toward a large planter on one corner of the street:

> There was only one thin sprig of plant growing out of it. I hid behind it. Can you imagine how small the plant was compared to the size of my body? But when those people came back, circling around on their motorbikes to find me, they couldn't see me. Emm . . . Look! I have goosebumps! [pointing to her left arm as she spoke, and as she did, I started to feel goosebumps too]. I was already covered in blood . . . The guy kept shouting, "Where is that waria? I will kill her! She should die!" But I was hiding in that spot all along—how could they not see me? Is that a mukjizat or what? I still think about it. If I had hidden behind this pot, you would think they could find me easily. Oh . . . I still can't understand it, it's a mukjizat. Trauma . . .

After the attackers left, Maya, bruised and battered, journeyed home by minibus. She didn't report the incident to the local police and she didn't go to the hospital to get treatment for her wounds. This perturbing narrative indicates the shift from experiencing trauma as an emotional response to physical and psychic injury to a complete submission to the divine grace of mukjizat.

Maya also invoked the term "mukjizat" when she recounted another story about when she was kidnapped by a group of men and taken to a forest outside a town in North Sumatra. Miraculously, she said, "I managed to escape by running so fast that it almost felt like I was floating through the thorny bushes." The association of trauma with miracle—two seemingly incommensurable terms—might be read as Maya's attempt to make sense of her encounters in the realm of the uncanny. Such an interpretation frames the work of trauma as an inexplicable aspect of violent experience and points to the operation of miracle as an "index of the transcendental," to borrow Deleuze's description.[33]

However, this interpretation does not fully explain why Maya so easily ties trauma to a perception of God's providence. In her narratives, traumatic and miraculous events are entangled as two sides of the same divine plan. This blending of trauma and miracle, symbolizing violent memories in Maya's accounts, reflects the everyday tribulations that circulate among the Indonesian Muslim community, commonly understood as the divine trial (*cobaan*).[34] The success or failure of a person when dealing with such a trial becomes a testament to their faith and determines whether they are worthy of God's protection.

For Maya, one of the most extraordinary outcomes of her traumatic experiences was the realization that despite her many shortcomings, she was given the chance to outlive them. Her narratives of trauma and miracle are deeply rooted in an affective repertoire that seeks to make sense of these violent events within an Islamic framework of divine providence and salvation. This approach allows Maya to view her survival not as a matter of mere chance but as a sign of divine affirmation.

Maya's narrative reminds me of Dina Georgis's concept of the better story.[35] The miraculous elements in Maya's account of her violent experiences suggest a more compelling narrative—not because these stories are inherently better but because they allow her to make meaning out of these traumatic events. In narrating her past and present traumas, Maya moves beyond the confines of victimhood, envisioning her journey as one that is interconnected with a larger spiritual constellation. This understanding—that her life is never solely her own—fueled her determination to navigate the weight of normative violence together with those closest to her. While many of these narratives convey solitary experiences shaped by memories of violence and fear of public hostility, the following vignette illustrates how she actively transforms these affective burdens into a collective modality for enduring seemingly hopeless situations alongside her community.

Having Just Enough

Maya had been living in Namu for four years when we met. When she first returned to Namu, she worked in various hair salons. After a year, she decided to start her own business, Salon Primadona, with the intention of providing better working conditions for her peers:

> I cook and provide food in the salon, so no one will go hungry, like I did while working for others. I've encouraged Yasmin, who currently has no salon skills, to start washing customers' hair. Since her own hair is still short, I suggested she wear a wig. I know who her true soul is [*aku tahu jiwa dia siapa*]. I asked her if she would prefer to wear makeup and long

hair or if she wanted to be a waria who looks more masculine. She said she prefers to wear makeup, so I gave her my old wig. I lent her my foundation and anything else she wanted to use, including dresses. I want to reverse all the pain I had to endure in the past—not out of revenge, but by making sure others don't have to experience what I went through.

Not all hair salon owners in Aceh allow their transpuan employees to express themselves according to their preferred gender. Maya told me that when she was still working in one particular hair salon in Banda Aceh, her employer prohibited her from wearing female attire or growing her hair long. She also mentioned a hair salon owner she worked for in Namu, a gay man who did not allow his employees to wear female clothing or makeup while on the job. Salon Primadona not only functions as a place of work but also as a space that allows Maya's circle of friends to express themselves according to their gendered soul (*jiwa*). This is an opportunity many do not have elsewhere, including at home. Maya's supportive gesture stems from her desire to avoid reproducing past harms.

Sometimes she lets her friends and their partners use her bedroom for sex. This decision could jeopardize her safety and the hair salon business, as it contravenes the moral control regulations that structure public life in Aceh. She describes how her "heart beats very fast" every time a crowd of friends gathers in her hair salon, fearing that people from the neighborhood might suddenly raid her place, as has happened in other hair salons run by transpuan in different parts of Aceh.

One evening, I asked Maya if she ever considered relocating from Aceh, given the intense violence she had experienced and had witnessed herself. She sighed and said, "It would be a pity [*kasihan*] to leave Aceh." She then spoke about the complex reasons that made her want to stay and endure, despite the constant threat of violence against transpuan bodies: "Although there is still zero acceptance for waria in this environment, I feel comfortable [*nyaman*] here." Another reason she could not leave was her hair salon business. It is not only her livelihood, but that of others too:

This has been our common rice pot [*belanga*]. Closing down the salon and leaving would mean a loss of livelihood for my friends. So let it stay as it is [*ya sudahlah begini-begini saja*]. The most important thing is that I have a decent job and enough to share with my family and friends.

This fragment of conversation with Maya encapsulates an ethics of endurance rooted in making do. Maya doesn't pretend to strive for political recognition or have grand aims for social transformation in her aspiration for the good life. At best, her hope boils down to the condition of *"begini-begini saja,"* or the promise of ordinary, everyday survival. This condition echoes Sara Ahmed's understanding of bearable life that "involves a relationship to suffering, to 'what' a life must endure."[36] At the same time, intimate attachments with friends and family and religious moral valuations contribute to shaping Maya's personal project of making everyday life more bearable, transforming it into an ethical engagement and practice of care toward others who share her experience of normative violence.

In turn, Maya's everyday entanglements with trauma and its sporadic manifestations as paralyzing fear ground the affective, moral, and material resources for taking care of community. Diane Reay refers to this as "emotional capital," which is "a variant of social capital generally confined within the bounds of affective relationships of family and friends and encompasses the emotional resources you hand on to those you care about."[37] However, as Reay also argues, emotional capital and emotional well-being are not neatly linked. The emotional cost of "being there for others" may sometimes constrain an individual's flourishing, as illustrated by Maya's anxieties over her safety. However, by accepting the likelihood of living with the ongoing threat of violence, her everyday engagement with a modest and almost non-eventful fantasy of a good life relationally overlaps with gestures of undoing harm.[38]

The subtle shifts and alterations of Maya's embodied experience of past violence and the recognition of interdependence as "essential to the existence of reliant and vulnerable beings" reveal the inextricable relations between affective meaning-making and an ethic of care in response to normative violence.[39] An ethic of care also requires an understanding that it cannot be practiced in the abstract.[40] It also demands attention to affective dimensions and to spatiotemporal and social contexts that shape the specifics of how care is performed in daily life.

* * *

In enduring normative violence, various affective dynamics emerge as both sources of and constraints on Muslim queer and trans worldmaking. Ali used expressions such as feeling down, feeling *marah* (enraged), feeling *malu* (ashamed), and being traumatized to describe his struggle growing up in a "normative" family. Ali also conveyed affective repertoires related to his past, his present circumstances, and his future expectations that depict more diffuse feelings. Among these were his feeling of comfort about being in between and his poetic invocation of a "home for the heart" as a state of well-being to aspire to, a goal paradoxically founded on painful memories of his coming of age within his birth family.

Maya, in contrast, experienced repeated abuse and discrimination from various levels of society, including her birth family, her school teachers, the people living in her hometown, and strangers she encountered away from home. The extent of violence she endured in everyday life speaks to the operation of normative frameworks that deem some lives livable while rendering others unintelligible. Faced with everyday violence, Maya experienced a range of feelings caused by injuries, from physical pain to fear. Like Ali, Maya verbalized the feeling of trauma. However, Maya's efforts to survive involve shifting trauma into an affective repertoire linked to miracles. A key aspect of her aspiration for the good life is deeply anchored in the material effects of personal achievement, represented the importance she assigns to family remittances, economic productivity, earning a livelihood, and providing daily sustenance for the transpuan community in Namu. Maya's life story lucidly depicts how enduring normative violence involves stepping sideways from affective paths of mourning and injury into tangible spaces of care. In the next chapter I will further examine how recurring encounters with the risk of violence transforms into efforts to attain and sustain communal belonging.

4

Promises of Belonging

When I first began staying at the Salon Primadona, I was easily startled. The slightest disturbance, like the screech of tires on the intercity road late at night, made me jump. I felt uneasy under the curious gaze of salon customers who saw me hanging around day after day. My apprehension was partly due to stories that were circulating of local young men and, sometimes, the local Shari'a police, or Wilayatul Hisbah (WH), raiding houses whenever an unmarried man and woman stayed inside too long after dark. The WH frequently visited and inspected salons due to rumors about adulterous conduct occurring inside transpuan hair salons, occasionally detaining their owners or staff for "moral education." At first I tried to suppress this anxiety, but then I decided to ask Maya what she told people or neighbors if they asked about who I was and what I was doing there. Casually, she said "Don't worry, I told them you're one of us, of course." At the time, I did not fully comprehend what she meant by saying I was "one of them." This ambiguity was somewhat clarified months later when I, Maya, and seven other transpuans went on an excursion after Ramadan to Medan, North Sumatra, in 2014.

Because our budget was tight, the nine of us squeezed into a couple of small rooms at a hotel outside Medan. One afternoon while we were all hanging out and chatting over snacks and cigarettes in the air-conditioned room while watching television, Maya decided to change her clothes. As she opened her bra and exposed her breasts, one of her friends, Luna, said something in Acehnese. I didn't realize at first that Luna was referring to me in her comment until Maya responded to Luna in Indonesian: "It's OK for me to change in front of him [pointing to me]." Luna replied: "But Ferdi is a man. You should be ashamed [*malu*] since he can see your breasts. It is impolite." I was caught off guard. Although I was aware that Maya was taking off her clothes, I had tried not to pay attention. Instead, I feigned interest in the Indian soap opera on the TV. I could feel all eyes on me while Maya smirked and answered back: "He is also like us, he is also LGBT, you know? He fucked men and also took it up in the ass like us." Luna looked at me with disbelief and let out a small laugh. In my peripheral vision, I could see that others in the room were smiling. What I recall from this experience is a sense of being enveloped by feelings of safety, care, and belonging—affective conditions that are necessary for the realization of queer and trans worldmaking projects.

Such projects are often deeply entrenched in normative violence when they materialize among Indonesian Muslim sexual and gender minorities. Keeping this in mind, this chapter explores the potential and limitations of such projects from the inside out. What do safety, care, and belonging mean when violence is a normative structure that shapes collective living? How does the interplay of these conditions forge and fracture bonds between community members? How does this affective dynamic complicate collective efforts to endure otherwise? This chapter explores these complex issues by examining how different Muslim queer and trans collectivities in Indonesia cultivate a sense of belonging that is held together by precarious care work and is continually tested by concerns about safety.

The Making and Breaking of Safe Spaces

Earlier I discussed the anti-LGBT campaign in Indonesian that began in early 2016. That campaign was sparked by the widespread publicity of a prohibited student-led initiative called Support Group and Research Centre (SGRC) at the University of Indonesia, the country's oldest state-run university. SGRC offered counseling services about gender and sexuality issues for students. Members of the group were at the center of the violent backlash in 2016 and have since then been targets of verbal intimidation, online persecution, and institutional harassment. On a local online platform, an SGRC member using the pseudonym ER expressed their support for SGRC as "a safe space to learn and discuss sexuality and gender, from sexual orientation all the way to gender disparity in everyday life."[1] ER's definition of safe space is consistent with similar understandings circulating among queer activist groups nationally and internationally.

In queer politics, the concept of a safe space—both physical and discursive—has contested meanings. Some scholars have called for a more nuanced understanding of the social settings and internal dynamics within these spaces.[2] Gilly Hartal's study of a queer community space in Jerusalem, for example, highlights how the discourse of queer safe space is embedded in a (Western) liberal logic that valorizes identity politics.[3] An ideal queer safe space is imagined as a "protected place, facilitating a sense of security, and recreating discourses of inclusion and diversity. It is a metaphor for the ability to be honest, take risks, share opinions, or reveal one's sexual identity."[4] However, this focus on identity politics can inadvertently lead to the reproduction of hegemonic power relationships, potentially resulting in unequal access to these "protected spaces" or even feelings of unsafety among the very community members these safe spaces seek to support. As Hartal concludes, the use of identity politics in the creation of queer safe space presents a paradox that requires attention from the various stakeholders.[5] Moreover, because safe spaces are always context specific, navigating this paradox also requires taking into account the social and material conditions that shape experiences of safety.[6]

In Indonesian, the term for a safe space is "*ruang aman*." In this grammatical construction, the noun "*ruang*" (space) precedes the adjective "*aman*," which carries the dual meanings of safety and security. Disparate meanings of the word "*aman*" require further exploration in order to understand the local concept of a safe space. Colloquially, both connotations of the word are used interchangeably in everyday situations. The first meaning refers to safety as being free from harm or risk, including in the psychic sense. The second meaning, security, is understood as a state of being free from danger and external threats. During Suharto's New Order authoritarian regime, the term "aman" and its corresponding noun, "*keamanan*," were often used to control public order and repress dissent.[7] In popular and sometimes politicized local interpretations, "aman" is often used in combination with two other Indonesian terms: *rukun* (roughly translated as social harmony) and *tenteram* (equanimity).[8]

Although the affective meanings of these three terms are not entirely interchangeable, they collectively imply the widely recognized rules that govern the cultural and moral rules about achieving personal well-being by avoiding conflict with others and maintaining a public image of harmony. The politicized, and ironically often violent, meanings related to "aman" can still be found in present-day Indonesia, particularly in how elites construct realities to maintain the status quo. The state apparatus, embodied by Indonesian police forces, commonly uses the euphemism "for reasons of security" (*demi alasan keamanan*) as a rationale for dispersing public gatherings or demonstrations.

Building upon Sara Ahmed's framework that examines "objects of feelings," wherein emotions are directed toward and engendered by objects, the term "aman" functions as both an emotive signifier that evokes and generates feelings of safety and security and a driving force that prompts the creation of structures and processes aimed at preserving these feelings.[9]

In the context of Muslim queer and trans worldmaking in Indonesia, safe spaces carry complex and layered meanings. Individuals and communities must navigate the tension between seeking protection and facing the constant risk of violence. I examine how Muslim sexual and gender minorities manage these overlapping relationships by reflexively and relationally engaging with each other. This chapter focuses on two archetypical safe spaces in my fieldwork: the Primadona hair salon in Namu and a queer youth camp held in Yogyakarta in 2014. These spaces relate to diverse interpretations and aspirations connected to the idea of safety. Within these domains, the actors involved articulate and enact often-conflicting affective registers, sometimes enabled by (hetero)normative tropes in Indonesian sociopolitical discourse and at other times constrained by them.

Tenuous Safety

By mid-Ramadan in June 2014, I had been living and conducting participant observation at Salon Primadona in Namu, Aceh, for several months. One afternoon, Nanda, one of the transpuans employed at the hair salon, asked me to accompany her to the market in town to buy snacks and food for the breaking of the fast. Achiel, a transpuan from a neighboring salon, joined us. We took to the streets of Namu on two motorbikes, me on my own, while Achiel and Nanda shared the other. Nanda, wearing tight jeans, full makeup, and a T-shirt adorned with a colorful scarf, sat on the back of Achiel's scooter. Achiel, who once told me that she disliked wearing women's clothes, chose not to wear women's makeup but accessorized with fashionable blue-framed sunglasses and high wedged shoes. Neither of them wore a helmet while riding the scooter.

When Nanda and Achiel asked me to accompany them to the market, I remembered the cautionary comments I had received from my peers and supervisors before embarking for Aceh. Many of these warnings were shaped by the fear and anxiety stoked by international media reports on the region's growing hostility toward visibly non-normative sexualities and genders in public spaces. But there I was, tagging along behind Achiel and Nanda on the road from Namu to a neighboring town farther south. We missed the turn that would take us directly to the market, but it seemed that Achiel and Nanda preferred a longer route to pass the time. I didn't object and continued following them. I felt my gaze shifting. The unfolding landscape felt like a slow-motion film scene. Nanda let the wind play with her bright red hair, dishing out smiles to passers-by while occasionally turning down her head bashfully. Meanwhile, Achiel drove the scooter single-handedly, waving her free hand sideways and giggling.

On the sidewalks, people were busy buying and selling food in preparation for breaking their fast, a traditional activity known as *ngabuburit* that is popular in many Indonesian towns and cities. I noticed people of all ages staring at my friends who are riding in front of me. Some looked surprised or laughed, others appeared indifferent, and a few frowned with contempt. People riding in the opposite lane turned their heads. A few even stopped, took a detour, and began trailing us. I could hear whistles and shouts addressed to the women and I could sense that a couple of young men on their fast-moving motorbikes were trying to catch up with Achiel. I was stunned when some of the chasers not only tried to chat with Nanda and Achiel as they passed by but even moved their vehicles dangerously close in order to touch or tap them. I feared that these hands were not just intrusive but potentially harmful. Meanwhile, gazes from every direction continued to follow us wherever we went, or to be more exact, wherever the scooter in front of me navigated. I blended in well with the other riders because of my gender-conforming appearance as a cis male: I was wearing ordinary clothes and the visor of my black helmet was closed.

When we got back from the market, I bombarded Nanda with questions. What was she doing? Wasn't she troubled by the boys who tried to touch her on the motorbike? Wasn't she afraid of being hit? She simply giggled and blamed Achiel: "It's all because of Achiel's blue sunglasses. The color is so flashy [*norak*] that people keep looking at us." She continued, "I'm from here, so I'm not worried. People here have known me since I was a child or have at least seen me before. They are quite used to me; they can accept me. If anyone tried to bother me it would most likely be someone who is not from here, a foreigner—someone who still sees me as something weird or the target for a joke. I'm pretty sure the local people would defend me if something like that happened."

Dissatisfied with Nanda's answer, I turned to Maya, with whom I felt a closer connection. I asked why she thought Nanda seemed to disregard her own safety. To my surprise, Maya sidestepped the question too, and said: "You have to understand. Nanda is still young and she has never lived outside of Namu before. She still has a strong desire to be seen— who else can appreciate all her efforts in making herself beautiful, wearing makeup and buying dresses, if no one is there to see her?" Maya continued, "I told her so many times to *jaga diri* [protect oneself], but she is still young, so what can I do?"

This vignette illustrates the tension between my concern for the safety of the Muslim trans women and their tendency to downplay it. Similar situations occurred throughout my fieldwork in Namu. However, this does not mean that matters of safety are taken lightly by the community members. Many of them have been subjected to harmful speech in public and to various forms of physical harassment, including in their own homes. Maya's account of living in Banda Aceh, the provincial capital, captures this reality well.

Abusive Security

Six years before I met her, Maya lived in Banda Aceh and worked full time at a hair salon. She shared a boardinghouse with fifteen other transpuan tenants in a working class neighborhood. One evening well past midnight, Maya returned home feeling tired. Some of her housemates were chatting in the hallway; others had retired to their rooms. Among those who were still up, only five had their full makeup on (*dandan*). Suddenly, Maya heard aggressive pounding at the front door. A group of men from the neighborhood was causing the disturbance.

They started to break through the doors: *gubraak debruk gubrak* [phonetic description of people breaking through the door] and shouting: "Everyone out! You sinners!" They ignored those among us with male appearances, targeting only those who looked like us, meaning those who are *dandan* and with long hair. There were five us. My door was left with a massive hole. One friend was slapped and they stole our belongings, including cell phones and cash. They dragged us to the *meunasah* [village prayer hall] and demanded our IDs, but none of us had them with us at the time. They wanted to "cleanse" us with sewage water, accusing us of committing sins during Ramadan. Just as they were about to hose us down with the filthy water, the police arrived and stopped them. We were taken to the police station, but the mob continued to follow, harassing us just like in protests we usually saw on TV [chuckling], shouting at the police to kill us. At the station, the police interrogated us one by one.

The next morning, the police released Maya and her housemates and told them to leave the neighborhood immediately. Maya continued: "The local people were watching us as we packed our stuff in a hurry. Many of them were brandishing big wooden sticks. But nothing happened that time. The police were there to ensure we were *aman* [safe]."

This incident occurred during the fasting month of Ramadan in 2008, three years after the local administration implemented Shari'a law. According to historian Michael Feener, during this early stage of the implementation of Shari'a law, the relationship between the Shari'a police and vigilante violence was still contentious.[10] Local officials argued that the implementation of the law through the Shari'a police, or WH, should be viewed as a preemptive measure to prevent vigilante violence. However, human rights advocates reported that the Islamic penal code actually encouraged local communities to police public morality in their own neighborhoods and carry out violent punishments to alleged violators of Shari'a-based norms. This included beatings, sexual harassment, and the practice of publicly "cleansing" accused wrongdoers with sewage water.

The notion of aman as an affective register that encompasses the double meanings of safety and security is inherently violent for those who do not conform to hetero- and cisnormative values. In Maya's story, when the police "secured" her and her friends from the angry mob, their motives were ambiguous. It was unclear whether they intended to protect Maya and her friends from harm or if they simply wanted to appease the mob and uphold the moral standards the mob claimed to represent.

In this instance, "security measures" had harmful consequences for Maya and her friends. When they were "saved" by being placed in local police custody, it led to interrogation rather than protection. This subjected them to the risk of being labeled instigators of public disorder instead of being acknowledged as victims of an injurious situation. Ultimately, the police reinforced public order by "securing" Maya and her housemates until they were effectively thrown out of the neighborhood. The word "aman" in Maya's recollection is not only saturated with the discourse of violence inherited from the previous political regimes, it also indicates the terms continued use to disserve and further marginalize transpuan.

Safe Space as Enclosure

When Maya returned to Namu in 2010, she worked in local hair salons for a few months before opening her own business. This period also marked the establishment of Rumoh Aceh, the transpuan community organization that Maya now leads. Maya conceived the idea to form a group after noticing the limited freedom of movement and access to public areas for transgender people in the district. As a peri-urban town, Namu has only a handful of places where residents can engage in leisure activities. Besides the beach located on the northern side of the town center, the only other leisure spot is an outdoor culinary area that I call the Taman Kerang market. This place attracts many people who come here in the late afternoon to hang out with friends and family and enjoy food from the street vendors. However, for months after returning from merantau (circular migration), Maya had difficulty convincing her friends to join her at Taman Kerang due to their fear of being harassed by other visitors. As Maya explained, this fear was not unfounded:

> In the beginning, as soon as we arrived at Taman Kerang, we would hear remarks like "the hellfire group is here" [*rombongan api neraka datang*]!" But I told my friends to ignore them. Confronting them would only get us banned from the place. So we kept coming, mostly just sitting around and

unwinding from the work at the salon. . . . Over time, more friends started to join us. I assured them there was no need to worry about the authorities. I gathered my courage and in doing so encouraged them. After all, this is our home. What reason is there to feel fear? We did nothing wrong. If we had misbehaved, then being afraid might make sense. But fear of stigma? That exists everywhere, not just in Aceh.

As Maya and her friends began socializing after work more frequently, they realized that their usual hangout spot, Taman Kerang, was no longer sufficient. Even though they were regulars there, their presence kept on drawing unwanted attention. At that time, Rumoh Aceh was still in the planning stages and the group needed a more suitable setting to discuss the details of the project. So Maya offered her hair salon as a meeting place.

The Primadona hair salon is located within a *ruko* building complex situated along the main road connecting Banda Aceh, the capital city of Aceh Province, to the city of Medan in neighboring North Sumatra Province. Ruko, which stands for *rumah-toko*, meaning "shop-house," is a common type of building in urban and suburban areas across Indonesia. A ruko complex generally consists of three to six single units of varying sizes, depending on the level of investment. Most units have two floors, with the first floor typically reserved for businesses and the second floor as living quarters. The ruko accommodates various small- to medium-sized commercial and official enterprises such as bank branches, dentists' offices, small restaurants, internet cafés, laundry businesses, cellphone repair shops, and local offices of political parties. Maya's hair salon is part of a smaller-sized ruko complex that is sandwiched between a motorbike repair shop and a small kiosk. The salon's front area is where Maya and her two employees greet clients. The middle section is for facials and hair washing, and the back serves as a kitchen and bathroom. The upstairs area has an empty hall with two rooms at the front where Maya and Alia, her housemate and employee, sleep.

During my stay in Namu, Maya, her friends, and I only occasionally ventured out of the salon during the day. Sometimes we would visit the town center to hang out at the food stall that stayed open very late in order to get some fresh air after a long day of work in the hair salon. On rare occasions like birthdays, we visited a small coffee shop located in a military complex in town to relax and sing karaoke. By only going out as a group in public during the late evening, the transpuans sought to avoid unwanted attention from the townspeople, as the streets usually quieted down after 10 p.m. Even then, on the journey between the salon and our usual hangout at the food stall, our presence could incite whistles and jeers from men still hanging around the street. This late-night routine highlights how the movements of the transpuans within the town were subject to watchful public scrutiny. As a result, they restricted themselves to certain times and to places like hair salons.

Within the transnational network of LGBT activism, which is mainly centered in urban areas, safe spaces usually operate through specific scripts. As Marie Thompson explains in her essay on grassroots feminist, queer, and antiracist activism mainly in the United States and the United Kingdom, safe spaces typically operate with "a set of principles, expectations, and 'ground rules' agreed by consensus, which seek to provide a supportive, compassionate environment in which participants can talk about issues, experiences, and resistive strategies; and in which harmful behavior is collectively addressed and met with consequences."[11] However, I noticed a distinct pattern in how Muslim transpuans in Namu organized themselves around the Primadona beauty salon and the Rumoh Aceh initiative. In these contexts, safety is relationally constructed through the continuous practice of attuning oneself to the ever-present risk of violence.

In response to the contingent nature of much of the violence that afflicts the social existence of transpuan in Namu, Maya and her friends have adopted a range of tactics for protecting themselves. When Maya discussed Nanda's behavior, she used the expression "jaga diri" (protecting oneself). This phrase is often used interchangeably with the phrases "buat-buat diri" (to behave oneself) and "jaga-jaga" (to be on alert) in casual interactions, before parting ways, or as a reprimand for trivializing concerns about safety. The phrase "jaga diri" means either self-protection or self-care, and in a relational context, it refers to the virtue of knowing one's place in the world. It also implies caution in presenting oneself to the world as exemplified by the term "buat-buat diri." The phrase "hanya jaga-jaga" carries a double meaning: to take precautions while actively anticipating the potential harm.

Practices such as this, in addition to the midnight excursion routines, framed my fieldwork interactions. When I made appointments with Maya to meet outside Salon Primadona during the daytime, for example at a coffee shop, it was not uncommon for her to change the rendezvous point at the last minute. She did this to jaga-jaga, which usually entails closely observing the coffee shop from a distance. If the crowd of men sitting at the designated coffee shop seemed unfriendly, she would suggest a new location to meet.

Safety in Muslim trans worldmaking includes an emotive aspect that is relationally produced and constantly (re)made and negotiated. In Namu, where transpuan people face many constraints, they must continuously adjust their routine to the risks they are willing to take based on the best available options and circumstances so they can continue living and engaging in communal pleasure and affective bonds. This embodied knowledge is crucial in their effort to endure persistent and chronic forms of violence. Places such as Salon Primadona and other sites transpuans frequent in Namu, such as Taman Kerang and the noodle shop, serve as safe enough spaces.[12] The term "safe enough" suggests that relative safety in these settings should not be assumed. This spatial formation is not always comfortable because it necessitates constant anticipation of and openness to potential crises that structure everyday life. By inhabiting these safe enough spaces, transpuans in Namu nourish a communal way of life amid normative violence by tapping into the political potential of self-preservation.

The Faith and Sexuality Activists' Camp

So far, I have described safe spaces in the peri-urban settings of Aceh through the experiences of Maya and the transpuan community in Namu. Now I shift the geographical focus to Yogyakarta, where I encountered a group of youths who had organized an activist camp called the Young Queer Camp on Faith and Sexuality (hereafter referred to as "the camp"). When I went to the camp in September 2014, it was in its third year. The camp was always held at a discrete location. This was because, contrary to Yogyakarta's reputation as a "city of tolerance," the city had become a volatile ground for vigilante violence, that includes xenophobic hostility and anti-LGBT campaigns.[13]

During the five-day camp, I primarily interacted with the organizers. I had agreed to limit my role to observing the camp's dynamics and taking notes of the process, keeping verbal engagement with the participants at a minimum. The organizers suggested this practice to accommodate the fact that I was outside the camp's stipulated age range of 18–30 years (I was 37 at the time). In addition to the camp participants and the fifteen-person committee, there were two volunteers who assisted with the day-to-day operation of the camp; they were mainly responsible for taking notes and documenting the event.

On the second day during lunch, I spoke with one of the coordinators, Sari, about who was participating in the camp. She explained that the camp aims to provide a safe space for young people to share experiences and express themselves, which is not an easy task. The coordinators had received over 120 applications that year. A committee had selected ninety applicants and conducted online interviews, cutting the list down to sixty. These were assigned to smaller online study groups facilitated by committee members from which forty passed through to a second interview that resulted in the final twenty-three applications who were selected. When I asked here about this seemingly elaborate and time-consuming procedure, Sari replied:

> Last year's selection process was more lenient; we accepted people from diverse backgrounds—LGBT activists, students from *pesantren* [Islamic boarding schools], theological schools, and public universities—through two processes: written applications and interviews. However, the results were disappointing. There was no real dialog during the camp, and most debates ended up becoming harmful. While sexuality and religion are sensitive subjects, the way they were discussed was not constructive. We did not get to the roots of the problems and there were no concrete outcomes. By the end of last year's camp, most participants returned to their own ideological bubbles. Only a few achieved the transformations we were aiming for.

The selection process described above allowed the camp's committee to establish rapport and shape group dynamics before the camp began. This permitted potential participants to familiarize themselves with each other earlier, and by initiating the online discussion, the organizing committee was able to anticipate any potential conflicts. This strategy also explains the committee's directive to me that I interact with camp participants

very minimally. Besides the obvious age difference between myself and
the young participants, my late arrival into the group and my role as a participant observer had the potential to disrupt the relationships among
participants that were developing.

The camp's aim to provide a space for young people to talk about issues
of sexuality and faith appeared in the camp's slogan: "The Circle of Love,
Diversity of Expressions." This slogan was printed on T-shirts the committee members wore and was made into huge banners that hung in the
Javanese *pendopo* (outdoor pavilion-style structure) where the main
sessions were held. Nestled within a lush green retreat complex located
in the hilly outskirts of Yogyakarta, the pendopo was surrounded by
wooden cabins where the participants and organizers stayed. The pendopo
functioned as the main location for most of the programmed activities,
including lectures, group discussions, and various games designed to foster group cohesion.

The camp organizers frequently used the feeling-word "comfort"
(*nyaman*) to foster a sense of safety within the camp, an emotive used by
some of the protagonists we encountered earlier. This sentiment was
conveyed by the camp mentors as instructive. They construed it as a
feeling-state that camp participants should strive to achieve when navigating faith and body-related issues. From day one of the camp, mentors
promoted comfort as they encouraged *penerimaan diri* (self-acceptance)
as an alternative to self-denial and coming in rather than coming out.
Mentors also suggested this perspective when participants inquired
about how to handle discrimination, intolerance, or bullying in their
environments. The camp mentors told participants that a way to achieve
comfort is through being honest with oneself about one's feelings and
sharing them openly with others.

This approach echoes Ruth Holliday's theory, which suggests that
comfort signifies the harmony between one's inner and outer self or, in
terms of how the inner as the "authentic" self is mapped onto the body,
comfort functions as a signifier of "what one feels from the degree of fit
between the outside of one's body and its inside."[14] The mentors' emphasis
on feelings of comfort as a way of fostering safety reflects their recognition and understanding of the participants' struggles with everyday
violence. However, some critics challenge the drive to normalize comfort as the only pathway to learning.[15] Sara Ahmed, for instance, argues

that promoting comfort can be a marketing strategy that seeks to make consumers feel comfortable at the expense of exploited labors.[16] In foregrounding comfort as the primary emotion in safe spaces, there is a risk of replicating hegemonic structures of privilege and exclusion. To further illustrate the consequences of overlooking these emergent paradoxes, I turn to an incident that occurred midway through the camp's week.

Fractured Comfort

On the third day of the camp, the morning session was dedicated to Sari's presentation on sexual orientation, gender identity, expressions, and bodies (SOGIEB) in local contexts.[17] This topic has become staple material in Indonesian queer activist education, and participants listened attentively Sari's explanation of the nuanced differences between sexual identity, orientations, gender, gender roles in society, and gender identities. All the participants were seated on the wicker mats rolled out on the pendopo floor, as was I. Anna, who I introduced in chapter 1, was sitting in a corner of the pendopo. She was the committee member who was responsible for filming the session. I noticed that from where she was sitting, she had a clear view of the entire event that enabled her to capture all the key moments on camera.

As Sari lectured, she projected images onto a screen to help illustrate traditional gender expressions in different ethnic cultures across Indonesia. Sari's presentation proceeded smoothly until she showed an image of a bare-chested Balinese woman from presumably the premodern period.

I was preoccupied with my own thoughts and was taking notes, so I was not paying too much attention to the scene that followed. Some members of the audience gasped, and I could hear some chuckles. And then I heard Anna shouting: "Hey, what did you do just now?" She pointed her finger at one of the young male participants, whom I will call Iwan. All eyes turned to Iwan, who was crawling back through the rows of participants sprawled on the floor. Anna demanded: "Repeat what you just did now! I did not get to see it clearly, what did you do?" Iwan, looking devastated, replied: "Nothing, it was just a joke. I did not mean to harass anyone; I know how it feels to be harassed." Despite his protest, Anna insisted he repeat his action. Reluctantly, Iwan returned to the front of the pendopo and mimed a gesture as if he was cupping the breasts of the Balinese woman's image projected onto the screen.

During the reenactment, total silence filled the room. Sari seemed flabbergasted by the situation; she had been looking the other way when Iwan made his gesture. Then Anna said, in a trembling voice,

> Okay, now I see it. I was not sure before as I was focusing on the camera. But you pointed to it yourself just now without me even asking. By saying it is not a kind of harassment, you are doing exactly the opposite.

A long, intense silence followed. Anna suggested that Sari continue her presentation and added that she would talk privately with Iwan during the break.

That night, as all participants returned to their cabins, the camp organizers gathered to evaluate the day's events and plan for the next. Anna reported that her intended one-on-one conversation with Iwan did not take place because he seemed to be avoiding her. The next morning when I entered the pendopo, I immediately sensed tension in the air. A committee member whispered to me that Iwan had left the camp. Throughout the rest of the day, I could see that Anna and a few core committee members seemed troubled. Both the participants and some of the organizers were whispering among themselves, blaming Anna for Iwan's hasty departure.

To address the tension, Sari and the core committee members decided to raise this issue with the entire group after lunch. They asked Anna to clarify her intervention from the previous day. When it was Anna's turn to speak, she stood up and said:

> Here I am speaking not on behalf of the committee, I only speak for myself. I would like to apologize for what happened yesterday. I realize it was disruptive to the running of the session. But I would like to point out that since all of us here agree that this is a safe space, I think what happened yesterday was a form of violence, and my reaction was also quite violent. I hope that this will never happen again.

The audience whispered among themselves and appeared unconvinced by Anna's apology. Suddenly, Dito, a volunteer who had been taking minutes of the session at the time of the incident, raised his hand. Dito is a trans man in his early twenties who worked in a local queer advocacy group in Yogyakarta. In a nervous tone, Dito spoke up:

> I want to apologize. I was quiet the entire time because I am not a part of the committee, I am only a volunteer. But I think I want to speak now on behalf of the person who is no longer here now. What happened yesterday was inappropriate. We all came here to learn, right?

"Yaaa!" some participants interjected. Dito continued:

> So if what happened yesterday was a mistake, the committee members should have reacted more wisely. They should not have treated the person in that way; it was understandable for him to feel humiliated and leave. What we need is an explanation and an apology from the committee, since what happened yesterday clearly is also an act of violence. After all, we are all still learning here.

When Dito put down the microphone, some camp participants applauded, but the situation remained unresolved. Anna stayed silent, leaving everyone waiting for her response. Sari then took the floor, saying the organizers would consider Dito's feedback and discuss how to proceed with the situation. The participants and mentors then moved on to the next lecture session.

This situation had complex layers. Anna had told me that her strong reaction to Iwan's action was due to personal trauma. The image of the Balinese woman presented on the screen reminded her of her mother, who had ended her life when Anna was still a teenager. She read Iwan's gesture as sexist, but more important to her, it triggered painful memories. However, Dito raised an important point when he hinted that Anna had abused her power when she humiliated Iwan in front of the other participants. This dynamic was particularly evident because Anna was one of the organizers of camp activities.

This incident relates to wider debates about callout culture. Activists often call out individuals who make offensive or discriminatory comments or actions, making the potential harm of their actions known to others. This approach isn't new, particularly among intersectional queer and feminist activists spaces, but it has gained attention with the rise of social media platforms. Opinions on calling out individuals in public vary. Some view the tactic as an effective way to hold people accountable and ensure that harmful acts are noticed.[18] Others criticize calling others out for its performative nature and its tendency to shut down dialogue by ignoring the complexities of the situations of individuals instead of engaging with them.[19] In my view, each of these positions make valid points; the challenges of callout culture are not inherent but relate to how it is practiced.

The discursive treatment of callout culture as a form of emotional expression within safe-space debates in Western activist circles has important implications for the phenomena I describe, especially given the growing connections between local and transnational activist scenes. However, my focus here is on understanding safe spaces in the context of Indonesian national history. This is because the category is tangled with the hegemonic discourse on *keamanan* (which conflates safety and security) and its entanglements with the affective register of *nyaman* (comfort) and the cultural prescriptions of *rukun* (social harmony) and *tenteram* (feelings of equanimity).

Iwan's avoidance of Anna after the incident, his abrupt departure during the night, and Anna's ineffective apology to the camp participants can be read against the predominance of social harmony as a cultural norm in the local context of Java in particular and Indonesia in general. In a social-cultural context where nyaman is often equated with a peaceful existence through avoiding open conflict, the crucial task for creating a safe space is to lay bare the processes in which power inequalities are reproduced through the idealization of comfort.

Marie Thompson advocates for a shift from normalizing comfort in safe spaces to creating safe(r) spaces alongside their inherent tension: "The perennial difficulty of safe(r) spaces means they are often far from comfortable. . . . Safer spaces may also be discomforting insofar as they require us to come face to face with uncomfortable truths about our own complicities and ignorances."[20] Thus, Anna's anger about Iwan's blatantly sexist joke, Iwan's display of shame and remorse after Anna called him out, and the participants' disappointment about Anna's impulsive reaction, as expressed by Dito, can all be viewed as processes of relearning ways to relate to each other that can get quite discomforting.

As an educational setting, the camp serves as a critical learning site not only for the person being excluded but also for other participants who experienced discomfort witnessing the fragility of safety when holding our peers accountable. This conflictual moment created an opportunity for the camp organizers to reflect and develop better ways of addressing similar situations, potentially building collective transformation over time. The challenge that Dito articulated can be read as a critical invitation to be mindful to the relational work involved in putting comfort and safety into practice.

In hindsight, I wonder what would have happened if Sari and her committee members had allowed more time to address the growing unease after Iwan left the camp instead of moving on to the next session. Although prolonging the discussion may have caused more discomfort and it might have been too late to resolve differences, I see potential in that critical moment. The organizers could have acknowledged that no space is free from domination and risk, a position that might have sparked thoughtful questions among both mentors and participants. They could have examined how issues of privilege, power, and difference play out in the camp in a discussion that connected those issues to broader social and political domains.

These are all, of course, my own speculations about how to counter the demotivating narratives—that is, the feelings of frustration, disillusionment, and exhaustion—that often arise in queer collective space-making when conflicts seem irresolvable or when structural inequalities persist. Drawing from scholars who emphasize the importance of negative affects in queer histories, I argue that the affective experience of impasse should be taken seriously as a crucial political category.[21] The unease resulting from a shared inability to arrive at a better solution might not be a shortcoming. Rather, it has the potential to demonstrate how conflicts in collective processes of queer and trans worldmaking can be primarily understood as the result of structural problems that present few opportunities for resolving conflict due to preexisting asymmetries.[22] The tension in the camp that developed after the incident during Sari's presentation can be seen as an opportunity to deal with power asymmetries collectively in ways that support individual needs. Configurations of power in this context shift away from a single individual or institutional actor and are distributed as care responsibilities among a diverse number of actors with varying roles, commitments, privileges, and vulnerabilities. The tension generated during the camp session thus could have been addressed with care, instead of attempting to diffuse discomfort with a harmonizing solution. Such situations signal an opportunity to change power relations in ways that highlight the role of conflict in constructing safer queer spaces and emphasize how incompatibilities between different positionings can be recognized and understood as opportunities for change.

Staying Put as Care

Beyond ensuring safety, care is a key aspect of communal belonging in Muslim queer and trans worldmaking in Indonesia. I now return to Namu, Aceh, where the care practices that Maya and her friends performed in the processes of becoming a community can be understood through lived experience. Maya's life story reveals the complex processes of her care practices, which are shaped by certain moral values, emotional valences, material conditions, and spiritual values.

As many feminist scholars have argued,[23] care is deeply entangled with its "messy worldliness" and "cannot be resolved in ready-made explanations."[24] Building on the various meanings of care in feminist thought regarding transformative justice, Nell Lake defines care as "a wide area of life and study comprising activities, institutions, ideologies, and emotional states concerned with meeting human need and suffering."[25] She contends that this broad meaning can be divided into three components: care as a moral value, care as emotion, and care as labor.

These three elements of care feature prominently in the narratives Maya conveyed. Because of their compelling character, some of the key points of her narratives bear repeating here. Despite increased raids and harassment by local authorities and people in her social surroundings, Maya refuses to leave her current location in order to become safer. Her decision to keep her hair salon open is rooted in her understanding that it provides not only a livelihood for her friends but also a safe space for them to express their inner gendered souls.

I had the privilege of witnessing how these complex meanings of care played out in the day-to-day interactions between Maya and her friends at the Primadona Salon. In the morning, employees would clean the salon and sweep and mop the floors and Maya or Alia would shop for the day, buying and cooking enough food to ensure that there was enough for everyone who would visit the salon throughout the day. Nanda, one of the salon workers, usually joined in the morning chores. Alia served as cashier and bookkeeper during the day, and balanced the books at the end of the business day. After all the morning chores were done, Maya and her employees took turns bathing. For about an hour, they would sit in front of the mirrors of the salon to put on their makeup and tend their hair.

Salon Primadona provides more services than cutting, washing, and styling hair. The staff also colors and smooths and rebonds hair on request, gives facial treatments, and applies makeup, among other services.[26] Prices vary based on the service and the quality of beauty products requested by the customer, but they are all relatively affordable by local standards. From time to time, prospective male clients, usually older, would enter the salon timidly and ask for a *khusuk* (massage) service, a covert term for sexual services. When they received such a request, Maya and her employers would assess their willingness or energy to perform the service for the extra income. The earnings from these services went solely to the individual providing the massage. Once terms were agreed upon, the client was escorted upstairs to a private area.

On rare occasions, certain clients received these services gratis, particularly if the masseuse was attracted to the client. However, I observed one incident when a prospective client got very upset because he got rejected even after he offered the right price, since neither Maya nor her employees found him attractive. When the man started to shout and make threats, a staff member took up his offer so there would not be a scene that would disturb the other customers.

As customers flowed into the salon throughout the day and evening, friends and relatives would also drop by. Some came for a cigarette break, others to pass the time, and some to deliver cakes or borrow something. During quieter times, such as sundown prayer time (Maghrib), everyone would relax on the couch in the salon, chatting while watching their favorite Indian soap opera on a small television set in the corner of the room. Guests would stop in during this time as well.

On one early evening, I noticed a group of young males gathering in the salon's parking lot. Even though they were invited in, they remained outside. According to Maya, they were planning to "transition" once they finished high school. "These boys are so naughty [*nakal*]," Maya told me. "They like to [sexually] experiment among themselves and with older men, but they usually don't use condoms. So when they come over, I always give them [condom] packages."

Friends visiting the salon would sometimes bring goods to sell, including designer handbags and clothing items (both genuine and counterfeit) to wigs and makeup tools. Tips and tricks about makeup techniques and instructions for creating a more "feminine curve" using body padding were shared. Occasionally, some of the transpuans would go into the room were facials were given at the back of the salon to inject each other with hormones obtained via the black market. This injections were usually administered by individuals who have past, albeit informal, "training" from local health care providers. While the injections were done in the salon, many also took birth control pills on their own as a part of broader hormone regimen.[27]

Care as Affective Labor

The neighborhood was accustomed to the fact that many people visited Salon Primadona throughout the day. One day I asked Maya how her neighbors perceived this, and she said she often had to explain herself:

> I would tell them that although I am like this, that doesn't mean that I'm trouble. I have never done anything to cause harm nor committed a crime. Sometimes I asked them. "I am only here to work and earn my own living— Why should *I* be in the wrong?" They would tell me [that] Islam forbids you to be like this, that it is a sin and so on. I would tell them I already know this, but being like this also has its own divine fortune [*rezeki*]. I don't really know how God perceives me but all I know is that by being like this I can still get my own livelihood. I'm not a burden to anyone. People would go quiet when I said this; I'm not sure if they still talk behind my back, but more important is that I just need to learn to get along with my family and society. I have been trying to convince my friends to do the same too. They need to be able to carry themselves [*bawa diri*] well.

Maya's pursuit of belonging is hindered by the religious and moral disapproval she receives because of her gender nonconformity. Despite this, she insists that being a transpuan does not prevent her from receiving divine fortune and contributing meaningfully to society. Her productivity, and that of her friends at Salon Primadona, contributes to the economic and social well-being of the neighborhood. Her story reveals how social recognition in Namu, or Aceh in general, operates through the norms that constitute moral behavior, which emphasize both a pious lifestyle and economic productivity as the grounds for acceptance.[28]

However, Maya frequently experiences resentment from others in her community. Her neighbors often admonish her by quoting passages from the Quran, which she finds particularly disturbing. She also discovered that despite her efforts to build amicable relations with her neighbors, they belittle her behind her back. This illustrates the challenges of using care and emotional labor to gain social recognition for transpuan in Namu. The dual nature of care is further illustrated by her mention of *bawa diri*—the need to master the art of conducting oneself. She uses this phrase to describe the practice of attuning one's everyday conduct to social norms to prevent further social exclusion and public ostracization.

My understanding of affective labor is indebted to the works of feminist scholars, notably the ethnographic research conducted by Samia Dinkelaker on the Indonesian labor migration program.[29] Dinkelaker defines "affective labor" as the nuanced skills expected of Indonesian migrant domestic workers.[30] She distinguishes between "affective labor for the employer" (work to ensure an employer's comfort and satisfaction) and "affective labor on the self" (managing personal emotions in a work environment where labor is devalued).

Dinkelaker's distinctions inspired my own understanding of "carrying oneself" as a prime example of both "affective labor for the neighbors" and "affective labor on the self." The former refers to the process by which transpuans constantly attune themselves to local norms in order to obtain social recognition. The latter illustrates the affective labor that transpuans perform on themselves to manage their feelings of insecurity and anguish when they are met by a lack of empathy from the people they seek acceptance from. Through "carrying oneself," they reveal the dual nature of care as affective labor that can be understood as a gesture of enduring otherwise. Their efforts to perform care labor as a means for "getting along" indicates both a precondition and a driving force in their efforts to attain and sustain belonging. It reveals that despite the constant negation of the social existence of transpuans in their social surrounding, they never gave up their ways of being in a world. Instead, they persist in reaching out to the very people that reject them. Through this behavior, the transpuan community in Namu crafted a sense of belonging as an affective state that demands continuous renewal.

Care at Its Limits

The full extent to which the Muslim transpuans bear the shifting values of care as an affective burden came to light in a conversation between Maya and Nanda. Maya and I were in the salon's back room one humid afternoon when Nanda stormed through the doorway, exclaiming the news she'd heard from Mami Paula's salon. Mami Paula, a transpuan elder and hair salon owner, had reportedly been spreading a rumor that Maya and Nanda were frequently seen at the municipal hospital because they were "ill," a euphemism for HIV infection. This rumor devastated both Maya and Nanda for a number of reasons. Nanda explained to me:

> The reason why we went to the hospital a lot is because we are helping those who need help in taking a voluntary HIV test there. We are there to facilitate the process and give moral support. And it is not specific to the HIV test only, we also assist those who need general medical support.

Maya surmised that Mami Paula instigated the gossip to smear Maya's reputation as an activist and to eliminate business competition:

> All of this causes me headache [*pening*], Fer. With all the trouble I've been through, going back and forth to the hospital every time people need to access treatments. But in the end, I am the one who has to deal with such gossip: I am the one who is ill, who is infected by AIDS. This sort of news will turn the hair salon customers away from me, you know? It's really bad for business.

The heated conversation continued well into the evening as I accompanied Maya to see Mami Yana, the well-respected transpuan elder

introduced in chapter 2. The purpose of the visit was to discuss the plan
for an upcoming assembly with members of Rumoh Aceh to get feedback
from community members about the idea of registering their group as a
legal entity. Still feeling upset by the rumor, Maya repeated Nanda's story
to Mami Yana. Mami Yana tried to console Maya and told her to ignore
the gossip. Maya lamented that such a rumor was so damaging to her,
especially because Mami Paula is not an outsider: "She knows really well
who I am and what I've been doing. She used to join our activities
[in Rumoh Aceh]." Mami Yana turned to me, and said to us both in a
calming tone:

> That's exactly why, Ferdi, we need to formalize Rumoh Aceh right away. So
> everything that we do is official. Later, others can also help you with what
> you are doing, Maya. You don't have to go to the hospital all the time any-
> more. We'll share the workload. Perhaps we could even use name tags like
> how other NGOs do it. This is important because then people like Mami
> Paula can see that we are doing this for no other reasons than work.

The assembly, which was attended by around thirty Rumoh Aceh members, took place two weeks later. The meeting concluded with a mandate
for Maya and a few other core members to initiate steps to register
the group as a legal entity. That was the last group meeting I attended
before departing from the fieldwork in Namu.

The key point to be gleaned from this vignette is the clarity with
which Maya expressed the predicament of care in Muslim queer and
trans worldmaking in Namu. The situation is shaped by the social and
political dynamics of (in)visibility and stigma around HIV/AIDS, particularly in Aceh and Indonesia more broadly.[31] Maya's routine visitations
to the hospital to help others access care inevitably invited rumors.
This aligns with Tom Boellstorff's findings on *penasaran* (anxious curiosity) that visible access to healthcare prompts among others. Based on
his research among people with HIV (known as orang dengan HIV, or
ODHIV, in Indonesia) Boellstorff notes how *penasaran* serves "as an
emotional counter to the fear [*takut*] that . . . prevented many persons
at risk from getting tested for HIV and that also shaped stigmatization
toward ODHAs."[32]

Maya's irritation about the rumor stemmed not from shame at being labeled a person living with HIV but from Mami Paula's alleged role in spreading it. Maya seemed more hurt about facing the news that a person like Mami Paula—someone she respected because of her social status as one of the community elders—shared a poor opinion of her.

While this vignette suggests a rivalry between Mami Paula and Maya regarding their salon businesses, I also read Maya's reaction as a sign of deep exhaustion from the lack of acknowledgment from the community members she served with her caring labor. The frustrating facet of care exemplified here aligns with what Maria Puig dela Bellacasa describes as the emotionally draining aspect of care. She writes: "In a world in which inequalities make of care a burden mostly carried by ones at the expenses of others, 'to care' can be devouring for women and other marginalized carers."[33]

The depletion of Maya's affective, moral, and material resources—what is typically understood in the context of caregiving practices around AIDS as burnout—is even more pronounced when she poses the question of what the ultimate value is of caring practices in the context of shared vulnerability to stigma.[34] What does it mean to care in a world of chronic social neglect?

A related paradox underlines the relational dimension of Maya's affective labor of communal care. Maya's anger at Mami Paula's misrecognition shows her need for community approval as motivation for her actions. This situation highlights tension within in-groups as a sign of nonbelonging. However, by engaging in *curhat* (a heart-to-heart talk) with Mami Yana about her frustration and disappointment with Mami Paula, Maya saw the importance of sharing the burden of care within community. Emotional support from people within the community offers Maya encouragement to continue her care labor. This demonstrates how relational affects form the basis for a communal care chain: one needs caring from the community in order to perform communal care.

Mami Yana, a respected community elder, advised Maya not to dwell on the rumor but to learn from it. She suggested that the problems caused by the precarious conditions of practicing care could be addressed through the formal institutionalization of Rumoh Aceh. This shift would allow the redistribution of Maya's personal burden of care *for* the community into a responsibility that is shared *together with* different members of the community.

The Longing to Belong

In her paper "Queer Belongings: Kinship Theory and Queer Theory," Elizabeth Freeman expands the notion of belonging beyond the desire to exist and connect with others.[35] She proposes that belonging also encompasses the desire to endure in a physical form over time. The longing to belong, or "being long" as Freeman puts it, "encompass not only the desire to impossibly extend our individual existence or to preserve relationships that will invariably end, but also to have something queer exceed its own time."[36]

Belonging in this context also involves enduring over time. This term can be difficult to translate directly into Indonesian, as it carries a distinct semantic structure. In Indonesian, belonging always has a passive connotation, implying a state of being owned or being a part of something. Grammatically, the phrase on an active voice only takes when the word "to belong" (*milik*) is combined with the Indonesian word "*rasa*" (roughly translated as "feeling" or "sense"), forming "*rasa memiliki*" (or feeling/sense of belonging). Alternatively, one might say, "I am a part of that" (*aku bagian dari itu*). These local expressions convey a heightened sense of ownership that stems from the interlocutors' connections to real or imagined material and personal possessions, not unlike the English term "belongings."

None of my research protagonists explicitly stated that they belong to something. Instead, they indicated belonging by saying that they felt attached, comfortable, or bound to a specific location or group of people. This indirect way of expressing the sense of "belonging to" suggests that it is not about individual claims of collective membership but about an experience of being within a social relation.[37] In other words, belonging *to* a collective is always about belonging *with*.

Thus far, I have examined belonging as a relation of being with others over time, which I have portrayed through stories of everyday collective engagements with safety and care. Through the lens of everyday practices of safety, we can draw an analytical distinction between the moral, practical, and affective modalities of safe space, safe enough space, and safer space. The communities' struggles for safety are constantly confronted by both external threats and internal conflict. These are complex and often painful affective terrains that limit and simultaneously sustain those involved in negotiating and fashioning relationships within their different social environments and, most important, between themselves.

The promise of belonging, which can never be guaranteed but must be secured through ongoing relational labor *to each other* and *with others* through caring enactments, emerges as another affective pattern of Muslim queer and trans communal life. The care labors of persisting under chronic violence are imbued with a complex set of affective dynamics that both complicate and enable endurance. The actors in this chapter did this by continually and collectively doing things a little differently than before. Through its promise of endless potential for renewal, the work of belonging in Muslim queer and trans worldmaking becomes synonymous with enduring otherwise.

Conclusion

Without an End

This book has argued that Muslim queer and trans worlds are continuously being made, unmade, and remade through ways of enduring everyday violence stemming from religious norms. These processes, when seen through the optic of affective dynamics, facilitate the agentive forces that characterize endurance as a mode of engaging with otherwise possibilities: an approach to living that recognizes its inherent harms yet remains committed to the question of what ought to be done differently to undo these harms.

The focus on different times, spaces, and ways affects, emotions, and feelings operate has provided us with an analytical route to disentangling the multiple pathways represented in the rich ethnographic material. By analyzing how affective dynamics unfold through the use emotives and affective repertoires in everyday settings, this book explores how protagonists engage with a complex relay between self-determination and normative structures in their personal and shared encounters with intersecting scenes of living. This process results in a montage of vernacular expressions that outlive the binary oppositions of accommodation and resistance.

Through the life stories of various Muslim queer and transgender protagonists, I have shown how prolonged social marginalization can profoundly affect psychological well-being, generating a structure of ambivalence patterned by diverse subjective experiences of inner conflict. The emotional turmoil the protagonists experienced while navigating the risks of normative violence and competing moral claims led to various distressing moments and debilitating sensations. At the same time, they remained committed to diverse conceptions of the good life through a range of affective practices. This process enabled some to endure difficult circumstances, although others were simply exhausted and wished to "stop." Some attempted to overcome these situations by either moving toward or away from Islamic tenets, while others failed altogether. Yet, ultimately, they all continued to seek ways to keep on going.

Through the life stories of Rizky, Tino, and Anna, I have contended that inner conflict is not exclusive to Muslim sexual and gender minorities. These three often struggled to reconcile the perceived tensions between their religion, their sexual orientation, and their gender identity. The range of affective dynamics involved in this process can differ substantially across personal biographies, individual desires, and what or who each person cares about. In affectively making what we are, who we were, and what we aspire to be, inner conflict not only creates a fragile and contingent moral self but also serves as a durable model for understanding how alternative possibilities for Muslim queer and trans worldmaking can be generated from fashioning, improvising, and attuning to different notions of a good life.

The second set of life stories, those of Ali and Maya, included traumatic encounters with the violent consequences of certain normative aspects of religion throughout their lives, and illuminated, above all, how they persist through them. This kind of narrative is compounded by religious understandings of spiritual faith exemplified by the belief in divine reward and salvation in the afterlife. However, some of the life stories indicated how the protagonists remained burdened by traumatic experiences related to strict religious precepts. Instead of attempting to adhere to them, they tried to find spiritual fulfillment by connecting with the divine in their everyday lives and surroundings.

Maya's story illustrates the most tragic circumstances. She endured repeated mental and physical abuse but also encountered unexpected moments of relief, or what she called "miracles." On one hand, "miracle" as an uncanny intervention indexes how Maya oscillates between the transcendental and the immanent in her process of coping with traumatic events. And on the other hand, it suggests how Maya is "enduring the impossible" by reworking past memories and present predicaments into everyday practices of undoing harm and remaking social life.[1] The impulse that animates both affective registers is hope.

Hope is also a recurring force in the narratives of other protagonists. However, this hopeful engagement does not simply mean holding onto an abstract promise of a happy ending or embodying an inner strength or human flourishing often characterized as "resilience." Instead, it necessitates engaging with damaging situations through arduous affective labor. For Muslim queer and trans worldmaking, everyday endurance is a different matter from fulfilling the need to survive. It involves affectively embodying and upholding moral and ethical visions of a good life in the face of ongoing crises and persistent injustice in larger societies. In this scenario, however, the future as a horizon of good life often appears capricious and thwarts endurance as more of an attempt to dwell in ambiguities of time. These are moments when future aspirations are often eclipsed by the ongoing struggle to grasp whatever life is offering as the only actions that can be taken in the time one has.

I have argued that enduring otherwise is also ingrained in and differentiated through the communal ways of life in Muslim queer and trans worldmaking. I looked at two types of collective practices—moral participation and community building—to understand the moments when the affective, relational dimension of enduring otherwise becomes perceptible.

While my ethnographic encounters with two communities in Aceh form the basis of much of this book's analysis, this should not be taken to overstate the uniqueness of queer and transgender communities in Aceh. Comparable moral quandaries affect many communities in other parts of the country. However, the richness of the empirical findings in Aceh regarding collective moral practices compelled me to reevaluate my stance toward the normalizing aspects of morality that can become oppressive. As a scholar-activist with life experiences embedded within queer feminist political work, it took me some time to comprehend how steadfastly moral claims were held by people rendered as morally abject in the hegemonic discourse. The research protagonists' collective engagement with moral values enacts a range of agentive capacities that challenge the preconceived notions that associate queer agency with resistance to or subversion of norms.

I showed through the case studies how the regulatory and oppressive power of moral norms continues to inform but never fully determines the ways moral lives are claimed, understood, and practiced among Muslim sexual and gender minorities. Moral participation as a form of enduring otherwise may take diverging paths in terms of format (formal or informal) and content (sinfulness or conversion). These differences are shaped by specific internal relationships and tensions and by power asymmetries.

However, there is a common thread: both forms of moral participation are permeated by affective articulations that ultimately blur the boundaries between categories of morality, ethics, and political imagination. Through shared experiences of marginalization, members of Muslim queer and trans communities are adopting the language of moralities often used against them. They participate in everyday attempts to answer the question of what is collectively *felt* as good and right. This ultimately entails knowing what possibilities are being opened up (and closed down) by attending to these shared feelings and what other possibilities should be pursued to ensure that such forms of togetherness continue to exist.

In distinct group settings, individuals often repeated the familiar teachings and values of the dominant religious moral discourse in their daily interactions by sharing and articulating what being moral and ethical means in relation to what is commonly understood as a good life. Simultaneously, these utterances are also sutured to Muslim queer and transgender vernacular practices and expressions. While the actors behind these repetitive actions are well aware that much of what they have shared and done within their respective community would not necessarily translate to better inclusion, they kept on going anyway. This determination is motivated by the intimate knowledge and experiences that can be gained from such a dynamic constellation, along with the awareness that through this activity, different ways of being moral and ethical can be collectively attained, assessed, and attested to.

I have shown how collective endurance is marked by tenacity and the courage to exist within the cracks of dominant political structures. Over time, friendships and communal living in a world filled with familial ostracization and social neglect become necessary foundations for creating safety, practicing care, and negotiating belonging. Hence, I argue that embodied and material processes are key to understanding the work of affective relationality of endurance in these communities. The practices of sharing common experiences of vulnerability include moments when material resources are exchanged with pleasure and support and feelings of sympathy and empowerment are reciprocated. However, often those practices are marred by failures, exhaustion, conflicts, and power dynamics. Past and present traumas linger and their wounds can still be traced through the bodies of community members and in their interpersonal relationships. In this type of communal living, enduring otherwise is not just about bringing together various actors to find ways to survive through coexistence; it is also about persisting through inevitable moments of dissonance by enacting different ways of being with each other.

There are times when hope is replaced by self-preservation, as happened when Maya and her friends fled Aceh. Still, it did not take long before they returned to Aceh although there was no guarantee of safety. They returned there possibly because of their deep attachments to the people and the place or maybe because they had nowhere else to go. What remains clear is their refusal to succumb to violent pressure.

Thus, enduring otherwise can be understood as a form of affective engagement with the moral, ethical, and political potential of inhabiting norms differently. Situated in tension with the multiple forms of chronic violence, the worldmaking processes of Muslim queer and trans people continue as they strive through by working on their capacity to persevere while holding on to the fragile hope that they can change their marginalized conditions.

Affirming Muslim Queer and Trans Worldmaking

When I embarked on my research more than a decade ago, I was primarily concerned with the apparent ruptures between religion, nonheterosexuality, and gender nonconformity. In popular discourse, living religiously has often been considered as incompatible or irreconcilable with living as queer or trans. My curiosity centered on how individuals navigate the tensions arising from conflicting identities and practices, particularly how they attempt to reconcile them. However, through the narratives of the protagonists in this book, I have come to understand that the coexistence of conflicting desires, practices, and discourses is not a problem to be solved. Instead of perceiving these contradictions as hurdles to overcome, I have learned that they are fundamental to how these people live, endure, and make meaning in their lives. I recognized that these contradictions are inherently human, and this led me to shift the focus of my study toward understanding how the protagonists stay with these contradictions without an end.

Muslim queerness and transness are not simply positions of exclusion or marginalization; they represent complex ways of life, of inhabiting these contradictions. Instead of striving to resolve the tensions between religiosity, nonheteronormativity, and gender nonconformity, many of the individuals and groups I encountered complicate these conflicting realms through various forms of moral participation and ethical relationship. In this context, I find the concept of "enduring otherwise" most adequate—not as an attempt to reconcile the irreconcilable but as a way to describe the dynamic spaces of possibility where a diverse array of moral, ethical, and political imaginations is enacted by those who experience contradictions the most acutely.

In many ways, the forms of endurance examined in this book align with the notion of affirmative ethics that Rosi Braidotti has proposed.[2] Rooted in posthumanism, feminist philosophy, and critical theory, her ethical framework emphasizes relationality, affect, and the creative transformation of lives shaped by social forces and harm. Braidotti argues that ethics should involve transforming negative passions into positive ones—not by ignoring pain, but by engaging with it actively. She asserts that "paradoxically, it is those who have already cracked up a bit, those who have suffered pain and injury, who are better placed to take the lead in the process of ethical transformation."[3] This perspective shares some resonances with the experiences of this book's protagonists, who continually reshape trauma, inner conflict, and social marginalization into something more bearable. Similar to Braidotti's ethics of affirmation, their endurance encompasses not just survival in the face of violence but also an affective commitment to envisioning alternative worlds.

However, I believe it is important to approach the overly positive tone of affirmative ethics with prudence. While Braidotti's framework highlights ethical transformation as a "qualitative leap through and across pain" toward positivity, the discussions in this book have revealed that the realities of endurance often manifest as slow burnout, chronic frustration, and further suffering.[4] These narratives reflect realities far removed from the defiant joy of challenging normative structures; they are instead characterized by gnawing feelings of uncertainty and deep ambivalences.

At the heart of the experience of enduring otherwise in Muslim queer and trans worldmaking lies the tenacity of faith, which serves as an impulse for pursuing a good life. This complexity complicates efforts to categorize whether enduring otherwise results in disempowerment or empowerment in relation to normative structures. The life stories of

Rizky, Tino, Anna, Ali, and Maya illustrate how individuals marginalized by religious discourse remain deeply connected to religious and moral frameworks, navigating a spectrum of experiences that include both pain and hope, disappointment and attachment, and rejection and salvation. Some strive for deeper piety or greater social acceptance while pursuing intimate relationships with same-sex partners. Some struggle with mental health challenges brought on by the sedimentation of bad feelings from the past, while others seek a more bearable existence by finding solace in "having just enough." Many of these aspirations are intertwined with the hope for a good afterlife, envisioned as a divine reward.

In their persistent pursuit of "the good life," the protagonists embody Berlant's notion of "cruel optimism," the condition of remaining attached to desires that ultimately impede well-being.[5] They navigate structures that obstruct the realization of their visions of a life worth living. These ideals, whether expressed through religious morality, spiritual growth, or communal belonging, offer potential promise and fulfillment while simultaneously perpetuating ambivalence and harm. This underscores the double bind of "cruel optimism" that complicates Muslim queer and trans worldmaking projects. Despite the potential harm associated with pursuing a good life dictated by normative structures, the protagonists remain committed to this pursuit—either because they perceive no viable alternatives or because these attachments provide a sense of stability and meaning. This is where the "otherwise" takes hold—a realm of affective possibilities in which existential problems like harmful social relations and attachments to problematic object of desires are perpetually reconfigured across time.

The possibilities for attachments to a good life appear to echo Braidotti's call to transcend pain through affirmative ethics. However, in its emphasis on transforming negative experiences into something "productive," the positive push in affirmative ethics runs the risk of underestimating both the difficulty and potential of staying with pain. As Sara Ahmed points out, the pressure to "get over" pain can generate new forms of suffering for those who are not yet ready or able to move on.[6] The protagonists in this book have spent their lives grappling with harm. Most of them show little sign of moving forward, and perhaps they never will. As I listened to their stories and engaged with their daily lives during my fieldwork, it became clear that our interactions had formed an ethics of witnessing, one that calls for staying with ruptures rather than rushing to transcend them. This is not about glorifying pain but about recognizing the importance of sitting with difficult emotions, bearing witness to them, and understanding that not everything broken can or should be repaired immediately. For many of the protagonists, the intention is not to transform suffering into something positive but rather to preserve their lives and sustain relational connections amid ongoing violence. Through these processes, they learn to understand how difficult affects have helped shape who they are. Ethical growth, in this sense, is not about getting rid of unwanted feelings in exchange for more desirable ones; rather, it involves cultivating a deep understanding and building a complex relationship with both, even when they don't align. In this process, the ruptures themselves become affective sites for engaging with the world differently.

Through the lens of Muslim queer and trans worldmaking, then, endurance takes form as an affirmative way of becoming otherwise. By attending to the limits and possibilities of staying with the pain of ongoing violence, individuals not only strive to overcome its damaging effects, they also cultivate the capacity to endure what might come next. This mode of living is a social project toward otherwise possibilities that is humbled by the constraints and resources of the world we inhabit. And by faithfully staying with *this* world, the protagonists ultimately transform the boundaries that it permits.[7]

The Endurance of Intellectual Labor

The exhaustive discussion on endurance has made me reflect on the lengthy process of writing this book. Throughout this process, I have experienced numerous personal losses and bereavements as well as chronic illnesses for myself and loved ones. There were times when I felt I could not write anymore. This was due not only to my own physical and emotional burdens, but also because many of those who had generously shared their deepest thoughts and feelings during my research were going through even more difficult times than when we first met.

While I was in Berlin, there was only so much I could do other than occasionally checking in electronically with the few research protagonists

I remained in contact with. During urgent situations, such as the harrowing event that happened to the trans women communities in Aceh, I tried my best to offer support, such as making solidarity calls or sending moral support to Maya and her friends whenever possible. But I am worlds away from their daily struggles with increasing risks of violence. These experiences caused a numbing feeling of helplessness and highlighted the futility of academic writing in the direst of circumstances. But in the end, I too had to keep on going with my writing. The main motivation to continue came from the insights generated by the empirical material, which illuminated how the different research protagonists were enduring forms of social life that continue to deny their right to exist. Not unlike facing a mirror, the durational process of staying attentive to the protagonists' narratives and enactments of endurance during fieldwork, analysis, and writing have, in turn, helped me endure various difficult moments in life as well.

I am not suggesting that only through my personal experience of endurance can the enactments of endurance in Muslim queer and trans worldmaking be understood. While there are perhaps some tangential overlaps, the gestures of endurance I encountered during my fieldwork are diverse, complex, and idiosyncratic and thus are not comparable with my personal experience. Instead, they have compelled me to think more carefully about how endurance as an ethnographic insight is intersubjectively woven by attending to both my personal affective experience and the embodied realities that constitute the "field."

One of the main affordances of doing affective ethnography is its focus on the points of convergence between the affects of the researcher and the research interlocutors in the field. Meanings and understandings are shared intersubjectively and co-produced through this approach. This methodological perspective reveals how affective encounters with moments of endurance at different phases of the research process can continue to implicate everyday academic practices.

This notion of endurance also raises questions concerning its application as a conceptual and methodological approach in affect studies. There have been some calls for what Margaret Wetherell describes as the "rubbishing of discourse,"[8] mainly among scholars in affect studies,[9] which is partly a backlash from the discursive or linguistic turn in the study of emotions in the 1980s.[10] This critique suggests that the focus on discourse or narratives in studying affects, emotions, and feelings has reached the point of exhaustion and expiration and therefore should be dismissed.[11]

While affects do circulate beyond words, as I have shown in this book, my observations and analysis of the empirical materials suggest that we should not give up on narratives just yet. This approach has gained even greater urgency in the age of post-truth, fake news, hate speech, and disinformation, in which the interplay of affects, emotions, and feelings in representational discourse and political rhetoric has heightened forms of social polarization and ideological contestation across different parts of the globe. The affective components of narratives within alternative social projects are increasingly being absorbed by neoliberal forces in order to perpetuate the status quo. On a different plane, heartfelt exchanges around political languages and other affective forms of expression have become some of the most vehement strains of various queer, trans, feminist, decolonial, and antiracist contemporary struggles. Given these dramatic shifts in the ways affective languages shape contemporary lives, critical attention to discourse and narrative remains indispensable.

Investigating the affective weight of particular aspects of social realities is always a slippery and arduous affair.[12] When possible, I attuned myself to plots, historical and biographical contexts, personal characters, tonalities, dictions, interruptions, interjections, bodily gestures, subjunctives, silences, and all kinds of visual shapes and colors as well as temporospatial arrangements. Such elements are inextricably linked with the spoken or written word, allowing us to feel the affective push when a story is narrated; the ineffability of narratives that cannot be reduced to simply linguistic and symbolic interpretations.

Scrutinizing the affective dimensions of narratives is physically and emotionally taxing. However, it can lead to a greater understanding: the very analytical labor of engaging with narratives in affective ethnography becomes a matter of endurance. In our work to engage with the thick messiness that "the world of affect brought into view," we must not limit our analysis to what is being said and written but extend our approach to diversify our perspectives and use context-specific methods to understand the affective composition of narratives.[13] This may involve enduring intense emotional experiences in the field that are born of the stories told, the persons telling them, and the temporal and spatial conditions of their emergence during ethnographic fieldwork. Later, during the writing stage, we might have to revisit these experiences as remnants of our memory, flashbacks, or other bodily sensations. But it does not end there. Our endurance as intellectual laborers will again be tested when the time comes to share, activate, and transform our ethnographic findings into knowledge that shapes different modes of becoming in other scenes of social, cultural, and political struggle.

No Way They Could Win

At the end of 2019, about a year and a half after the incident that opens this book, I told Maya over WhatsApp that I was heading to Medan, North Sumatra, for a few days of work. Even though a flight to Aceh would take only an hour, the time between my visit to Medan and my return flight to Berlin was insufficient for a stopover in Namu. "Unfortunately, I won't be able to visit you in Namu this time," I told her. She replied saying she would come to Medan on those particular dates to meet me. I knew that making such a trip would cost her time, energy, and money, but I did not try to dissuade her. After all, it had been almost four years since we last saw each other and I was excited to see her again in person.

On the appointed date, we met just outside a glitzy restaurant located in the city's main square. She came with two other transpuans: Yasmin, who seemed to have grown more confident since we had last met in 2014, and Chandra, a new acquaintance for me. We took a seat at one of the restaurant's outside tables, ordered our food, and immediately started catching up. Then I began asking about our mutual friends back in Namu.

I was aware that Alia, Maya's employee and housemate, had moved to another town in Aceh to open up her own hair salon business. "But what about Nanda?" I asked. All three went silent, then Yasmin raised her left thumb, lightly pressing it under her lips to signal that Nanda had been using crystal meth, known as *shabu-shabu* in Indonesia. Seeing my perplexed reaction, Maya added:

> She quit her job at the salon. She's not the only one using drugs these days; there are others [she mentioned a few familiar names]. It all started not long after returning from the safe house last year. Some of us just couldn't

handle it anymore. Initially, they did it to take their mind off everything that was going on. Now it seems that they cannot stop.

I paused, taken aback by the news, then continued: "What about Dara? We have been in contact quite regularly via social media until about three months ago. But I could not find her online profile anymore. How is she doing?" Maya looked agitated by my question and told me that it was around that time also Dara packed up all of her stuff from the salon and just left without any explanation. Dara also cut communication with all members of Rumoh Aceh. "Going on a journey of self-discovery, maybe," said Yasmin testily. It struck me that things had deteriorated much more than I had anticipated. Substance abuse and mental health problems that had seemed so distant five years earlier had become prevalent in the transpuan community. It seemed that many were succumbing to exhaustion, despair, and further isolation.

Unwilling to dwell on this morbid thought, I asked Maya a question I had asked countless times before: "So, after all of this, you still want to continue staying in Aceh?" The tone of her response included rancor: "Of course I have to stay! If I leave then they will become the winner! I refuse to lose! There is no way I could let them win this!" It was evident that Maya's resolve was now fueled by defiance, compounded by a layer of fortitude. If previously her persistence in holding her ground in Namu was colored by a compassionate sense of belonging to her community, at that moment it was inflected by a desire to work against a "them" who remained nameless. She seemed to have reached a juncture in her life where withstanding an extended present in the shadow of violence had forged a form of refusal to give up, to admit defeat, to collapse under its pressures.

My last in-person interaction with Maya and her companions in Medan once again solidified the narrative of endurance. Even though their resolve has been tested by more violent trials and tribulations, the threads of enduring otherwise remained unscathed, but perhaps further radicalized. They remain tenacious in their efforts to open up possibilities for a world where no one will ever have to endure the unendurable anymore.

ACKNOWLEDGMENTS

This book has been over ten years in the making. In many ways, the writing process itself was a test of endurance. I could not have finished it without the abundant contributions and support from those I have encountered along the way. Foremost, I am profoundly grateful to the interlocutors whose experiences and knowledge shape these pages. Although confidentiality keeps many unnamed, their insights are at the heart of this body of work. I am indebted to their openness, patience, and generosity in welcoming me into their lives. They allowed me to bear witness to, participate in, and learn from how Muslim queer and trans worldmaking is affectively scaffolded by forms of enduring otherwise. It is through these connections that this book finds its grounding and meaning.

This book began as a doctoral dissertation, and I benefited immensely from the mentorship and advice of Thomas Stodulka and Birgitt Rötgger-Rössler at Freie Universität Berlin. Their guidance has profoundly shaped my approach to thinking about and practicing anthropology. I would like to express special thanks to Thomas Stodulka for his genial support throughout my research journey and for being a constant source of inspiration. To me, Thomas is more than just a mentor; I am proud to have him as a close friend and collaborator. I especially thank him for opening up opportunities to pursue a scholarly life in Berlin, for offering empathetic guidance when necessary, and for continuously encouraging me to find my footing as a scholar. Likewise, I am indebted to Birgitt Röttger-Rössler, who has generously supported my research since its earliest stages. She has graciously helped me carve out mindful ethnographic research conduct, and she helped me navigate bureaucratic hurdles in the early stages of the research. I also thank Christian von Scheve, Beate Binder, and Nasima Selim for their invaluable support as members of my PhD defense committee.

This research was made possible by the scholarship from the German Academic Exchange Service (DAAD) Scholarship. I am grateful to the

Volkswagen Foundation for supporting my involvement as an affiliated researcher in the Researchers' Affects Project, a collaborative initiative between social and cultural anthropology, literary studies, and primatology based at Freie Universität Berlin and the University of Bern, Switzerland. I would also like to express my gratitude to the project leaders, Katja Liebal, Oliver Lubrich, and Thomas Stodulka, for making this collaboration both possible and pleasurable. I particularly valued the stimulating interdisciplinary exchange with my peers in the project: Julia Keil, Mira Shah, and Fermin Suter. A special word of thanks goes to Samia Dinkelaker, who is not only an astute fellow scholar at the Researchers' Affects Project but has proven many times to be an invaluable friend and ally who deeply engaged with my theoretical musings and empirical work. I thank her for galvanizing me with her healthy and willful outlook on life, especially when it was at its most bleak.

Thanks to those who listened, commented, and generously engaged with me during my doctoral studies at the Institute of Social and Cultural Anthropology at Free Universität Berlin: Mechthild von Vacano, Hansjörg Dilger, Victoria Kumala Sakti, Irina Savu-Cristea, Florin Cristea, Leilani Hermiasih, Anita von Poser, Eric Anton Heuser, Marcos Andrade Neves, Rosa Cordillera Castillo, Ronja Eberle, Dominik Mattes, and Omar Kasmani. I also would like to extend my deep appreciation to colleagues in the Elite Graduate Program "Standards of Decision-making Across Cultures" at Friedrich-Alexander-Universität Erlangen-Nürnberg, particularly Dominik Müller, Viola Thimm, Mingqing Yuan, Jean-Baptiste Pettier, and Oleg Vasilchenko. I am also grateful to Farish A. Noor, who served as a guest professor in the program for a year. The last two years I have spent in this supportive working environment have allowed me to focus on bringing this book to fruition.

Special thanks to the outstanding editorial team at NYU Press—Jennifer Hammer, Brianna Jean, and Ellen Chodosh—and to the esteemed editors of the Hauntings: Queer/Trans Studies in Religion series: Melissa M. Wilcox, Ashon T. Crawley, and Tamara C. Ho, whose exquisite guidance was crucial in steering my work through the publishing process. Several anonymous reviewers appointed by NYU Press also contributed greatly to this work's completion. Their thoughtful feedback helped me strengthen and improve the book immensely. I am very grateful to Cecil Mariani for permitting me to display her artwork: *Silver Shadow series, Number 2*, as the cover of this book, which not only enhances the book's visual appeal but also captures the soul of the narratives contained within. I thank Kate Babbitt for her attuned engagements in the copyediting process. I would also like to thank Rebecca Conroy for her delightfully surgical approach to editing the earlier draft of the book, which was key in refining the language and sharpening the clarity while keeping its nuance intact. Any shortcomings are mine alone.

Some earlier versions of the chapters in this book have appeared in other publications, and I thank the respective publishers for granting permission to reprint the materials here in modified form. Part of the introduction was published in *Queer Southeast Asia* (edited by Shawna Tang and Hendri Yulius Wijaya). Some portion of it is also featured in "Following the Hearts: Ethics of Doing Affective Ethnography in Vulnerable Research Settings," *International Quarterly for Asian Studies* 53, no. 4 (2022); and "Discordant Emotions: The Affective Dynamics of Anti-LGBT Campaigns in Indonesia," *Indonesia and the Malay World* 50, no. 146 (2021). Part of chapter 4 appeared in "The Making and Breaking of Indonesian Muslim *Queer* Safe Space," *borderlands e-journal* 17, no 1 (2018). I deeply appreciate the guidance and insight of the editors and special issue editors in these and other publications; they have significantly shaped the arguments presented in this book.

Throughout the research stages, I have been supported by various intellectual companions working and living in Berlin, Yogyakarta, and elsewhere in between. These include Annemarie Samuels, Benjamin Hegarty, Jan Simon Hutta, Ben Murtagh, Bart Barendregt, AbdouMaliq Simone, David Kloos, Sylvia Tidey, Dede Oetomo, Sharyn Graham Davies, Saskia Wieringa, Yasmeen Arif, Tom Boellstorff, Peter A. Jackson, Ed Green, Saskia Schaeffer, David Seitz, Francis Seeck, Antke Antek Engel, Nikita Dhawan, Maria do Mar Castro Varela, Gilly M. Hartal, Ruth Preser, Mike Laufenberg, Christopher Sweetapple, and Rachmi Diyah Larasati.

Countless formidable collaborators and confidantes have left their marks on this book in ways too numerous to list here. Among them, I am especially grateful to Rully Mallay, Amar Alfikar, Annette Krauss, Kabelo Malaitse, Sabine Mohammed, Andy Fuller, Aicha Diallo, Wendelien van Oldenborgh, Marnie Badham, Wong Binghao, Suza Husse, Nino Halka, Yulia "Edith" Dwi Andriyanti, Rosalia Engchuan, Molemo Moiloa, Teesa

Bahana, Gertrude Flentge, Bina Choi, Yolande Zola Zoli van der Heide, Conal McStravick, and Cannach MacBride.

Fellow comrades of the KUNCI Study Forum and Collective have been playing the pivotal role of becoming my intellectual muses in completing this book. I thank Nuraini Juliastuti, Syafiatudina, Brigitta Isabella, Antariksa, Fiky Daulay, Gatari Surya Kusuma, Hayyi Al Qayyumi, Rifki Akbar Pratama, Very Handayani, and Maria Uthe. The countless hours of working, studying and hanging out both physically and virtually with the group of people who belong to this nondisciplinary collective have instilled in me the commitment to unsettle as soon as things are settling down and to reflexively reposition myself wherever possible contingencies and oversights arise.

I would also like to extend my deep appreciation to my close circles of friends, mostly outside academia, who have sustained and grounded me with much love and support over the years. In no particular order, I thank Abraham Soekarno Poespo, Eva Streifeneder, Ratna Mufida, Suryani Liauw, Reza Caropeboka, Didit Saptadi, Imelda Taurina Mandala, Lisabona Rahman, Sebastian Winkels, and Alex Head for their unwavering friendship through thick and thin. This book is also dedicated to the memory of friends who are no longer with us: Patricia Elida Tamalagi, Rusmadian Karyani, and Arip Rahman (Arga) Hakim.

Last but not least, I reserved my thanks to my family of origins, each of whom has supported and nurtured me in their own distinct ways: my mother, Njai Raden Koesnajanti; my late father, Teuku Zulfansyah Thajib; and my sister, Risthy Z. Thajib, and her family. My life in Berlin has also been further nourished by the priceless comfort offered by my "found family": Doris Müller-Ziem, Michael Ziem, and Leoni Ziem. I am ever so grateful to my partner, Bernd Müller, for his warm companionship and his quietly comforting, humorous, and patient support. I cannot thank him enough for allowing me to feel love and loved in the most concrete and grounded way possible. It is ultimately his courageous endurance that instills in me enough courage to endure whatever life may present.

NOTES

INTRODUCTION

1 The term "*waria*," which is an acronym of the Indonesian words *wanita* (woman) and *pria* (man), was commonly used in local and national everyday speech by both ingroups and outgroups during my fieldwork in 2013–2015. Today, however, "transpuan" is gradually replacing the term in an effort to promote more self-determination and broader social justice. I asked Maya, a transgender woman who is one of this book's main protagonists, about her preferred term of description in response to a recent debate in Indonesian social media regarding the use of "waria" or "transpuan." She advised me to use the term "transpuan" to educate the public, even though she acknowledged that the term "waria" is still used in her community today.

2 Throughout this book, all names are pseudonyms and details about persons, places, and situations have been altered for safety reasons.

3 Browne, Munt, and Yip 2010; Taylor and Snowdon 2014.

4 Jamal 2001; Yip 2005; Kugle 2010, 2014.

5 Boellstorff 2004a; Oetomo 2001.

6 Blackwood 2007.

7 Boellstorff 2005a, 223.

8 Berlant 2011, 10.

9 Das 2007; Kleinman 2000.

10 S. Davies 2010.

11 Garcia Rodriguez 2023; Safitri 2011.

12 Zuhri 2006; Dzulkarnain 2006.

13 Merriam-Webster online 2023.

14 Povinelli 2011.

15 Povinelli 2011, 32.

16 Baraitser 2017, 182.

17 Povinelli 2011, 128.

18 Agamben 1998.

19 Van Doorn 2015, 636.

20 Simone 2016.

21 Bracke 2016, 62.

22 Simone 2016.

23 Feldman 2015, 429.

24 Feldman 2015, 429.
25 Feldman 2015, 443.
26 Weiss 2022.
27 Hage 2015.
28 Bracke 2003; Mahmood 2005; Braidotti 2008a; Singh 2015.
29 Mahmood 2005.
30 Mahmood 2005, 15, italics in original.
31 Mahmood 2005, 34, 2–3.
32 Ahmed 2004.
33 Ahmed 2004, 155, italics in original.
34 Braidotti 2008a, 15.
35 Braidotti 2008a, 15.
36 Mahmood 2005; Ahmed 2004; Braidotti 2008a, 2008b; Muñoz 1999; Povinelli 2011.
37 Simone 2013, n.p.
38 See King, Navarro, and Smith 2020.
39 Crawley 2017, 2, italics in original.
40 "*Keyakinan*" means faith or belief in the Indonesian language. In everyday parlance, this word is used interchangeably with "*kepercayaan*" and "*iman*," both of which mean faith or conviction. While there is no significant difference of meaning between keyakinan, kepercayaan, and iman, the former two can be applied to nonreligious contexts. Iman, which can be translated as "recognition with the heart," is a word that derives from Islamic theology. For Muslims, iman is built on six pillars: belief in Allah, the angels, the books, the prophets, the Day of Judgment, and Allah's predestination.
41 Yip 2010.
42 Goh 2020, 178.
43 Braidotti 2012, 2008b.
44 Mahmood 2005.
45 Das 2007; Mahmood 2005; Berlant 2011.
46 Love 2007; Ngai 2005; Cvetkovich 2003; Ahmed 2010.
47 Puar 2007; Massad 2002, 2007.
48 Dhawan 2013.
49 Rao 2020.
50 Rao 2020, 52.
51 Behar 1996.
52 Following Feldman (2015, 430), I am aware that a focus on endurance can raise ethical concerns akin to those raised by Andrea Muehlebach, in her critique of "resilience." Muehlebach argues that resilience can "perform a kind of violence as those with the privilege of detecting 'resilience' in others seem to be telling themselves a soothing story: the poor are strong (no matter how we batter them); they can withstand (no matter how much we exploit them); they will bend and rebound (but not rise up)" (Muehlebach 2013, 301). However, I argue that

attending to endurance reveals what romanticized narratives of resilience often obscure—not just the capacities of individuals and communities to persist but also the toll exacted by enduring structural violence. This perspective moves away from a self-contained view of human agency, emphasizing instead its relational entanglement with the structural conditions that necessitate endurance in the first place.

53 See Frjida 1986; Stodulka, Dinkelaker, and Thajib 2019.
54 Massumi 2002.
55 Burkitt 2014; Wetherell 2012.
56 Gould 2009; Stodulka 2017.
57 Stodulka, Dinkelaker, and Thajib 2019, 283.
58 Damasio 1994, 1999; Stanghellini and Rosfort 2013; Gould 2009.
59 Cromby 2007; Burkitt 2014.
60 See Geertz (1959) 1974; Wikan 1990, 1992; Heider 1991.
61 Magnis-Suseno 1998, 130–131. Tr.: "*perasaan jasmani inderawi, perasaan akan kedudukannya dalam medan interaksi, perasaan kesatuan dengan alam semesta.*" In addition to Franz Magnis-Suseno's ethical understanding of *rasa*, its significant role in Javanese spiritual cultures has also been addressed in the work of Paul Stange (1984) and Niels Mulder (1992).
62 See Blackman and Cromby 2007.
63 See Röttger-Rössler and Markowitsch 2009.
64 Reddy 2001, 270.
65 Berlant and Warner 1998, 558.
66 Muñoz 1999, 121.
67 Schielke and Debevec 2012; Marsden and Retsikas 2013; George 2010; Peletz 1997.
68 Houben 2015; Hefner 2010.
69 Heryanto 2008.
70 Subijanto 2011; Jones 2010.
71 Kloos 2017; Rudnyckyj 2011; Simon 2009.
72 Wilcox 2021, 43.
73 Namaste 2000; Stryker 2004.
74 Munir 2014; Paramaditha 2018.
75 Blackwood 2005, 237.
76 Quoted in Munir 2011, 116, italics in original.
77 Hegarty 2022.
78 See Simone 2022.
79 Blackwood 2005; Peletz 2009; Lim 2013.
80 Boellstorff 2005a; Wieringa 2009.
81 Tom Boellstorff (2005a) wrote *gay* and *lesbi* in italics in his ethnographic work on Indonesia to signal that these terms are locally used and locally meaningful identity categories, not simply direct translations of the English "gay" and "lesbian."
82 Blackwood 2010.

83 Blackwood 2007.
84 Hegarty and Thajib 2016.
85 Thajib 2021.
86 Paramaditha 2016; see Siegel 2006 and Boellstorff 2004a.
87 Bevins 2021.
88 Simone 2022, 28.
89 Gherardi 2019; Rai 2019.
90 Rabinow 1977; Clifford and Marcus 1986.
91 Lutz 1988; Visweswaran 1994; Wolf 1996.
92 Davies 2010; Spencer 2010; Svašek 2010.
93 Thajib, Dinkelaker, and Stodulka 2019, 15.
94 Stewart 2017, 197.
95 This is a transcultural translation because in the Indonesian and broader Malay-speaking world, "*hati*" literally means the liver while the English word "heart" translates as *jantung*. But in Indonesian popular culture, "hati" is understood as the heart, which is metaphorically expressed in various world languages as the seat of emotions.
96 Massumi 2002, 5.
97 Marcus 1995.
98 See Samuels 2019.
99 See Kloos 2017.
100 See chapter 3 for details.
101 Stodulka, Dinkelaker, and Thajib 2019.
102 Dickson-Swift quoted in Liamputtong 2007, 72.
103 See Samuels 2016; Lovell 2007.
104 Kirby and Corzine 1981; Liamputtong 2007.
105 Juliastuti 2006; Anderson 1966.
106 Hegarty 2022.
107 See Slama 2010.
108 Van Maanen 1988.
109 See Spencer 2010.
110 Clifford and Marcus 1986; Faubion and Marcus 2009.

CHAPTER 1. INHABITING INNER CONFLICT

1 See Geertz 1984; Simon 2009.
2 Gould 2009.
3 Georgis 2013.
4 Schielke 2009a, 2009b.
5 See Simon 2009.
6 Mattingly 2013.
7 Arendt 1958.
8 Mattingly 2013, 308.
9 Zigon 2007; Lambek 2010; Fassin 2012.

10 Fassin 2012, 7–8.

11 Lambek 2010, 8.

12 See Fassin 2012, 2013.

13 Schotten 2018, 2.

14 Dave 2008.

15 From Surah Al'Baqara (The Cow) 9 verse 286 in the Quran.

16 Heryanto 2003.

17 Kantjasungkana and Wieringa 2016, 69.

18 Kloos 2017, 2015.

19 Bennett 2007, 375–376.

20 Jamal 2001; Yip 2004; Yip and Khalid 2010; Siraj 2012; Boellstorff 2005b.

21 Boellstorff 2005a.

22 Jankowiak and Paladino 2008.

23 This particular hadith says: "Ibn 'Umar reported: Messenger of Allah said, "A Muslim is a brother of Muslim, he neither wrongs him nor does hand him over to one who does him wrong. If anyone fulfills his brother's needs, Allah will fulfill his needs; if one relieves a Muslim of his troubles, Allah will relieve his troubles on the Day of Resurrection." (Al Bukhari and Muslim in Riyad as-Salihin 244). Scott Siraj al-Haqq Kugle (2007) writes something similar within the mystic tradition of same-sex love among Sufi poets.

24 In Indonesia, people commonly say "motor" to refer to both scooters and motorcycles/ motorbikes. Here, I use "motorbike" interchangeably with "motorcycle" and "scooter" to encompass the wide range of two-wheeled vehicles—both automatic scooters and semi-manual motorcycles—that dominate daily transportation. This contrasts with the United States, where "motorcycle" usually means large, powerful bikes, and "scooter" refers to smaller, often recreational vehicles.

25 Geertz 1973; Keeler 1983; Stodulka 2009; Boellstorff and Lindquist 2004; Fessler 2004.

26 Röttger-Rössler 2013, 408.

27 Scheff 1990.

28 See Fessler 2004.

29 Collins and Bahar 2000, 42, italics in original.

30 Sedgwick 2003; Halberstam 2005; Munt 2007; Love 2007; Ahmed 2004; Warner 1999.

31 Ahmed 2004, 107.

32 Valentine, Skelton, and Butler 2003; Britt and Heise 2000.

33 Boellstorff 2004a, 477.

34 Fatah 2004.

35 Jauhola 2012; Blackwood 2010.

36 Boellstorff 2005b, 98–99.

37 Nguyen 2014, 6–7.

38 Nguyen 2014, 12.

39 Hamudy and Hamudy 2020.
40 Mahmood 2005.
41 "Istikharah" refers to a supplication performed by Muslims seeking divine guidance regarding a concern or a decision in their life.
42 Ahmed 2010, 6.
43 See Lukens-Bull 2007.
44 See Colombetti and Ratcliffe 2012; Colombetti 2011.
45 These are: Islam, Protestantism, Catholicism, Hinduism, Buddhism, and Confucianism
46 Yip and Khalid 2010, 98.
47 Good and Good 1994, 868.
48 Butler 1990.
49 Holliday 1999, 481.
50 Siegel 1998; Boellstorff 2005a; Hegarty 2022.
51 Hegarty 2022, 133.
52 Hegarty 2022, 88.
53 Connell 1995, 35.
54 Sedgwick 2003; Kasmani 2022.
55 M. Jackson 1989, 149.
56 Berlant 2011, 199.

CHAPTER 2. MORAL PARTICIPATION AT THE MARGINS
1 Boellstorff 2005b.
2 Heryanto, Huat, and Varney 2015.
3 Gandhi 2006; Joseph 2002; Ahmed and Fortier 2003, 254 (quote).
4 Berlant 2016.
5 See Pine 2008.
6 See Schaefer 2015.
7 Siapno 2002.
8 Quoted in Deeb and Harb 2013, 8.
9 See Hegarty 2022 for the shifting historical meaning of the term.
10 The temporality of these gendered expressions is closely tied to the living conditions of many younger transpuans. While feminine attributes may be embraced or tolerated within the salon, they are often removed before returning to family homes and neighborhoods where such expressions are met with disapproval or hostility.
11 *Sari tilawah* (ritual prostration) is one component of three activities of Musabaqah Tilawatil Quran (MTQ), an Indonesian Islamic religious festival aimed at the glorification of the Quran. At this festival, participants compete at reciting Al-Qur'an, employing specific methodologies, including a *sari tilawah* competition that involves a poetization of interpretation or exegesis of the Quran. The tradition of MTQ was initiated by the largest Islamic organization in Indonesia, Nahdatul Ulama, and has been officiated by the state as a national

event since 1968. A series of smaller scale competitions are held in different regions, leading to an annual event held at the national level.

12 "*Bencong*" is a derivative of the word "banci."

13 *Junub* is an Arabic-Islamic term meaning ritually impure due to sexual intercourse or seminal discharge. A person in such a state needs to take a bath in order to become ritually pure and be able to perform one's prayers. *Husnul khotimah* is an Islamic concept meaning a good end to life.

14 The term "emosi" has a negative connotation that means "upset" or "emotional."

15 See Wieringa 2022b.

16 Kloos 2015.

17 See Bowen 1989.

18 Kloos 2015; Bowen 1989.

19 See Mahmood 2005.

20 Mahmood 2005; Hirschkind 2006.

21 Yentriyani and Affiah 2017.

22 *Aurat* refers to the parts of the body that must be modestly covered in Islam, generally the whole body except the face and hands for women, and from the navel to the knees for men.

23 See Yip and Khalid 2010.

24 From Surah Al-Hujurat (The Dwellings) verse 49–11 in the Quran.

25 White 1994; Lutz 1988; Geertz 1984.

26 These emotional registers conjure the prevailing social imaginations of the Acehnese as an "exceptionally" pious people. David Kloos (2017) points out that while this essentialist portrayal is in many ways problematic, this image and its concomitant stereotypes of fanaticism and Islamic militancy are historically rooted in precolonial times in Aceh. This idea has since then been continuously invoked, from the Acehnese struggle against Dutch colonial power to the sectarian conflict in postcolonial Indonesia.

27 Lutz 1988, 3.

28 Lutz 1988, 73–75.

29 Röttger-Rössler 2013.

30 Beatty 2005, 28.

31 Heider 1991, 46.

32 Stodulka 2017.

33 Boellstorff 1999, 2005a.

34 Boellstorff 1999, 482.

35 Crosby 2013, 61.

36 Anderson 1978, 284.

37 Dangdut is a popular folk-pop genre known for its mix of demure and sensual dance movements.

38 "Kristenisasi" literally means Christianization, a vernacular term for proselytization.

39 Crouch 2014.

40 Asad 1986, 15–16.
41 Schielke 2009a, 2009b.
42 Mahmood 2005, 15.

CHAPTER 3. IN THE SHADOW OF VIOLENCE

 1 Knight 2016.
 2 Hegarty and Thajib 2016.
 3 Wieringa 2022a; Listiorini, Asteria, and Sarwono 2019; Davies 2018; Garcia Rodriguez and Murtagh 2022.
 4 Thajib 2021.
 5 Blackwood 2007.
 6 Hegarty 2022.
 7 Murtagh 2013.
 8 Slama and Barendregt 2018; Hefner 2010; Platt, Davies, and Bennett 2018.
 9 See Oetomo 2001.
10 See Boellstorff 2004a.
11 S. Davies 2010; Jauhola 2012.
12 Boellstorff 2005a, 223.
13 Thajib 2021.
14 Butler 2004, 42.
15 Quoted in Mills 2007, 140.
16 Boellstorff 2005a; Hegarty 2022.
17 A *slametan* is a ritualized feast central to the Javanese experience due to its symbolic values (Geertz 1960; Beatty 2005, 1999; Boellstorff 2005a; Stodulka 2017). In *the Religion of Java*, Clifford Geertz notes that "a slametan can be given in response to almost any occurrence one wishes to celebrate, ameliorate, or sanctify. . . . There is always the special food[,] . . . the Islamic chant, and the extra-formal high-Javanese speech of the host. . . . Most slametans are held in the evening" (1960, 11–13).
18 Samuels 2016.
19 Boellstorff 2009; Stodulka 2017; Samuels 2016.
20 Valentine, Skelton, and Butler 2003; Oswin 2014.
21 Boellstorff 2005a, 136–137.
22 See Boellstorff 2005a.
23 In *Gay Archipelago*, Tom Boelstorff describes the common use of metaphors of "opening" and "closing" among sexual minorities: "like the Western metaphor of being 'in' or 'out' of the closet, this spatial metaphor is bi-directional: one can be in a state of being opened or closed (*terbuka, tertutup*) and can open or close oneself (*membuka diri, menutupi diri*). . . . Like the concept of world (*dunia*), the concept of being open (*buka*) or closed (*tutup*) originates in the normal world" (2005a, 70–71).
24 *Mu'allimin* is a colloquial term for Madrasah Muallimin, an institution for the study of Islamic theology and religious law founded by Muhammadiyah, the second largest Islamic organization in Indonesia, after Nahdatul Ulama.

25 "Kuala Batee" is a pseudonym.
26 Boellstorff 2005a; Hegarty 2022.
27 P. Jackson 1995, 113.
28 Lindquist 2013.
29 In Aceh- and Malay-speaking contexts, the terms "Mamak Ayam" (Mother Chicken) and "Bapak Ayam" (Father Chicken) are euphemisms used to refer to individuals who operate prostitution businesses, while sex workers are colloquially referred to as "chickens."
30 Samuels 2019, 104.
31 Cvekovitch 2003, 3.
32 Green 1994.
33 Caruth 1996; Deleuze quoted in Das 2007, 91.
34 Samuels 2019.
35 Georgis 2013.
36 Ahmed 2010, 97.
37 Reay 2004, 60.
38 Berlant 2011.
39 Puig de la Bellacasa 2017, 70.
40 Lawson 2007.

CHAPTER 4. PROMISES OF BELONGING

1 Online comment by a SGRC member, accessed February 20, 2016.
2 Fox and Ore 2010; Hartal 2017; The Roestone Collective 2014.
3 Hartal 2017.
4 Hartal, David, and Pascar 2014 quoted in Hartal 2017, 14.
5 Hartal 2017, 17.
6 The Roestone Collective 2014.
7 Mundayat 2005; Sebastian 2006.
8 Stodulka 2017, 60.
9 Ahmed 2004.
10 Feener 2012.
11 Thompson 2017, n.p.
12 See Stengel 2010.
13 Stodulka 2017.
14 Holliday 1999, 481.
15 hooks 1994; Stengel 2010.
16 Ahmed 2004, 149.
17 According to Hendri Yulius Wijaya (2019, 144) this term and similar acronyms like SOGIE (sexual orientation, gender identity, and gender expression) or SOGIESC (sexual orientation, gender identity and expression, and sex characteristics) are popular among queer activists in Indonesia. They promote a more pluralistic view of sexual and gender plurality and also avoid the term "LGBT," which has a negative connotation among the public.

18 See Uprichard 2013.
19 Ahmad 2015; O'Neill 2016.
20 Thompson 2017, np.
21 Ahmed 2004; Cvetkovich 2003; Love 2007.
22 Thajib, Seeck, and Engels 2020.
23 Tronto 1993; Puig de la Bellacasa 2011, 2017; Zelizer 2005; Dinkelaker 2019; Ticktin 2011; Von Poser 2017.
24 Puig de la Bellacasa 2017, 10 (first quote); Puig de la Bellacasa 2011, 96 (second quote).
25 Lake 2023, 588.
26 Smoothing and rebonding are two techniques for straightening hair.
27 See Boellstorff 2004b.
28 See Hegarty 2018.
29 Weeks 2007; Gutiérrez-Rodríguez 2010; Dinkelaker 2019.
30 This notion is a significant departure from Michael Hardt and Antonio Negri's broad definition of affective labor as something that "produces or manipulates affects such as a feeling of ease, wellbeing, satisfaction, excitement, or passion. One can recognize affective labor, for example, in the work of legal assistants, flight attendants, and fast-food workers (service with a smile)" (2004, 18).
31 Samuels 2016.
32 Boellstorff 2009, 359.
33 Puig de la Bellacasa 2017, 163.
34 Cvetkovich 2003.
35 Freeman 2007.
36 Freeman 2007, 299.
37 See Probyn 1996.

CONCLUSION

1 Badiou 2008, n.p.
2 Braidotti 2012, 2008a, 2008b.
3 Braidotti 2008b, 23.
4 Braidotti 2008b, 23.
5 Berlant 2011.
6 Ahmed 2010, 215.
7 Simone 2022.
8 Wetherell 2012, 19.
9 Massumi 2002; Thrift 2008.
10 Lutz and Abu-Lughod 1990; Lutz and White 1986.
11 See Barad 2003.
12 Stewart 2017.
13 Stewart 2017, 192.

REFERENCES

Agamben, Giorgio. 1998. *Homo Sacer. Sovereign Power and Bare Life.* Stanford University Press.

Ahmad, Asam. 2015. "A Note on Call-Out Culture." *briarpatch*, March 2. https://briarpatchmagazine.com/articles/view/a-note-on-call-out-culture

Ahmed, Sara. 2004. *The Cultural Politics of Emotion.* Routledge.

———. 2010. *The Promise of Happiness.* Duke University Press.

Ahmed, Sara, and Anne-Marie Fortier. 2003. "Re-Imagining Communities." *International Journal of Cultural Studies* 6 (3): 251–59.

Anderson, Benedict R. O. G. 1966. "The Languages of Indonesian Politics." *Indonesia* 1: 89–115.

———. 1978. "Cartoons and Monuments: The Evolution of Political Communication Under the New Order." In *Political Power and Communications in Indonesia*, edited by Karl D. Jackson and Lucian W. Pye. University of California Press.

Arendt, Hannah. 1958. *The Human Condition.* University of Chicago Press.

Asad, Talal. 1986. "The Idea of an Anthropology of Islam." Occasional Papers Series. Center for Contemporary Arab Studies, Georgetown University.

Badiou, Alain. 2008. "The Communist Hypothesis." *New Left Review* 49, January/February. https://newleftreview.org/issues/ii49/articles/alain-badiou-the-communist-hypothesis

Barad, Karen. 2003. "Posthumanist Performativity: Toward an Understanding of How Matter Comes to Matter." *Signs: Journal of Women in Culture and Society* 28 (3): 801–31.

Baraitser, Lisa. 2017. *Enduring Time.* Bloomsbury.

Beatty, Andrew. 1999. *Varieties of Javanese Religion. An Anthropological Account.* Cambridge University Press.

———. 2005. "Emotions in the Field: What Are We Talking About?" *Journal of Royal Anthropological Institute* 11: 17–35.

Behar, Ruth. 1996. *The Vulnerable Observer: Anthropology That Breaks Your Heart.* Beacon Press.

Bennett, Linda R. 2007. "Zina and the Enigma of Sex Education for Indonesian Muslim Youth." *Sex Education* 7 (4): 371–86. https://doi.org/10.1080/14681810701635970

Berlant, Lauren. 2011. *Cruel Optimism.* Duke University Press.

Berlant, Lauren, and Michael Warner. 1998. "Sex in Public." *Critical Inquiry* 24 (2): 547–66.

Bevins, Vincent. 2020. *The Jakarta Method: Washington's Anticommunist Crusade & the Mass Murder Program That Shaped Our World.* PublicAffairs, Hachette Book Group.

Blackman, Lisa, and John Cromby. 2007. "Editorial: Affect and Feeling." *International Journal of Critical Psychology* 21: 5–22.

Blackwood, Evelyn. 2005. "Transnational Sexualities in One Place: Indonesian Readings." *Gender and Society* 1 (2): 221–42. https://doi.org/10.1177/0891243204272862

———. 2007. "Regulation of Sexuality in Indonesian Discourse: Normative Gender, Criminal Law and Shifting Strategies of Control." *Culture, Health, and Sexuality* 9 (3): 293–307. https://doi.org/10.1080/13691050601120589

———. 2010. *Falling into the Lesbi World: Desire and Difference in Indonesia.* University of Hawai'i Press.

Boellstorff, Tom. 1999. "The Perfect Path: Gay Men, Marriage, Indonesia." *GLQ: Journal of Lesbian and Gay Studies* 5 (4): 475–510. https://doi.org/10.1215/10642684-5-4-475

———. 2004a. "The Emergence of Political Homophobia in Indonesia: Masculinity and National Belonging." *Ethnos* 69 (4): 465–86. https://doi.org/10.1080/0014184042000302308

———. 2004b. "Playing Back the Nation: *Waria*, Indonesian Transvestites." *Cultural Anthropology* 19 (2): 159–95. https://doi.org/10.1525/can.2004.19.2.159

———. 2005a. *Gay Archipelago: Sexuality and Nation in Indonesia.* Princeton University Press.

———. 2005b. "Between Religion and Desire: Being Muslim and *Gay* in Indonesia." *American Anthropologist* 107 (4): 575–85. https://doi.org/10.1525/aa.2005.107.4.575

———. 2009. "Nuri's Testimony: HIV/AIDS in Indonesia and Bare Knowledge." *American Ethnologist* 36 (2): 351–63. https://doi.org/10.1111/j.1548-1425.2009.01139.x

Boellstorff, Tom, and Johan Lindquist. 2004. "Bodies of Emotion: Rethinking Culture and Emotion Through Southeast Asia." *Ethnos* 69 (4): 437–44. https://doi.org/10.1080/0014184042000302290

Bowen, John. 1989. "Salat in Indonesia: The Social Meanings of an Islamic Ritual." *Man* 24 (4): 600–19.

Bracke, Sarah. 2016. "Bouncing Back: Vulnerability and Resistance in Times of Resilience." In *Vulnerability in Resistance*, edited by Judith Butler, Zeynepp Ganbetti, and Letitia Sabsay. Duke University Press.

Braidotti, Rosi. 2008a. "In Spite of the Times: The Postsecular Turn in Feminism." *Theory, Culture & Society* 25 (6): 1–24. https://doi.org/10.1177/0263276408095542

———. 2008b. "Affirmation, Pain and Empowerment." *Asian Journal of Women's Studies* 14 (3): 7–36. https://doi.org/10.1080/12259276.2008.11666049

———. 2012. "Nomadic Ethics." In *The Cambridge Companion to Deleuze*, edited by Daniel W. Smith and Henry Somers-Hall. Cambridge Companions to Philosophy. Cambridge University Press.

Britt, Lory, and David Heise. 2000. "From Shame to Pride in Identity Politics." In *Self, Identity, and Social Movements* edited by Sheldon Stryker, Timothy J. Owens, and Robert White. University of Minnesota Press.

Browne, Kath, Sally R. Munt, and Andrew Kam-Tuck Yip, eds. 2010. *Queer Spiritual Spaces: Sexual and Sacred Places.* Ashgate.

Burkitt, Ian. 2014. *Emotions and Social Relations.* Sage.

Butler, Judith. 1990. *Gender Trouble: Feminism and the Subversion of Identity*. Routledge.
———. 2004. *Undoing Gender*. Routledge.
Caruth, Cathy. 1996. *Unclaimed Experience: Trauma, Narrative, and History*. John Hopkins University Press.
Clifford, James, and George E. Marcus. 1986. *Writing Culture: The Poetics and Politics of Ethnography*. University of California Press.
Collins, Elizabeth F., and Ernaldi Bahar. 2000. "To Know Shame: Malu and Its Uses in Malay Societies." *Crossroads: An Interdisciplinary Journal of Southeast Asian Studies* 14 (1): 35–69.
Colombetti, Giovanna. 2011. "Varieties of Pre-Reflective Self-Awareness: Foreground and Background Bodily Feelings in Emotion Experience." *Inquiry: An Interdisciplinary Journal of Philosophy* 54: 293–313.
Colombetti, Giovanna, and Matthew Ratcliffe. 2012. "Bodily Feeling in Depersonalization: A Phenomenological Account." *Emotion Review* 4: 145–50.
Connell, Raewyn. 1995. *Masculinities*. Polity Press.
Crawley, Ashon T. 2017. *Blackpentecostal Breath: The Aesthetics of Possibility*. Fordham University Press.
Cromby, John. 2007. "Toward a Psychology of Feeling." *International Journal of Critical Psychology* 21: 94–118.
Crosby, Alexandra. 2015. "Relocating Kampung, Rethinking Community: Salatiga's 'Festival Mata Air.'" In *Performing Contemporary Indonesia: Celebrating Identity, Constructing Community*, edited by Barbara Hatley and Brett Hough. Brill.
Crouch, Melissa. 2014. *Law and Religion in Indonesia: Conflict and the Courts in West Java*. Routledge.
Cvetkovich, Ann. 2003. *An Archive of Feelings: Trauma, Sexuality, and Lesbian Public Cultures*. Duke University Press.
Damasio, Antonio R. 1994. *Descartes' Error: Emotion, Reason and the Human Brain*. London: Picador.
———. 1999. *The Feeling of What Happens: Body, Emotion and the Making of Consciousness*. William Heinemann.
Das, Veena. 2007. *Life and Words: Violence and the Descent into the Ordinary*. University of California Press.
Dave, Naisargi N. 2008. "Between Queer Ethics and Sexual Morality." In *The Sarai Reader 07: Frontiers*, edited by Monica Narula, Shuddhabrata Sengupta, Jeebesh Bagchi, and Ravi Sundaram. The Director, Center for the Study of Developing Studies.
Davies, James. 2010. "Disorientation, Dissonance, and Altered Perception." In *The Anthropology and Psychology of Fieldwork Experience*, edited by James Davies and Dimitrina Spencer. Stanford University Press.
Davies, Sharyn G. 2010. *Gender Diversity in Indonesia: Sexuality, Islam and Queer Selves*. Routledge.
———. 2018. "Turning the Rising Tide of Anti-LGBT Sentiment in Indonesia." *East Asia Forum*, February 21. http://www.eastasiaforum.org/2018/02/21/turning-the -rising-tide-of-anti-lgbt-sentiment-in-indonesia/.

Deeb, Lara, and Mona Harb. 2013. *Leisurely Islam: Negotiating Geography and Morality in Shi'ite Beirut.* Princeton University Press.

Dhawan, Nikita. 2013. "The Empire Prays Back: Religion, Secularity and Queer Critique." *boundary 2* 40 (1): 191–222.

Dinkelaker, Samia. 2019. "Negotiating Respect(ability). A Transnational Ethnography of Indonesian Labor Brokerage." Unpublished dissertation, University of Osnabrück, Germany.

Dzulkarnain, Iskandar. 2006. "Perilaku Homoseksual di Pondok Pesantren" [Homosexual practices in an Islamic boarding school]. Unpublished thesis, Faculty of Sociology, Gajah Mada University Graduate School, Yogyakarta.

Fassin, Didier. 2012. "Introduction: Toward a Critical Moral Anthropology." In *A Companion to Moral Anthropology,* edited by Didier Fassin. Wiley-Blackwell.

———. 2013. "On Resentment and Ressentiment: The Politics and Ethics of Moral Emotions." *Current Anthropology* 54 (3): 249–67.

Fatah, Eep S. 2004. *Mencintai Indonesian dengan Amal: Refleksi atas Fase Awal Demokrasi* [Loving Indonesia with piety: Reflections on the early phases of democracy]. Republika.

Faubion, James D., and George E. Marcus. 2009. *Fieldwork: Learning Anthropology's Method in a Time of Transition.* Cornell University Press.

Feener, Michael. 2012. "Social Engineering Through Shari'a: Islamic Law and State-Directed Da'wa in Contemporary Aceh." *Islamic Law and Society* 19 (3): 275–312.

Feldman, Ilana. 2015. "Looking for Humanitarian Purpose: Endurance and the Value of Lives in a Palestinian Refugee Camp." *Public Culture* 27 (3): 427–47. https://doi.org /10.1215/08992363-2896171

Fessler, Daniel M. T. 2004. "Shame in Two Cultures: Implications for Evolutionary Approaches." *Journal of Cognition and Culture* 4 (2): 207–62.

Flam, Helena. 2005. "Emotion's Map: A Research Agenda." In *Emotions and Social Movements,* edited by Helena Flam and Deborah King. Routledge.

Fox, Catherine O., and Tracy E. Ore. 2010. "(Un)Covering Normalized Gender and Race Subjectivities in LGBT 'Safe Spaces.'" *Feminist Studies* 36 (3): 629–49.

Freeman, Elizabeth. 2007. "Queer Belongings: Kinship Theory and Queer Theory." In *A Companion to Lesbian, Gay, Bisexual, Transgender, and Queer Studies,* edited by George E. Haggerty and Molly McGarry. Blackwell Publishing.

Frijda, Nico H. 1986. *The Emotions.* Cambridge University Press.

Gandhi, Leila. 2006. *Affective Communities: Anticolonial Thought, Fin-De-Siècle, Radicalism, and the Politics of Friendship.* Duke University Press.

Garcia Rodriguez, Diego. 2023. *Gender, Sexuality and Islam in Contemporary Indonesia: Queer Muslims and Their Allies.* Routledge.

Garcia Rodriguez, Diego, and Ben Murtagh. 2022. "Situating Anti-LGBT Moral Panics in Indonesia." *Indonesia and the Malay World* 50 (146): 1–9.

Geertz, Clifford. 1960. *The Religion of Java.* University of Chicago Press.

———. 1973. *The Interpretation of Cultures.* Basic Books.

———. 1984. "'From the Native's Point of View': On the Nature of Anthropological Understanding." In *Culture Theory: Essays on Mind, Self, and Emotion*, edited by Richard A. Shweder and Robert A. LeVine. Cambridge University Press.

Geertz, Hildred. (1959) 1974. "The Vocabulary of Emotion: A Study of Javanese Socialization Processes." In *Culture and Personality*, edited by Robert A. LeVine. Aldine.

Georgis, Dina. 2013.*The Better Story: Queer Affects from the Middle East*. SUNY Press.

Gherardi, Silvia. 2019. "Theorizing Affective Ethnography for Organization Studies." *Organisation* 26 (6): 741–60. https://doi.org/10.1177/1350508418805285.

Goh, Joseph N. 2020. *Becoming a Malaysian Trans Man: Gender, Society, Body and Faith*. Palgrave Macmillan.

Good, Byron. J., and Mary-Jo D. V. Good. 1994. "In the Subjunctive Mode: Epilepsy Narratives in Turkey." *Social Science & Medicine* 38 (6): 835–42. https://doi.org/10.1016/0277-9536(94)90155-4.

Gould, Deborah. 2009. *Moving Politics: Emotion and ACT UP's Fight against AIDS*. University of Chicago Press.

Green, Linda. 1994. "Fear as a Way of Life." *Cultural Anthropology* 9 (2): 227–56. https://doi.org/10.1525/can.1994.9.2.02a00040.

Gutiérrez-Rodríguez, Encarnación. 2010. *Migration, Domestic Work and Affect: A Decolonial Approach on Value and the Feminization of Labor*. Routledge Research in Gender and Society. Routledge.

Hage, Ghassan. 2015. *Alter-Politics: Critical Anthropology and the Political Imagination*. Melbourne University Press.

Halberstam, Jack. 2005. "Shame and White Gay Masculinity." *Social Text* 23: 219–33. https://doi.org/10.1215/01642472-23-3-4_84-85-219.

Hamudy, Nurul A., and Moh. Ilham A. Hamudy. 2020. "Hijrah Movement in Indonesia: Shifting Concept and Implementation in Religiosity." *JSW (Jurnal Sosiologi Walisongo)* 4 (2): 133–50.

Hardt, Michael, and Antonio Negri. 2004. *Multitude: War and Democracy in the Age of Empire*. Penguin.

Hartal, Gilly. 2017. "Fragile Subjectivities: Constructing Queer Safe Spaces." *Social & Cultural Geography* 19 (8): 1053–72. https://doi.org/10.1080/14649365.2017.1335877

Hartal, Gilly, Yossi David, and Lital Pascar. 2014. Safe space. *Mafte'akh—Lexical Review of Political Thought* 8: 93–120 (Hebrew).

Hefner, Robert W. 2010. "Religious Resurgence in Contemporary Asia: Southeast Asian Perspectives on Capitalism, the State, and the New Piety." *Journal of Asian Studies* 69 (4): 1031–47.

Hegarty, Benjamin. 2018. "Under the Lights, onto the Stage: Becoming Waria through National Glamour in New Order Indonesia." *TSQ: Transgender Studies Quarterly* 5 (3): 355–77. https://doi.org/10.1215/23289252-6900738.

———. 2022. *The Made-Up State: Technology, Trans Femininity, and Citizenship in Indonesia*. Cornell University Press.

Hegarty, Benjamin, and Ferdiansyah Thajib. 2016. "A Dispensable Threat." *Inside Indonesia* 124, June 13. https://www.insideindonesia.org/archive/articles/benjamin -hegarty-and-ferdiansyah-thajib.

Heider, Karl. G. 1991. *Landscapes of Emotion: Mapping Three Cultures of Emotion in Indonesia*. Cambridge University Press.

Heryanto, Ariel. 2003. "Public Intellectuals, Media and Democratization: Cultural Politics of the Middle Classes in Indonesia." In *Challenging Authoritarianism in Southeast Asia: Comparing Indonesia and Malaysia*, edited by Ariel Heryanto and Sumit K. Mandal. RoutledgeCurzon.

———. 2008. "Pop Culture and Competing Identities." In *Popular Culture in Indonesia: Fluid Identities in Post-Authoritarian Politics*, edited by Ariel Heryanto. Routledge.

Heryanto, Ariel, Chua Beng Huat, and Denise Varney. 2015. "Identity, Community and the Marketplace in Contemporary Indonesian Performance." In *Performing Contemporary Indonesia: Celebrating Identity, Constructing Community*, edited by Barbara Hatley with Brett Hough. Brill.

Hirschkind, Charles. 2006. *The Ethical Soundscape: Cassette Sermons and Islamic Counterpublics*. Columbia University Press.

Holliday, Ruth. 1999. "The Comfort of Identity." *Sexualities* 2 (4): 475–91. https://doi.org /10.1177/136346099002004007.

hooks, bell. 1994 *Teaching to Transgress: Education as the Practice of Freedom*. Routledge.

Houben, Vincent. 2015. "Islam and the Perception of Islam in Contemporary Indonesia." *Heidelberg Ethnology*, Occasional Paper 3. https://doi.org/10.11588 /hdethn.0.0.25362.

Jackson, Michael. 1989. *Path Toward a Clearing: Radical Empiricism and Ethnographic Inquiry*. Indiana University Press.

Jackson, Peter A. 1995. *Dear Uncle Go: Male Homosexuality in Thailand*. Bua Luang Books.

Jamal, Amreen. 2001. "The Story of Lot and the Quran's Perception of the Morality of Same-Sex Sexuality." *Journal of Homosexuality* 41 (1): 1–88. https://doi.org/10.1300 /J082v41n01_01.

Jankowiak, William R. and Thomas Paladino. 2008. "Desiring Sex, Longing for Love: A Tripartite Conundrum." In *Intimacies: Love and Sex across Cultures*, edited by William R. Jankowiak. Columbia University Press.

Jauhola, Marjaana. 2012. "'Natural' Sex Difference? Negotiating the Meanings of Sex, Gender and *Kodrat* Through Gender Equality Discourse in Aceh, Indonesia." *Intersections: Gender and Sexuality in Asia and the Pacific* 30. http://intersections .anu.edu.au/issue30/jauhola.htm.

Jones, Carla. 2010. "Materializing Piety: Gendered Anxieties about Faithful Consumption in Contemporary Urban Indonesia." *American Ethnologist* 37 (4): 617–37. https://doi.org/10.1111/j.1548-1425.2010.01275.x.

Joseph, Miranda. 2002. *Against the Romance of Community*. University of Minnesota Press.

Juliastuti, Nuraini. 2006. The Language of Punkasila. Insert leaflet for Punkasila album *Acronym Wars*. Accessed March 10, 2019. https://pineappledonut.org/2010/12/27/punkasila.

Kantjasungkana, Nursyahbani and Saskia E. Wieringa. 2016. *Creeping Criminalisation: Mapping of Indonesia's National Law and Regional Regulations that Violates Human Rights of Women and LGBTIQ People*. Outright Action International.

Kasmani, Omar. 2022. *Queer Companions: Religion, Public Intimacy, and Saintly Affects in Pakistan*. Duke University Press.

Keeler, Ward. 1983. "Shame and Stage Fright in Java." *Ethos* 11 (3): 152–65.

King, Tiffany Lethabo, Jenell Navarro, and Andrea Smith. 2020. *Otherwise Worlds: Against Settler Colonialism and Anti-Blackness*. Duke University Press.

Kirby, Richard, and Jay Corzine. 1981. "The Contagion of Stigma: Fieldwork Among Deviants." *Qualitative Sociology* 4 (1): 3–20.

Kleinman, Arthur. 2000. "The Violences of Everyday Life: The Multiple Forms and Dynamics of Social Violence." In *Violence and Subjectivity*, edited by Veena Das, Arthur Kleinman, Mamphela Ramphele and Pamela Reynolds. University of California Press.

Kloos, David. 2015. "Sinning and Ethical Improvement in Contemporary Aceh." In *Islam and the Limits of the State: Reconfigurations of Practice, Community and Authority in Contemporary Aceh*, edited by Michael Feener, David Kloos and Annemarie Samuels. Brill.

———. 2017. *Becoming Better Muslims: Religious Authority and Ethical Improvement in Aceh, Indonesia*. Princeton University Press.

Kugle, Scott A. 2007. *Sufis and Saints' Bodies: Mysticism, Corporeality, and Sacred Power in Islam*. The University of North Carolina Press.

———. 2010. *Homosexuality in Islam: Critical Reflection on Gay, Lesbian, and Transgender Muslims*. One World Publication.

———. 2014. *Living Out Islam: Voices of Gay, Lesbian, and Transgender Muslims*. NYU Press.

Knight, Kyle. 2016. *"These political games ruin our lives": Indonesia's LGBT Community Under Threat*. Human Rights Watch, August 10. https://www.hrw.org/report/2016/08/11/these-political-games-ruin-our-lives/indonesias-lgbt-community-under-threat.

Lake, Nell. 2023. "Double-Edged Care: Toward a Politics of Care Justice." *Signs: Journal of Women in Culture and Society* 48 (3): 585–605.

Lambek, Michael. 2010. "Introduction" In *Ordinary Ethics: Anthropology, Language, and Action*, edited by Michael Lambek. Fordham University Press.

Lawson, Victoria. 2007. "Geographies of Care and Responsibility." *Annals of the Association of American Geographers* 97 (1): 1–11. https://doi.org/10.1111/j.1467-8306.2007.00520.x.

Liamputtong, Pranee. 2007. *Researching the Vulnerable. A Guide to Sensitive Research Method*. Sage.

Lim, Eng-Beng. 2013. *Brown Boys and Rice Queens: Spellbinding Performances in the Asias*. New York University Press.

Lindquist, Johan. 2013. "Rescue, Return, in Place: Deportees, 'Victims,' and the Regulation of Indonesian Migration." In *Return: Nationalizing Transnational Mobility in Asia*, edited by Xiang Bao, Brenda S. A. Yeoh, and Mika Toyota. Duke University Press.

Listiorini, Dina, Donna Asteria, and Billy Sarwono. 2019. "Moral Panics on LGBT Issues: Evidence from Indonesian TV Program." *Jurnal Studi Komunikasi* 3 (3). https://doi.org/10.25139/jsk.v3i3.1882.

Love, Heather. 2007. *Feeling Backward: Loss and the Politics of Queer History*. Harvard University Press.

Lovell, Anne M. 2007. "When Things Get Personal: Secrecy, Intimacy, and the Production of Experience in Fieldwork." In *The Shadow Side of Fieldwork: Exploring the Blurred Borders Between Ethnography and Life*, edited by Athena McLean and Annette Leibing. Blackwell.

Lukens-Bull, Ronald A. 2007. "Lost in a Sea of Subjectivity: The Subject Position of the Researcher in the Anthropology of Islam." *Contemporary Islam* 1: 173–92. https://doi.org/10.1007/s11562-007-0014-y.

Lutz, Catherine A. 1988. *Unnatural Emotions: Everyday Sentiments on a Micronesian Atoll and their Challenge to Western Theory*. University of Chicago Press.

Lutz, Catherine A., and Lila Abu-Lughod, eds. 1990. *Language and the Politics of Emotion*. Cambridge University Press.

Lutz, Catherine A., and Geoffrey M. White. 1986. "The Anthropology of Emotions." *Annual Review of Anthropology* 1: 405–36.

Magnis-Suseno, Franz. 1988. *Etika Jawa* [Javanese ethics]. Gramedia Pustaka Utama.

Mahmood, Saba. 2005. *Politics of Piety: The Islamic Revival and the Feminist Subject*. Princeton University Press.

Marcus, George E. 1995. "Ethnography in/of the World System: The Emergence of Multi-Sited Ethnography." *Annual Review of Anthropology* 24: 95–117.

Marsden, Magnus and Konstantinos Retsikas, eds. 2013. *Articulating Islam: Anthropological Approaches to Muslim Worlds*. Springer.

Massad, Joseph. 2002. "Re-Orienting Desire: The Gay International and the Arab World." *Public Culture* 14 (2): 361–85.

———. 2007. *Desiring Arabs*. The University of Chicago Press.

Massumi, Brian. 2002. *Parables for the Virtual: Movement, Affect, Sensation*. Duke University Press.

Mattingly, Cheryl. 2013. "Moral Selves and Moral Scenes: Narrative Experiments in Everyday Life." *Ethnos* 78 (3): 301–327. https://doi.org/10.1080/00141844.2012.691523.

Mills, Catherine. 2007. "Normative Violence, Vulnerability, and Responsibility." *Difference: A Journal of Feminist Cultural Studies* 18 (2): 133–56. https://doi.org/10.1215/10407391-2007-005.

Muehlebach, Andrea. 2013. "On Precariousness and the Ethical Imagination: The Year 2012 in Sociocultural Anthropology." *American Anthropologist* 115 (2): 297 311. https://doi.org/10.1111/aman.12011.

Mulder, Niels. 1992. *Individual and Society in Java*. Gajah Mada University Press.

Mundayat, Aris Arif. 2005. "Ritual and Politics in New Order Indonesia: A Study of Discourse and Counter-Discourse in Indonesia." Unpublished dissertation, School of Social and Life Sciences, Swinburne University of Technology.

Munir, Maimunah. 2011. "Queering the Epistemology of 'Coming Out': The Representation of Male Same-Sex Relationship in Nia Dinata's Arisan." *Jati* 16: 113–29.

———. 2014. "Memahami Teori Queer di Budaya Populer iIndonesia: Permasalahan dan Kemungkinan" [Understanding Queer Theory in Indonesian Popular Culture: Problems and Possibilities]. *Lakon: Jurnal Kajian Sastra Dan Budaya* 3 (1): 43–69. https://doi.org/10.20473/lakon.v3i1.1926.

Muñoz, José Esteban. 1999. *Disidentifications: Queers of Colors and the Performance of Politics*. University of Minnesota Press.

Munt, Sally R. 2007. *Queer Attachments: The Cultural Politics of Shame*. Routledge.

Murtagh, Ben. 2013. *Genders and Sexualities in Indonesian Cinema: Constructing Gay, Lesbi and Waria Identities on Screen*. Routledge.

Namaste, Vivian K. 2000. *Invisible Lives: The Erasure of Transsexual and Transgendered People*. University of Chicago Press.

Nawawi, Imam. 2014. *Riyad As-Salihin: The Gardens of the Righteous*. Tughra Books.

Ngai, Sianne. 2005. *Ugly Feelings*. Harvard University Press.

Nguyen, Tan Hoang. 2014. *A View from the Bottom: Asian American Masculinity and Sexual Representation*. Duke University Press.

Oetomo, Dede. 2001. "Gay Men in the Reformasi Era: Homophobic Violence Could Be a By-Product of the New Openness." *Inside Indonesia* 66, July 30. https://www.insideindonesia.org/editions/edition-6641/gay-men-in-the-reformasi-era.

O'Neill, Michael. 2016. "The Pitfalls of Call-Out Culture." *Brown Political Review*, May 6. https://brownpoliticalreview.org/26760/.

Oswin, Natalie. 2014. "The Modern Model Family at Home in Singapore: A Queer Geography." *Transactions of the British Institute of Royal Geographers* 35 (2): 256–68.

Paramaditha, Intan. 2016. "The LGBT Debate and the Fear of 'Gerakan.'" *The Jakarta Post*, February 27.

———. 2018. "Q! Film Festival as Cultural Activism: Strategic Cinephilia and the Expansion of a Queer Counterpublic." *Visual Anthropology* 31 (1–2): 74–92. https://doi.org/10.1080/08949468.2018.1428015.

Peletz, Michael G. 1997. "'Ordinary Muslims' and Muslim Resurgents in Contemporary Malaysia: Notes on an Ambivalent Relationship." In *Islam in an Era of Nation-States: Politics and Religious Renewal in Muslim Southeast Asia*, edited by Robert Hefner and Patricia Horvatich. University of Hawai'i Press.

———. 2009. *Gender Pluralism: Southeast Asia Since Early Modern Times*. Routledge.

Pine, Jason. 2008. "Contact, Complicity, Conspiracy: Affective Communities and Economies of Affect in Naples." *Law, Culture and the Humanities* 4: 201–223. https://doi.org/10.1177/1743872108091474.

Platt, Maria, Sharyn G. Davies, and Linda R. Bennett. 2018. "Contestations of Gender, Sexuality and Morality in Contemporary Indonesia." *Asian Studies Review* 42 (1): 56–68. https://doi.org/10.1080/10357823.2017.1409698.

Povinelli, Elizabeth A. 2011. *Economies of Abandonment: Social Belonging and Endurance in Late Liberalism.* Duke University Press.

Probyn, Elspeth. 1996. *Outside Belongings.* Routledge.

Puar, Jasbir. 2007. *Terrorist Assemblages: Homonationalism in Queer Times.* Duke University Press.

Puig de la Bellacasa, Maria. 2011. "Matters of Care in Technoscience: Assembling Neglected Things." *Social Studies of Science* 41 (1): 85–106. https://doi.org/10.1177/0306312710380301.

———. 2017. *Matters of Care: Speculative Ethics in More Than Human Worlds.* University of Minnesota Press.

Rabinow, Paul. 1997. *Reflections on Fieldwork in Morocco.* University of California Press.

Rai, Amit S. 2019. *Jugaad Time: Ecologies of Everyday Hacking in India.* Duke University Press.

Rao, Rahul. 2020. *Out of Time: The Queer Politics of Postcoloniality.* Oxford University Press.

Reay, Diane. 2004. "Gendering Bourdieu's Concepts of Capitals? Emotional Capital, Women and Social Class." In *Feminism After Bourdieu*, edited by Lisa Adkins and Beverley Skeggs. Blackwell.

Reddy, William M. 2001. *The Navigation of Feeling. A Framework for the History of Emotions.* Cambridge University Press.

The Roestone Collective. 2014. "Safe Space: Towards a Reconceptualization." *Antipode* 46 (5): 1346–65.

Röttger-Rössler, Birgitt. 2013. "The Eyes of the Others: Shame and Social Conformity in Contemporary Indonesia." In *Shame Between Punishment and Penance: The Social Usages of Shame in the Middle Ages and Early Modern Times*, edited by Bénédicte Sere and Jörg Wettlaufer. Microligus Library.

Röttger-Rössler, Birgitt and Hans Jürgen Markowitsch, eds. (2009). *Emotions as Bio-cultural Processes.* Springer.

Rudnyckyj, Daromir. 2011. "Circulating tears and managing hearts: Governing through affect in an Indonesian steel factory." *Anthropological Theory* 11(1): 63–87. https://doi.org/10.1177/1463499610395444.

Safitri, Dian M. 2011. "Tolerance of Minorities and Cultural Legitimacy: The Case of Pesantren Khusus Waria Al-Fattah Senin-Kamis Yogyakarta." *Jurnal Ilmu Sosial dan Ilmu Politik* 15 (2): 154–67.

Samuels, Annemarie. 2016. "Seeing AIDS in Aceh: Sexual Moralities and the Politics of (In)Visibility in Post-Reconstruction Times." *Indonesia* 101: 103–20. https://doi.org/10.5728/indonesia.101.0103.

———. 2019. *After the Tsunami: Disaster Narratives and the Remaking of Everyday Life in Aceh.* University of Hawai'i Press.

Schaefer, Donovan O. 2015. *Religious Affects: Animality, Evolution, and Power.* Duke University Press.

Scheff, Thomas. 1990. "Socialization of Emotion: Pride and Shame as Casual Agents." In *Research Agendas in the Sociology of Emotion*, edited by Theodore D. Kemper. SUNY Press.

Schielke, Samuli. 2009a. "Being Good in Ramadan: Ambivalence, Fragmentation, and the Moral Self in the Lives of Young Egyptians." *Journal of the Royal Anthropological Institute* 15: S24–S40.

———. 2009b. "Ambivalent Commitments: Troubles of Morality, Religiosity and Aspiration Among Young Egyptians." *Journal of Religion in Africa* 39 (2): 158–85.

Schielke, Samuli, and Liza Debevec, eds. 2012. *Ordinary Lives and Grand Schemes: An Anthropology of Everyday Religion*. Berghahn Books.

Schotten, C. Heike. 2018. "Nietzsche and Emancipatory Politics: Queer Theory as Anti-Morality." *Critical Sociology* 45 (2): 1–14. https://doi.org/10.1177/0896920517752071

Sebastian, Leonard C. 2006. *Realpolitik Ideology: Indonesia's Use of Military Force.* Institute of South East Asian Studies.

Sedgwick, Eve Kosofsky. 2003. *Touching Feeling: Affect, Pedagogy, Performativity.* Duke University Press.

Siapno, Jacqueline A. 2002. *Gender, Islam, Nationalism and the State of Aceh: The Paradox of Power, Co-optation and Resistance.* Routledge Curzon.

Siegel, James T. 1998. *A New Criminal Type in Jakarta: Counter-Revolution Today.* Duke University Press.

———. 2006. *Naming the Witch.* Stanford University Press.

Simon, Gregory M. 2009. "The Soul Freed of Cares? Islamic Prayer, Subjectivity, and the Contradictions of Moral Selfhood in Minangkabau, Indonesia." *American Ethnologist* 36 (2): 258–75. https://doi.org/10.1111/j.1548-1425.2009.01134.x.

Simone, AbdouMaliq. 2013. "Endurance, Not Survival." *Cityscapes Magazine* 3. Archived September 25, 2021, at the Wayback Machine, https://web.archive.org/web/20210925101309/https://cityscapesmagazine.com/articles/endurance-not-survival.

———. 2016. "The Uninhabitable? In Between Collapsed Yet Still Rigid Distinctions." *Cultural Politics* 12 (2): 135–54. https://doi.org/10.1215/17432197-3592052.

———. 2022. *The Surrounds: Urban Life Within and Beyond Capture.* Duke University Press.

Singh, Jakeet. 2015. "Religious Agency and the Limits of Intersectionality." *Hypatia* 30 (4): 657–74. https://doi.org/10.1111/hypa.12182.

Siraj, Asifa. 2012. "'I Don't Want to Taint the Name of Islam': The Influence of Religion on the Lives of Muslim Lesbians." *Journal of Lesbian Studies* 16 (4): 449–67. https://doi.org/10.1080/10894160.2012.681268.

Slama, Martin. 2010. "The Agency of the Heart: Internet Chatting as Youth Culture in Indonesia." *Social Anthropology/Anthropologie Sociale* 18 (3): 316–30. https://doi.org/10.1111/j.1469-8676.2010.00110.x.

Slama, Martin, and Bart Barendregt. 2018. "Introduction: Online Publics in Muslim Southeast Asia." *Asiascape: Digital Asia* 5 (1–2): 3–31.

Spencer, Dimitrina. 2010. "Emotional Labour and Relational Observation in Anthropological Fieldwork." In *Anthropological Fieldwork: A Relational Process*, edited by Dimitrina Spencer and James Davies. Cambridge Scholars Publishing.

Stange, Paul. 1984. "The Logic of Rasa in Java." *Indonesia* 38: 113–34.

Stanghellini, Giovanni, and René Rosfort. 2013. *Emotions and Personhood: Exploring Fragility: Making Sense of Vulnerability*. Oxford University Press.

Stengel, Barbara. 2010. "The Complex Case of Fear and Safe Space." *Studies in Philosophy and Education* 29 (6): 524–40.

Stewart, Kathleen. 2017. "In the World That Affect Proposed." *Cultural Anthropology* 32 (2): 192–98. https://doi.org/10.14506/ca32.2.03.

Stodulka, Thomas. 2009. "'Beggars' and 'Kings': Emotional regulation of shame among street youths in a Javanese city in Indonesia." In *Emotions as Bio-cultural Processes*, edited by Birgitt Röttger-Rössler and Hans Jürgen Markowitsch. Springer.

———. 2017 *Coming of Age on the Streets of Java: Coping with Marginality, Stigma and Illness*. Transcript Verlag.

Stodulka, Thomas, Samia Dinkelaker, and Ferdiansyah Thajib. 2019. "Fieldwork, Ethnography, and the Empirical Affect Montage." In *Analyzing Affective Societies*, edited by Antje Kahl. Routledge.

Stryker, Susan. 2004. "Transgender Studies: Queer Theory's Evil Twin." *GLQ A Journal of Lesbian and Gay Studies* 10 (2): 212–15. https://doi.org/10.1215/10642684-10-2-212

Subijanto, Rianne. 2011. "The Visibility of a Pious Public." *Inter-Asia Cultural Studies* 12 (2): 240–53. https://doi.org/10.1080/14649373.2011.554651.

Svašek, Maruška. 2010. "'The Field': Intersubjectivity, Empathy and the Workings of Internalised Presence." In *Anthropological Fieldwork: A Relational Process*, edited by Dimitrina Spencer and James Davies. Cambridge Scholars Publishing.

Taylor, Yvette, and Ria Snowdon, eds. 2014. *Queering Religion: Religious Queers*. Routledge.

Thajib, Ferdiansyah. 2017. "Kaleidoscopic Feelings: Faith Narratives Among Indonesian Muslim *Queers*." *Emotion, Space and Society* 25: 127–35. https://doi.org/10.1016/j.emospa.2016.11.007.

———. 2018. "The Making and Breaking of Indonesian Muslim *Queer* Safe Space." *borderlands e-journal* 17 (1): 1–24. https://www.jstor.org/stable/48782588.

———. 2021. "Discordant Emotions: The Affective Dynamics of Anti-LGBT Campaigns in Indonesia." *Indonesia and the Malay World* 50 (146): 10–32. https://doi.org/10.1080/13639811.2022.2005312.

———. 2022a. "Following the Heart: Ethics of Doing Affective Ethnography in Vulnerable Research Settings." *International Quarterly for Asian Studies* 53 (4): 533–51. https://doi.org/10.11588/iqas.2022.4.20798.

———. 2022b. "Endurance as Queer Worldmaking in Northern Aceh of Indonesia." In *Queer Southeast Asia*, edited by Shawna Tang and Hendri Yulius Wijaya. Routledge.

Thajib, Ferdiansyah, Samia Dinkelaker, and Thomas Stodulka. 2019. "Affective Dimensions of Fieldwork and Ethnography: Introduction." In *Affective Dimensions of Fieldwork and Ethnography*, edited by Thomas Stodulka, Samia Dinkelaker and Ferdiansyah Thajib. Springer.

Thajib, Ferdiansyah, Francis Seeck, and Antke Engels. 2020. "Konflikte Umsorgen: Queere Praktiken künstlerischer Kollaboration" [Caring for conflict: Queer practices of artistic collaboration]. *Feministiche Studien* 2 (20): 309–321. https://doi.org /10.1515/fs-2020-0027.

Thompson, Marie. 2017."The Discomfort of Safety." *Society & Space*, February 14. https://www.societyandspace.org/articles/the-discomfort-of-safety/.

Thrift, Nigel. 2008. *Non-Representational Theory: Space, Politics, Affect*. Routledge.

Ticktin, Miriam. 2011. *Casualties of Care: Immigration and the Politics of Humanitarianism in France*. University of California Press.

Tronto, Joan C. 1993. *Moral Boundaries: A Political Argument for an Ethic of Care*. Routledge.

Uprichard, Lucy. 2013. "In Defence of Call-Out Culture." *Huffington Post*, December 27. http://www.huffingtonpost.co.uk/lucyuprichard/call-out-culture_b_4507889.html.

Valentine, Gill, Tracey Skelton, and Ruth Butler. 2003. "Coming Out and Outcomes: Negotiating Lesbian and Gay Identities with, and in, the Family." *Environment and Planning D: Society and Space* 21 (4): 479–99. https://doi.org/10.1068/d277t.

Van Doorn, Niels. 2015. "Forces of Faith: Endurance, Flourishing and the Queer Religious Subject." *GLQ A Journal of Lesbian and Gay Studies* 21 (4): 635–66. https:// doi.org/10.1215/10642684-3123725.

Van Maanen, John. 1988. *Tales of the Field: On Writing Ethnography*. University of Chicago Press.

Visweswaran, Kamala.1994. *Fictions of Feminist Ethnography*. University of Minnesota Press.

Von Poser, Anita. 2017. "Care as Process: A Life-Course Perspective on the Remaking of Ethics and Values of Care in Daiden, Papua New Guinea." *Ethics and Social Welfare* 11 (3): 213–29. https://doi.org/10.1080/17496535.2017.1300303.

Warner, Michael. 1999. *The Trouble with Normal: Sex, Politics, and the Ethics of Queer Life*. Harvard University Press.

Weeks, Kathi. 2007. "Life Within and Against Work: Affective Labor, Feminist Critique, and Post-Fordist Politics." *Ephemera* 7 (1): 233–49.

Weiss, Hadas. 2022. "From Desire to Endurance: Hanging On in a Spanish Village." *Cultural Anthropology* 37 (1): 45–68. https://doi.org/10.14506/ca37.1.07.

Wetherell, Margaret. 2012. *Affect and Emotion: A New Social Science Understanding*, Sage.

White, Geoffrey. M. 1994. "Affecting Culture: Emotion and Morality in Everyday Life." In *Emotion and Culture: Empirical Studies of Mutual Influence*, edited by Shinobu Kitayama and Hazel R. Markus. American Psychological Association.

Wieringa, Saskia E. 2009. "Postcolonial Amnesia: Sexual Moral Panics, Memory and Imperial Power." In *Moral Panics, Sex Panics; Fear and the Fight over Sexual Rights*, edited by Gilbert Herdt. New York University Press.

———. 2022a. "Nationalism and Two Moral Panics in Indonesia." In *Local Responses to Global Challenges in Southeast Asia: A Transregional Studies Reader*, edited by Lina

Knorr, Andrea Fleschenberg, Sumrin Kalia, and Claudia Derichs. World Scientific Press.

———. 2022b. "Dorce Gamalama's Burial and Indonesia's Transgender Traditions." *Inside Indonesia* 149, August 2. https://www.insideindonesia.org/archive/articles /dorce-gamalama-s-burial-and-indonesia-s-transgender-traditions.

Wijaya, Hendri Yulius. 2019. "Localising Queer Identities: Queer Activisms and National Belonging in Indonesia." In *Contentious Belonging: The Place of Minorities in Indonesia*, edited by Greg Fealy and Ronit Ricci. ISEAS–Yusof Ishak Institute.

Wikan, Uni. 1990. *Managing Turbulent Hearts*. Chicago: University Press.

———. 1992. "Beyond the Words: The Power of Resonance." *American Ethnologist* 19 (3): 460–82.

Wilcox, Melissa M. 2021. *Queer Religiosities: An Introduction to Queer and Transgender Studies in Religion*. Rowman & Littlefield.

Wolf, Diane L., ed. 1996. *Feminist Dilemmas in Fieldwork*. Westview Press.

Yentriyani, Andy and Neng Dara Affiah. 2017. "Women's Sexuality and the Debate on the Anti-Pornography Bill in Democratizing Indonesia." In *Sexual Politics in Muslim Societies*, edited by Pinar Ilkkaracan and Rina Athar. GAYa NUSANTARA and CSBR.

Yip, Andrew K. T. 2010. "Coming Home from the Wilderness: An Overview of Recent Scholarly Research on LGBTQI Religiosity/Spirituality in the West." In *Queer Spiritual Spaces: Sexuality and Sacred Places*, edited by Kath Browne, Sally Munt, and Andrew K. T. Yip. Ashgate.

Yip, Andrew K. T. 2005. "Religion and the Politics of Spirituality/Sexuality: Reflections on Researching British Lesbian, Gay, and Bisexual Christians and Muslims." *Fieldwork in Religion* 1 (3): 271–89.

Yip, Andrew K. T., and Amna Khalid. 2010. "Looking for Allah: Spiritual Quests of Queer Muslims." In *Queer Spiritual Spaces: Sexuality and Sacred Places*, edited by Kath Browne, Sally R. Munt, and Andrew K. T. Yip. Ashgate.

Zelizer, Viviana A. 2005. *The Purchase of Intimacy*. Princeton University Press.

Zigon, Jared. 2007. "Moral Breakdown and the Ethical Demand: A Theoretical Framework for an Anthropology of Moralities." *Anthropological Theory* 7 (2): 131–50. https://doi.org/10.1177/1463499607077295.

Zuhri, Saifuddin. 2006. "Dalaq di pesantren" [Dalaq in Islamic boarding schools]. Unpublished thesis, Faculty of Comparative Religion Studies, Gajah Mada University Graduate School Yogyakarta.

INDEX

Aceh, 1, 106; banning of gender nonconformity in, 2; and climate of discretion,
25; criminal bylaw in (Qanun Jinayat),
1; ancestral roots of, 22; fieldwork in,
5, 21, 24–25, 43–45, 68, 73, 122–23, 148;
dilemma about staying or leaving,
116, 150, 157; gender discourse in, 48;
implementation of Shari'a law, 1, 22;
moral control in, 40, 116; Muslim
layperson in, 39, 78; Namu and
Rancong in, 23; postconflict and post-
disaster, 22, 25, 112; public leisure in,
83–84; stereotypes about, 22, 169n26;
transpuan's life in, 73–78, 82, 129, 154
affect: centrality in research, 20;
definitions of, 14
affective dynamics, 10, 13, 18; definition
of, 14–15; of inner conflict, 28;
of moral and ethical engagements, 28
affective ethnography: definitions of,
20–21; methodological applications
of, 22–27
affective experiences: beyond binary, 11;
damaging, 12; as epistemic research
tools, 26–27, 154; of impasse, 3, 136;
of Muslim queer subjectivities, 33;
transformative, 65, 106
affective labor: care as, 139, 43; definition of,
140, 172n30; of endurance, 12, 145, 148
affective repertoire, 68, 80, 146; of brotherly love, 43; definition of, 15; of fear
of feeling guilty, 38; of fear of being
alone, 64; of feeling always wrong, 56;
of home-making, 106, 118; of safety, care,

and belonging, 28; of self-comfort, 57;
of trauma and miracle, 112–15, 118
affirmative ethics, definition and critiques
of, 151–52
agency: critique of, 8–9; queer, 148; of
religious women, 8–9; as unhappy
consciousness, 9
Ahmed, Sara: 9, 47, 132, 152
Ali, 28, 94–106, 111–12, 117–18, 147, 158
aman (safety and security): double meaning of, 121–22; *ruang* (space), 121;
vernacular use of, 125–26. *See also*
emotives: keamanan; safe; safety;
security
ambivalence, 3, 54, 151; as emotive, 64;
spaces of, 3; structures of, 30–31
Anggun, 85–88
Anna, 27, 30, 54–65, 67, 104, 147, 152 ; in
queer youth camp, 132–36
Anti Pornography Law (2008), 93
anti-communism: and nationwide
massacres, 58; politics of, 18–19
anti-LGBT campaign, 19, 91–93
antiretroviral therapy, 97, 100
authenticity: and discourse of citizenship,
61; of gender, 62, 76, 79, 88; Muslim,
86; of the self, 60, 131

banci, bencong: as derogatory term, 74–75,
109, 169n12, as reclaimed term in the
community, 73
Banda Aceh, Indonesia, 22, 43, 44, 69, 71,
107, 110, 113, 116, 124, 127
Bandung, West Java, 33

ABOUT THE AUTHOR

Ferdiansyah Thajib is senior lecturer in the Elite Graduate Program "Standards of Decision-Making Across Cultures" at Friedrich-Alexander-Universität Erlangen-Nürnberg, Germany. His work on queer religiosity has been published in various journals and he is coeditor of *Embracing Faith and Desire: Queer and Feminist Engagements with Islam and Christianity as Lived Religions* (Routledge, 2025) and *Affective Dimensions of Fieldwork and Ethnography* (Springer, 2019).